INTRODUCTION TO e-GOVERNANCE

AUTHOR

Dr. Kamal Kant Verma

Professor, IILM University, Knowledge Park-II

Greater Noida, Uttar Pradesh-201306

REVIEWER

Prof. Dulu Patnaik

Principal, Government College of Engineering (GCE), Kalahandi

Bhawanipatna, Orissa- 766003

KHANNA BOOK PUBLISHING CO. (P) Ltd.

4C/4344, Ansari Road, Darya Ganj,
New Delhi, India

All India Council for Technical Education

Nelson Mandela Marg, Vasant Kunj,
New Delhi, India

Dear Readers,

To prevent the piracy, this book is secured with HIGH SECURITY HOLOGRAM on the front title cover. In case you don't find the hologram on the front cover title, please write us to at contact@khannabooks.com or whatsapp us at +91-99109 09320 and avail special gift voucher for yourself.

Specimen of Hologram on front Cover title:

Moreover, there is a SPECIAL DISCOUNT COUPON for you with EVERY HOLOGRAM.

How to avail this SPECIAL DISCOUNT:

Step 1: Scratch the hologram

Step 2: Under the scratch area, your "coupon code" is available

Step 3: Logon to www.khannabooks.com

Step 4: Use your "coupon code" in the shopping cart and get your copy at a special discount

Step 5: Enjoy your reading!

ISBN: 978-93-5538-429-4

Book Code: DIP496EN

Introduction To e-Governance

by Dr. Kamal Kant Verma

First Edition: 2026

Originally Published by:

All India Council for Technical Education, Ministry of Education, GOI

Exclusively Published & Distributed by:

Khanna Book Publishing Co. (P) Ltd.
4C/4344, Ansari Road, Daryaganj,
New Delhi (INDIA)

Visit us at: **www.khannabooks.com**

Write us at: **contact@khannabooks.com**

To view complete list of books,
Please scan the QR Code:

KPH

Printed in Bharat.

प्रो. टी. जी. सीताराम
अध्यक्ष
Prof. T. G. Sitharam
Chairman

सत्यमेव जयते

आज़ादी का अमृत महोत्सव

अखिल भारतीय तकनीकी शिक्षा परिषद्
(भारत सरकार का एक सांविधिक निकाय)
(शिक्षा मंत्रालय, भारत सरकार)
नेल्सन मंडेला मार्ग, वसंत कुंज, नई दिल्ली–110070
दूरभाष : 011–26131498
ई–मेल : chairman@aicte-india.org

ALL INDIA COUNCIL FOR TECHNICAL EDUCATION
(A STATUTORY BODY OF THE GOVT. OF INDIA)
(Ministry of Education, Govt. of India)
Nelson Mandela Marg, Vasant Kunj, New Delhi-110070
Phone : 011-26131498
E-mail : chairman@aicte-india.org

FOREWORD

Engineers are the backbone of any modern society. They are the ones responsible for the marvels as well as the improved quality of life across the world. Engineers have driven humanity towards greater heights in a more evolved and unprecedented manner.

The All India Council for Technical Education (AICTE), have spared no efforts towards the strengthening of the technical education in the country. AICTE is always committed towards promoting quality Technical Education to make India a modern developed nation emphasizing on the overall welfare of mankind.

An array of initiatives has been taken by AICTE in last decade which have been accelerated now by the National Education Policy (NEP) 2020. The implementation of NEP under the visionary leadership of Hon'ble Prime Minister of India envisages the provision for education in regional languages to all, thereby ensuring that every graduate becomes competent enough and is in a position to contribute towards the national growth and development through innovation & entrepreneurship.

One of the spheres where AICTE had been relentlessly working since past couple of years is providing high quality original technical contents at Under Graduate & Diploma level prepared and translated by eminent educators in various Indian languages to its aspirants. For students pursuing 2nd year of their Engineering education, AICTE has identified 87 books, which shall be translated into 12 Indian languages - Hindi, Tamil, Gujarati, Odia, Bengali, Kannada, Urdu, Punjabi, Telugu, Marathi, Assamese & Malayalam. In addition to the English medium, books in different Indian Languages are going to support the students to understand the concepts in their respective mother tongue.

On behalf of AICTE, I express sincere gratitude to all distinguished authors, reviewers and translators from the renowned institutions of high repute for their admirable contribution in a record span of time.

AICTE is confident that these outcomes based original contents shall help aspirants to master the subject with comprehension and greater ease.

T. G. Sitharam

(Prof. T. G. Sitharam)

ACKNOWLEDGEMENT

I am grateful to the authorities of AICTE, particularly Prof. T.G. Sitharam, Chairman; Dr. Abhay Jere, Vice-Chairman; Prof. Rajive Kumar, Member Secretary; Dr. Sunil Luthra, Director, and Reena Sharma, Hindi Officer Training and Learning, for their planning to publish this book on Introduction to e-Governance. I am deeply grateful to Prof. Dullu Patnaik of Government Engineering College Bhawanipatna, Orissa who promptly and thoroughly reviewed this book.

His review significantly improved the presentation. The mini project report format for evaluation of e-governance projects are due to his suggestions and guidance. I am thankful to AICTE Graphics Team for designing the cover page nicely.

Special thanks to my family specially my beloved wife Yogita Panwar and sweet daughter Pranshi Verma for their patience and understanding during the countless hours I spent immersed in writing. Your encouragement and love have been my greatest strength.

To my colleagues and peers, thank you for your valuable insights, discussions, and constructive criticism. Your diverse perspectives have enriched this book in ways I could not have imagined.

I extend my gratitude to IILM University Greater Noida (Uttar Pradesh) and COER University Roorkee (Uttarakhand) for providing the resources and support necessary to conduct the writing process.

Lastly, I am grateful to my readers. Your interest and enthusiasm inspire me to continue exploring and sharing new ideas. I hope this book resonates with you and sparks meaningful conversations.

This book is an outcome of various suggestions of AICTE members, experts and authors who shared their opinion and thought to further develop the engineering education in our country. Acknowledgements are due to the contributors and different workers in this field whose published books, review articles, papers, photographs, footnotes, references and other valuable information enriched us at the time of writing the book.

Dr. Kamal Kant Verma

PREFACE

In the rapidly evolving landscape of the digital age, the concept of governance has undergone significant transformation. e-Governance, the application of information and communication technologies to the processes of government functioning, has emerged as a powerful tool to enhance the efficiency, transparency, and accessibility of public services. This book, "Introduction to e-Governance," aims to provide a comprehensive understanding of the principles, practices, and potential of e-governance. It is divided into five units, each of which is based on previous unit.

The first unit consists of various emerging trends in Information & Communication Technology as well as design and implementation of e-governance project and their life cycle. In the subsequent units from two to four, consist of basics of e-governance concepts such as Government Process Re-engineering (GPR), National e-governance Plan (NeGP), SMART Governance, architecture and model of e-governance and various initiative taken by governance for citizen welfare. Together, all four units provide the fundamental understanding of e-governance services. In fifth unit students are advised to submit the mini project based on evaluated report of various national and state level e-governance projects. The book also addresses critical issues such as cybersecurity, data privacy, and the digital divide, which are integral to the successful implementation of e-governance. I encourage the reader to thoroughly comprehended every topic for deeper understanding and see the exercise mentioned at the end of each unit. I also recommend to browse the website of Ministry of Electronics and Information Technology for further understanding of allied topics.

It is my hope that this book will serve as a valuable resource and inspire further exploration and innovation in the field of e-governance. As we navigate the complexities of the digital era, let us embrace the potential of e-governance to create more inclusive, efficient, and transparent systems of governance for the benefit of all.

Dr. Kamal Kant Verma

OUTCOME BASED EDUCATION

For the implementation of an outcome-based education the first requirement is to develop an outcome-based curriculum and incorporate an outcome-based assessment in the education system. By going through outcome-based assessments, evaluators will be able to evaluate whether the students have achieved the outlined standard, specific and measurable outcomes. With the proper incorporation of outcome-based education there will be a definite commitment to achieve a minimum standard for all learners without giving up at any level. At the end of the programme running with the aid of outcome-based education, a student will be able to arrive at the following outcomes:

Programme Outcomes (POs) are statements that describe what students are expected to know and be able to do upon graduating from the program. These relate to the skills, knowledge, analytical ability attitude and behavior that students acquire through the program. The POs essentially indicate what the students can do from subject-wise knowledge acquired by them during the program. As such, POs define the professional profile of an engineering diploma graduate. National Board of Accreditation (NBA) has defined the following seven POs for an Engineering diploma graduate:

National Board of Accreditation (NBA) has defined the following seven POs for an Engineering diploma graduate:

PO1. Basic and Discipline specific knowledge: Apply knowledge of basic mathematics, science and engineering fundamentals and engineering specialization to solve the engineering problems.

PO2. Problem analysis: Identify and analyses well-defined engineering problems using codified standard methods.

PO3. Design/ development of solutions: Design solutions for well-defined technical problems and assist with the design of systems components or processes to meet specified needs.

PO4. Engineering Tools, Experimentation and Testing: Apply modern engineering tools and appropriate technique to conduct standard tests and measurements.

PO5. Engineering practices for society, sustainability and environment: Apply appropriate technology in context of society, sustainability, environment and ethical practices.

PO6. Project Management: Use engineering management principles individually, as a team member or a leader to manage projects and effectively communicate about well-defined engineering activities.

PO7. Life-long learning: Ability to analyse individual needs and engage in updating in the context of technological changes.

COURSE OUTCOMS

At the end of the course students are expected to learn the following:

CO-1: To understand emerging ICT trends in e-governance and life cycle of e-governance.

CO-2: To critically analyze Government Process Re-engineering (GPR) in e-governance.

CO-3: To evaluate e-governance architectural models and role of PPP.

CO-4: To analyze the challenges in e-governance, including corruption, resistance, and e-Security.

CO-5: To assess the impact of Indian e-Governance initiatives through case studies.

CO-6: To develop mini project report based on various e-governance initiatives.

The mapping of the course outcomes with program outcomes to be done as per the following matrix given below:

Course Outcomes	**Expected Mapping with Programme Outcomes** (*1- Weak Correlation; 2- Medium correlation; 3- Strong Correlation*)						
	PO-1	**PO-2**	**PO-3**	**PO-4**	**PO-5**	**PO-6**	**PO-7**
CO-1	3	2	1	2	1	1	2
CO-2	2	3	1	2	2	1	2
CO-3	2	3	2	3	2	1	2
CO-4	2	3	1	2	3	2	2
CO-5	2	2	1	2	3	3	2
CO-6	2	2	3	3	2	3	3

GUIDELINES FOR TEACHERS

To implement Outcome Based Education (OBE) knowledge level and skill set of the students should be enhanced. Teachers should take a major responsibility for the proper implementation of OBE. Some of the responsibilities (not limited to) for the teachers in OBE system may be as follows:

- Within reasonable constraint, they should manoeuvre time to the best advantage of all students.
- They should assess the students only upon certain defined criterion without considering any other potential ineligibility to discriminate them.
- They should try to grow the learning abilities of the students to a certain level before they leave the institute.
- They should try to ensure that all the students are equipped with the quality knowledge as well as competence after they finish their education.
- They should always encourage the students to develop their ultimate performance capabilities.
- They should facilitate and encourage team work to consolidate newer approach.
- They should follow Blooms taxonomy in every part of the assessment.

Bloom's Taxonomy

Level	Teacher should Check	Student should be able to	Possible Mode of Assessment
Create	Students ability to create	Design or Create	Mini project
Evaluate	Students ability to justify	Argue or Defend	Assignment
Analyze	Students ability to distinguish	Differentiate or Distinguish	Project/Lab Methodology
Apply	Students ability to use information	Operate or Demonstrate	Technical Presentation/ Demonstration
Understand	Students ability to explain the ideas	Explain or Classify	Presentation/Seminar
Remember	Students ability to recall (or remember)	Define or Recall	Quiz

GUIDELINES FOR STUDENTS

Students should take equal responsibility for implementing the OBE. Some of the responsibilities (not limited to) for the students in OBE system are as follows:

- Students should be well aware of each UO before the start of a unit in each and every course.
- Students should be well aware of each CO before the start of the course.
- Students should be well aware of each PO before the start of the programme.
- Students should think critically and reasonably with proper reflection and action.
- Learning of the students should be connected and integrated with practical and real-life consequences.
- Students should be well aware of their competency at every level of OBE.

ABBREVIATIONS AND SYMBOLS

List of Abbreviations

General Terms			
Abbreviations	**Full form**	**Abbreviations**	**Full form**
ICT	Information Communication Technology	HIPAA	Health Insurance Portability and Accountability Act
IOT	Internet of Things	AR	Augmented Reality
AIML	Artificial Intelligence Machine Learning	VR	Virtual Reality
SDG	Sustainable Development Goals	ADAS	Advanced Driver Assistance System
WHO	World Health Organization	FIFO	First-In First-Out
EMR	Electronic Medical Record	3GPP	3rd Generation Partnership Project
EHR	Electronic Health Record	ITU	International Telecommunication Union
MPS	Mobile Payment System		
NFC	Near Field Communication	IEEE	Institute of Electrical and Electronics Engineers
QRC	Quick Response Code		
P2P	Peer-to-Peer	ETSI	European Telecommunications Standards Institute
AT	Assistive Technology		
TTS	Text-to-Speech	eMBB	Enhanced Mobile Broadband
AAC	Augmented and Alternative Communication	uRLLC	Ultra-Reliable Low-Latency Communication
WCAG	Web Content Accessibility Guidelines	V2X	vehicle-to-infrastructure
SGDs	Speech Generated Devices	mMTC	Massive Machine-Type Communication
CAT	Cognitive Assistive Technology		
RFID	Radio-Frequency Identification	NLP	Natural Language Processing
CPU	Central Processing Unit	DLT	Distributed ledger technology
MQTT	Message Queuing Telemetry Transport	PoW	Proof of Work
CoAP	Constrained Application Protocol	PoS	Proof of Stake
HTTp	Hyper Text Transfer Protocol	NASM	Netwide Assembler
LPWAN	Low-Power Wide-Area Network	NOP	No Operation
NB-IoT	Narrowband IoT	CAD	Computer-aided design
LoRaWAN	Low Range Wide Area Network	FDM	Fused Deposition Modeling
API	Application Programming Interface	SLA	Service Level Agreement
IIOT	Industrial IOT	RAM	Random Access Memory
HDFS	Hadoop Distributed File System	SLS	Selective Laser Sintering
CRM	Customer relationship management	MFA	Multi-factor authentication
ETL	Data Extraction, Transformation, and Loading	IDPS	Intrusion detection and prevention systems
VPN	Virtual private networks	DBMS	Database Management Systems
IDS	Intrusion Detection Systems	CMS	Content Management Systems
NIC	National Informatics Centre	CMDB	Configuration Management Databases

General Terms

Abbreviations	Full form
UIDAI	Unique Identification Authority of India
NAIM	National Artificial Intelligence Mission
DBT	Direct benefit transfers
RFP	Request for Proposal
GPR	Government Process Re-engineering
NeGP	National e-governance Plan
BPR	Business Process Reengineering
DMAIC	Define Measure Analyze Improve Control
DFSS	Design for Six Sigma
MMP	Mission Mode Project
SWAN	State Wide Area Network
DIT	Department of Information Technology
UT	Union Territory
SDC	State Data Centre
CSC	Common Service Centre
PPP	Public Private Partnership
IVFRT	Immigration, Visa, and Foreigners Registration & Tracking
MCA	Ministry of Corporate Affairs
NGO	Non-Governmental Organization
CCTNS	Crime and Criminal Tracking Network & Systems
EDI	Electronic Data Interchange
VLE	Village Level Entrepreneurs
IAM	Identity and Access Management
SIEM	Security Information and Event Management
WAF	Web Application Firewall
EDR	Endpoint Detection and Response
RBAC	Role-based access controls
SSO	Single Sign-On
DRM	Digital Rights Management
UMANG	Unified Mobile Application for New-age Governance
NSP	National Scholarships Portal
VO	Voluntary Organization
NCoG	National Center of Geo-informatics
PMJDY	Pradhan Mantri Jan Dhan Yojana
ERP	Enterprise Resource Planning
DMS	Document Management Systems
WPA	Workflow and Process Automation
BI	Business Intelligence
GIS	Geographic Information Systems
MDM	Master Data Management
CIO	Chief Information Officer
PMO	Project Management Offices
KPI	Key Performance Indicators
G2C	Government-to-Citizen
G2B	Government-to-Business
BRS	Australia's Business Registration Service
GeM	India's Government e-Marketplace
G2G	Government-to-Government
G2E	Government-to-Employee
C2G	Citizen-to-Government
G2P	Government-to-Partner
UNDP	United Nations Development Programme
BOT	Build-Operate-Transfer
DBFO	Design-Build-Finance-Operate
LDO	Lease-Develop-Operate
TNA	Training Needs Analysis
LMS	Learning Management Systems
CSF	Critical Success Factor
ROI	Return on Investment
DDOS	Distributed Denial of Service
SME	Small and medium enterprises
EKVI	E-Agricultural Marketing
RAP	Rural Authorized Person
B2C	Business to consumer
MTS	Money Transfer Service
PAN	Permanent Account Number
GST	Goods and Services Tax
ITR	Income Tax Return
TDS	Tax Deduction at Source
PSK	Passport Seva Kendras
MEA	Ministry of External Affairs

General Terms			
Abbreviations	**Full form**	**Abbreviations**	**Full form**
SECC	Socio-Economic Caste Census	POPSK	Post Office Passport Seva Kendra
HWC	Health and Wellness Centres	PCC	Police Clearance Certificate
RTC	Record of Rights, Tenancy and Crops	ECNR	Emigration Check Not Required
KMS	Knowledge Management System	NFSA	National Food Security Act
CPIS	Centralized Personnel Information System	PRI	Panchayati Raj Institutions
PMVVY	Pradhan Mantri Vaya Vandana Yojana	NJDG	National Judicial Data Grid
IGNOAPS	Indira Gandhi National Old Age Pension Scheme	AEPS	Aadhar Enabled Payment System
		NDLM	National Digital Literacy Mission
FIF	Financial Inclusion Fund	KAVERI	Karnataka Valuation and e-Registration
FLCC	Financial Literacy and Credit Counseling Centers	CCC	Citizen Care Centres
		AMRUT	Atal Mission for Rejuvenation and Urban Transformation
NLRMP	National Land Records Modernization Programme		

LIST OF FIGURES

Unit 1: Introduction to e-Governance

Unit 2: Government Process Re-engineering

LIST OF TABLES

TABLE OF CONTENT

1 Introduction to e-Governance

UNIT SPECIFIES

Through this unit we discuss the following aspects:

- *Exposure to emerging trends in ICT for development*
- *Understanding of design and implementation of e-Government projects*
- *e-governance lifecycle*

RATIONALE

This introductory units gets reader acquainted with the exposure to emerging trends in ICT including current and related topics on main ICT trends along with their applications have been discussed. Then in subsequent section, understanding the design and implementation of e-Government projects is discussed which improves accessibility, transparency, and citizen engagement while reducing costs. We end this unit by introducing the e-governance lifecycle which ensure a structured, risk-managed approach, continuous improvement, stakeholder involvement, and optimal resource utilization.

PRE-REQUESITE

None

UNIT OUTCOMES

List of the outcomes of this unit is as follows:

U1-O1: To understand the basics of various ICT trends

U1-O2: To understand the design and implementation of e-governance projects

U1-O3: To analyze the various e-governance project initiatives

U1-O4: To understand the e-governance project life cycle

Unit-1 Outcomes	**Expected Mapping with Programme Outcomes** (*1- Weak Correlation; 2- Medium correlation; 3- Strong Correlation*)					
	CO-1	**CO-2**	**CO-3**	**CO-4**	**CO-5**	**CO-6**
U1-O1	3	1	1	1	1	0
U1-O2	2	2	1	1	1	1
U1-O3	2	1	3	2	2	2
U1-O4	3	1	2	2	2	3

1.1 Exposure to emerging trends in ICT for development

The term *"Information and Communication Technologies" (ICTs)* refers to any digital device, tool, content, resource, forum, and service, as well as those that can be converted into or delivered through digital platforms, that can be used to achieve the objectives of learning and teaching, improving resource access and reach, developing capacities, and managing the educational system.

This is not only containing hardware components linked to the computer program and software, but also contain digital interactive content, satellite-based communications tools, internet, television and other interactive communications ways such as telecommunication services other interactive discussion forums, management information systems, and learning management system.

The main agenda for sustainable development in 2024 is to deliver an action plan that can achieve environmentally, socially and economically sustainable future. Information and Communication Technologies (ICTs) play an important role for 2030 agenda of sustainable development. Their adoption and spread throughout society's domains offer new methods to persistent development problems.

It becomes really critical for government officials and policymakers to properly aware of recent trends and technologies in order to fully utilize the potential benefits of ICT in rapid changing environment as soon as a new technology came into existence along with its increased connectivity.

The purpose of this section is to present and pertinent information on the main ICT trends along with its implications.

1. Digital Healthcare
2. Mobile Payments
3. Assistive Technologies
4. Internet of Things (IOT)
5. 5th Generation Mobile Networks
6. Artificial Intelligence and Machine Learning
7. Blockchain and Shared Ledgers
8. 3D Printing
9. Big Data Analytics
10. Cybersecurity Measures

The topic included in this section are chosen because they are important to attaining the Sustainable Development Goals (SDGs). A broad representative sample encompassing a variety of technical domains, including hardware, software, networking, and data, as well as application domains (such as healthcare, finance, and disability), is another goal of the themes chosen.

Every topic first begins with an overview of the technology's importance and components and then it describes the significant use cases and application areas. Furthermore, a discussion of the policy implications pertaining to standards & regulations, and connections to the SDGs is mentioned. Each topic may differ significantly to emphasis important points.

1.1.1 Digital Healthcare

The need for healthcare has grown rapidly. However, due to the shortage of infrastructure, financial resources, and human resources, the population's needs for healthcare have not been met by the healthcare system. Government spending on public health has remained mostly unchanged, despite an increase in out-of-pocket medical expenses. Statistics from the World Health Organization (WHO) show that approximately half of health spending in countries including Afghanistan, Cambodia, India, Myanmar, and Pakistan goes towards out-of-pocket costs. Moreover, fewer than one physician for every 1000 people is estimated to be in poor condition in 44% of WHO member countries. Developments in digital healthcare can aid in addressing the issues the healthcare industry is currently facing, especially with reference to these trends in healthcare and the rapidly expanding and evolving field of information and communication technology(ICT). Figure 1.1 shows the different stakeholders involved in digital healthcare ecosystem.

Figure 1.1: Intersection of Various Stakeholders in the Digital Healthcare Ecosystem

a) Digital Healthcare and SDGs

The Sustainable Development Goal (SDG) is all about well-being and good health. This goal's objectives include preventing HIV/AIDS-related mortality, putting an end to numerous epidemics and infectious diseases, and enhancing access to medications and vaccinations. In order to meet these objectives and provide universal health coverage—a point that the World Health Organization has emphasized—nations have been developing strategies and putting plans into action to enhance healthcare accessibility. The use of ICT in healthcare has proven a crucial tactic in this approach. In actuality, a WHO report promotes electronic health, or e-health, as a way to advance the SDGs and the objective of reaching universal health coverage.

b) Digital Healthcare Definition and Scope

ICTs have been considered to be crucial in the last several decades in the areas of "health and health-related fields, including healthcare services, monitoring of health, health literature, and health education, knowledge, and research". Although the majority of work in this field have been focused on enhancing the present healthcare service delivery systems, efforts have also been made to build technology that might offer stand-alone healthcare services. These changes have an impact on how the three primary participants in the health system—providers, patients, and payers—interact with one another.

c) Various Components in Digital Healthcare

i. m-health Solutions

Mobile computing and communication technologies are being used more and more in public health and healthcare as a result of the development of mobile technologies and the rise in worldwide mobile data usage over time. The vast array of m-health initiatives and implementations across the globe attests to the fact that mobile health, or m-health, has emerged as a significant element of digital healthcare.

The most popular features to use when creating m-health solutions are messaging via text capabilities. Additional features contain voice, video, multimedia messaging apps, add-ons (like a glucometer), and native applications. These are usually employed for consultations, handling emergencies, education and information dissemination, monitoring and surveillance of health, and interaction among healthcare providers and patients. Several m-health solutions and devices have encountered obstacles, even if some have been effectively scaled up throughout the health system.

ii. Telemedicine

The practice of providing healthcare treatments to patients remotely via telecommunications is known as telemedicine. This could involve patient monitoring and many types of clinical diagnostics. The phrase has become synonymous with the word "telehealth" over time, encompassing the use of ICT for non-clinical tasks related to the healthcare system. The individual receiving medical care and the healthcare professional can communicate via phone, electronic mail, or a videoconferencing, and the connection can be asynchronous (store and forward) or real-time. The various telemedicine projects that were reported comprise teleradiology, tele-dermatology, telepathology, telepsychiatry, and monitoring patients remotely, according to WHO's third worldwide assessment on e-health.

Like m-health, telehealth also refers to projects that aim to increase knowledge and understanding accessibility, offer a forum for stakeholder networking and collaboration, assist in policy development, promote health training and education, and enhance public accountability within the healthcare system.

iii. Health Information System

A health information system of a country includes data production, compilation, communication, analysis and synthesis. The health information systems are designed to provide the effective decision-making at various levels such as individual, facility and country levels of any health system. It is anticipated that the development of strong and robust health information system will facilitate improved research and planning, illness and pandemic management, health & facility management, and assessment & tracking.

iv. Electronic Medical Records and Medical Practice Management Software

An electronic m record (EMR) is used to maintain the medical history of patients through a specific healthcare facility. The main reason of this change is attributed primarily to ease of storage and retrieval. With the use of medical practice management software, healthcare providers and other staff members may monitor the patients who come into their facility and give patients access to pertinent information. One such programs is Practo

Ray, which has functions for patient appointment reminders in addition to handling patient records. It also manages billing and accounts for administrative and financial purposes.

v. Electronic Health Record

Compared to an EMR, an electronic health record (EHR) has an extensive record of the patient's health history since it incorporates information from other physicians who are participating in the patient's treatment. Updates and exchanges of patient information, including prescriptions, diagnoses, and doctor's notes, are possible for authorized medical practitioners.

Patients and doctors at various locations can easily access patient medical record items due to a well-organized EHR system. EHR systems provide individuals with the necessary medical information through previous interactions within the health system, allowing them to transfer across medical facilities as long as they adhere to the required interoperability standards.

This increases the effectiveness of healthcare delivery by preventing unnecessary repetition of effort on the part of physicians and other healthcare providers when they create treatment plans that are suitable for their patients. Additionally, by using aggregated patient data from the EHR system, physicians, and other healthcare providers, the government can gain a better understanding of illness trends and health-related behaviors of the people for whom the data is available.

The use of EMRs and EHRs introduces a number of important issues, including ownership and access, security, confidentiality and privacy of health data, and the legal ramifications of maintaining such information. There are additional difficulties in implementing the systems, which needs modifying the behavior and methods of medical practitioners. The deficiency of system standardization and compatibility, as well as the high deployment and maintenance costs, are further obstacles. As a result of all these difficulties, the WHO published a handbook on the deployment of EHRs for developing nations.

Table 1.1 Some of the benefits of Digitizing Healthcare for Patients, Player and Providers

	Patients	Providers	Payers
Electronic Medical Record (EMR)	Easier to read and understand	Easy storage and retrieval; improved efficiency and productivity	Streamlined processes and faster service
Electronic Health Record (EHR)	Better diagnosis and treatment	Coordination and informed decision-making	Faster reimbursement
Personal Health Records	Personal wellness management	Consistency of information	Links to healthcare plans and lower claims
Remote Diagnostics	Reduces duplicated tests and referrals	Easy access	Lower cost
Remote Monitoring	Patient-centric integrated care	Reduce emergency and re-admissions	Lower cost

Telecare	Access to specialist care	Improves productivity and reduces burden of healthcare resources	Lower cost
mHealth applications	Greater patient engagement and saves time	Proactive and targeted care	Enhanced patient management and reduced claim costs
Big Data Analytics	Accurate diagnosis, better treatment	Improves diagnostics and accuracy of treatment	Lower cost

a) Possible benefits of ICT in Health

According to a comprehensive review about 100 studies on telehealth showed the enhancements in quality of healthcare is due to the major impact of employing in healthcare sectors. This was followed by developments in accessibility and cost-minimization.

Digital health technology has benefited medical professionals by decreasing paper documentation, admissions to hospitals, bed days, and enhancing face-to-face patient time. Many of these technologies minimize the usage of medical facilities that can be prevented, encourage patient independence, and emphasis on preventative care. Each of these improves the results for patients. Under such circumstances, patients are enabled to engage with their medical providers through different communication channels, training, and self-management. This suggests that the "paternalistic model of healthcare" will give way to a model of "empowered patient sharing ownership." Table 1.1 shows some benefits of using various types of digital healthcare technologies. After carefully seeing the table, better quality and cost saving are the main benefits of using healthcare technologies.

b) Digital Health Strategies and Policies

With the increase of various kind of healthcare technologies, there is an urgent requirement of well-defined legislative and regulatory structures addressing the numerous aspects of e-health systems. These regulations are necessary on a worldwide scale in addition to inside individual nations. Every region and nation require a policy framework that takes into account the environment in which ICT is being used. This is crucial, particularly for poor nations where it might be difficult to replicate or model effective ICT initiatives from rich nations if the context is overlooked.

The Broadband Communication for Sustainable Development established a Group on Digital Health in 2015. It released a documented report in 2017 that focused on financing, governance, and the establishment of national frameworks which take into account various points such as connectivity, interoperability, and common standards. The report also highlighted the role of government leadership and cooperation in improving the role of ICTs in healthcare.

In a survey conducted by the WHO Global Observatory for eHealth, 73 countries that participated out of 125 that responded (or around 58 percent) said they had some kind of e-health plan in place. Nonetheless, a greater proportion (about 66%) stated that they had a plan in place for a health information system. Regarding privacy laws, about 78% of these nations have said to have any regulations governing personally identifiable information.

Although, these regulations may sometimes have an unclear and imprecise goal. Some Asian countries such as Singapore, Thailand, Korea, China, India, Indonesia, Malaysia, and Singapore, have national e-health policies in place. But since they have only been in place for a few years, it is still too early to determine their effects. The use of e-health methods by countries from 1990 to 2015 is shown in Figure 1.2.

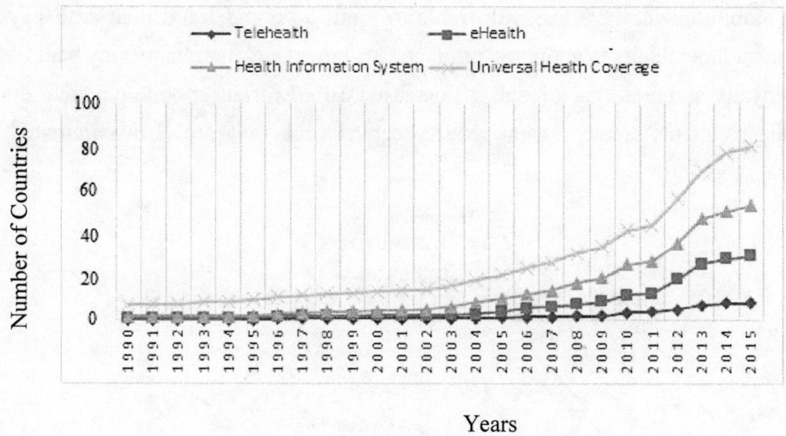

Figure 1.2: Shows the Universal health coverage, eHealth, Health Information System and Telehealth policies for various countries from 1990 to 2015.

1.1.2 Mobile Payment

The crucial element of any standard financial system consists of platforms, methods, regulations and defined procedures to "enable the settlement and clearing of financial transactions and money related services. The conventional method of payment is cash. Simultaneously, a number of physical and digital payment methods, such as credit and debit cards, facilitate cashless transactions globally. Technological advancements and banking improvements have impacted how the financial system—particularly the payment system—and its users/stakeholders communicate with one another.

a) Advantages of Mobile Payment Systems

The introduction of digital payment technologies has increased the momentum towards the goal of establishing a cashless society. According to research studies, handling cash has significant both direct and indirect costs that are unsafe to society, especially for the community belonging to lower income category. Several methods of cashless payment have been encouraged by this, particularly when employing digital or mobile payment technologies. The online and mobile payment systems have been connected with the current cashless payment methods, such as credit and debit cards.

It is expensive to provide gain access to traditional financial services, particularly in remote locations. On the other hand, the widespread use of cell phones has made it possible to reach out to underprivileged and unbanked populations as well as the general public with a variety of financial services. For instance, banks can save an enormous amount of money because fewer ATMs are needed when using mobile phones for banking and transferring cash. The use of smartphones for payment has made sending financial transfers and making cross-border payments more affordable and convenient. Such money transfers are expected to promote growth through increased transactions and money transfers between countries. Mobile operators can also get cost benefits as tapping the potential for mobile payments market in the rural and developing regions is expected to improve their average revenue per user. The reduction in transaction costs and improved efficiency (that enables speed and liquidity of money) have been major factors in improving productivity.

Since the majority of mobile payment systems come with appropriate security safeguards, it is thought that payments made via mobile devices are less vulnerable to theft, loss, and fraud than cash payments. This encourages customers and merchants to adopt the product. Customers and merchants may benefit from value-added services like loyalty and credit as a result of increased use of certain mobile payment options. Since electronic and mobile payments create a clear record-keeping trail, they are also anticipated to increase accountability and transparency.

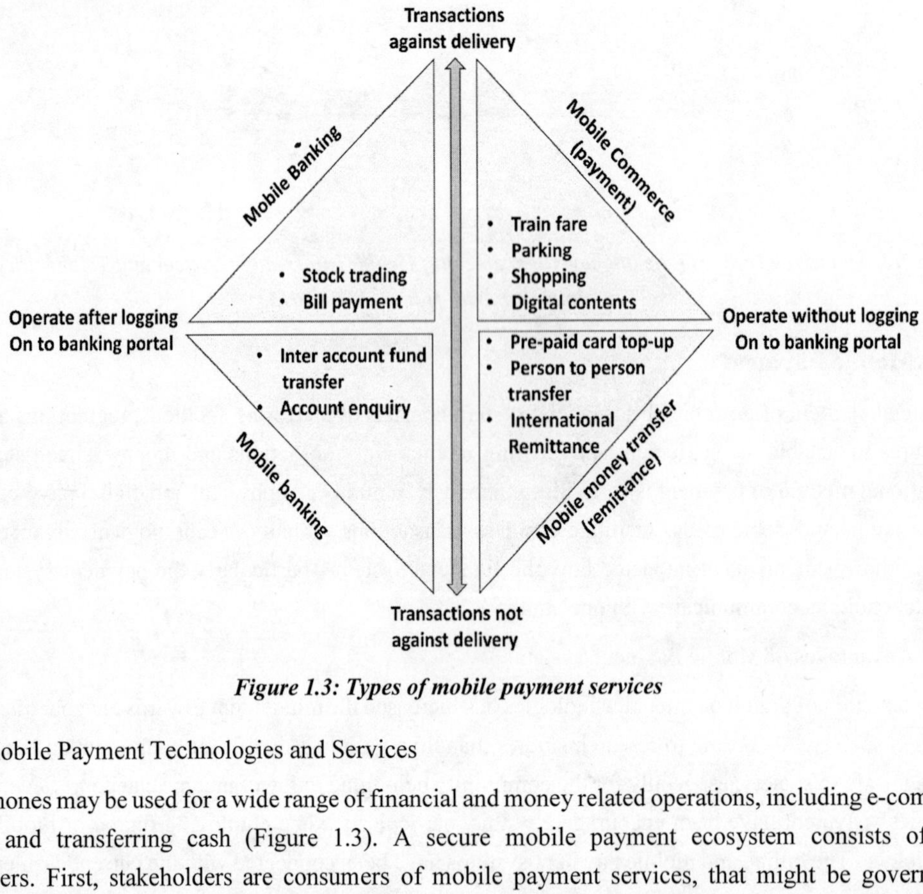

Figure 1.3: Types of mobile payment services

b) Mobile Payment Technologies and Services

Mobile phones may be used for a wide range of financial and money related operations, including e-commerce, banking, and transferring cash (Figure 1.3). A secure mobile payment ecosystem consists of many stakeholders. First, stakeholders are consumers of mobile payment services, that might be governments, companies, retailers, and individuals. Second, may be providers of mobile payment services that includes non-banking organizations such as mobile operators, mobile money stores, and cryptocurrency trading platforms, as well as financial firms and banks. Thirdly, stakeholders are those who provide required infrastructure and support services. This category includes policymakers and technology suppliers.

Mobile payment technologies and services refer to the systems and methods that enable users to make financial transactions using their mobile devices, such as smartphones or tablets. These technologies have gained significant popularity due to their convenience, security, and accessibility. Here are some key aspects of mobile payment technologies and services:

i. Near Field Communication (NFC): NFC enables two devices to communicate when they are in close proximity (usually within a few centimeters). This technology is commonly used in contactless payment systems where the mobile device is tapped or waved near a compatible terminal to complete a transaction. Examples include Apple Pay, Google Pay, and Samsung Pay.

ii. QR Code Payments: QR (Quick Response) codes are two-dimensional barcodes that can be scanned using a smartphone camera. QR code payment systems allow users to make payments by scanning a QR code displayed at the point of sale. Popular examples include Alipay and WeChat Pay in China.

iii. Mobile Wallets: Mobile wallets are digital versions of traditional wallets that store payment card information, loyalty cards, tickets, and more. Users can make payments by accessing their mobile wallet app and selecting the desired payment method. Examples include Apple Wallet, Google Wallet (now Google Pay), and Samsung Pay.

iv. Peer-to-Peer (P2P) Payments: P2P payment services allow individuals to transfer money directly to one another using their mobile devices. These services are often used for splitting bills, repaying debts, or sending money to family and friends. Popular P2P payment apps include Venmo, Cash App, and PayPal.

v. Mobile Banking Apps: Many banks offer mobile banking apps that allow customers to manage their accounts, transfer funds, pay bills, and make purchases directly from their mobile devices. These apps often integrate mobile payment functionalities, providing users with a convenient way to conduct financial transactions on the go.

vi. Biometric Authentication: Mobile payment services increasingly incorporate biometric authentication methods such as fingerprint scanning, facial recognition, or iris scanning to enhance security and streamline the payment process. Biometric data adds an extra layer of protection against unauthorized access to sensitive financial information.

vii. Tokenization: Tokenization replaces sensitive card information (such as credit card numbers) with unique digital tokens during transactions, reducing the risk of fraud. Mobile payment systems often utilize tokenization to secure payment data transmitted between the mobile device and the payment terminal.

Overall, mobile payment technologies and services continue to evolve rapidly, offering consumers and businesses innovative ways to conduct financial transactions securely and conveniently using their mobile devices.

a) Benefits of Mobile Payments:

i. Convenience: No need to carry cash or physical cards.

ii. Speed: Transactions are processed quickly and efficiently.

iii. Security: Mobile wallets often use tokenization, where a unique digital identifier is used instead of your actual card number, reducing the risk of fraud.

iv. Rewards: Some mobile wallets offer loyalty points or cashback programs.

b) Things to Consider:

i. Smartphone Compatibility: Ensure your phone has the necessary features like near field communication (NFC) for contactless payments.

ii. App Availability: Not all merchants accept all mobile payment methods.

iii. Security: While generally secure, be cautious about using public Wi-Fi for transactions and keep your phone's software updated.

1.1.3 Assistive Technology

Assistive Technology (AT) in the realm of Information and Communication Technology (ICT) refers to the utilization of technology to facilitate access to digital information and communication for individuals with disabilities. It encompasses a broad range of hardware, software, and services designed to mitigate barriers and enable equal participation in the digital world.

ICT-based assistive technology aims to address various disabilities, including visual, auditory, physical, cognitive, and speech impairments. Here's an overview of some key aspects:

Accessibility Features: Many mainstream ICT devices, software, and online platforms incorporate built-in accessibility features to accommodate diverse user needs. These features include screen readers, magnification tools, speech recognition, captioning, keyboard shortcuts, and adjustable display settings. By activating these features, individuals with disabilities can interact with digital content more effectively.

Screen Readers and Text-to-Speech (TTS): Screen readers are software applications that convert on-screen text into synthesized speech or braille output, enabling individuals with visual impairments to access digital content. Text-to-Speech (TTS) technology also plays a vital role in converting written text into spoken words, enhancing accessibility for users who have difficulty reading.

Augmentative and Alternative Communication (AAC) Systems: AAC systems leverage ICT to support individuals with speech and language disabilities in expressing themselves. These systems encompass various tools, such as communication apps, speech-generating devices, picture boards, and symbol-based communication software, empowering users to communicate effectively in different contexts.

Adaptive Input Devices: Adaptive input devices modify standard computer peripherals to accommodate the needs of users with physical disabilities. Examples include alternative keyboards, switches, joystick controllers, trackballs, and mouth-operated input devices, which enable individuals with limited mobility to navigate digital interfaces and input commands.

Specialized Software and Applications: A wide range of specialized software and applications cater to specific accessibility needs. This includes screen magnification software, closed-captioning tools, alternative web browsers optimized for accessibility, voice recognition software, and cognitive assistance tools designed to support individuals with learning disabilities.

Web Accessibility Standards: Web accessibility guidelines, such as the Web Content Accessibility Guidelines (WCAG), outline best practices for making digital content accessible to individuals with disabilities. These standards cover aspects such as content structure, navigation, multimedia accessibility, color contrast, and keyboard operability, ensuring that websites and web applications are usable by all users, regardless of their abilities.

Assistive Mobile Apps: Mobile applications offer a wide range of assistive features for smartphones and tablets, including screen readers, magnifiers, voice assistants, text-to-speech converters, AAC apps, and accessible navigation tools. These apps empower users to access information, communicate, and perform tasks on portable devices conveniently.

By leveraging ICT-based assistive technology, individuals with disabilities can overcome barriers to accessing and using digital resources, participate more fully in education, employment, social interactions, entertainment, and enhance their overall quality of life. Additionally, as technology continues to advance, the potential for innovation in ICT-based assistive solutions continues to expand, offering new opportunities for inclusivity and accessibility in the digital age.

a) Need of Assistive Technology

The need for Assistive Technologies (AT) in the realm of Information and Communication Technology (ICT) is critical for several reasons:

Accessibility for All: ICT has become ubiquitous in modern society, with digital platforms and services playing an increasingly central role in education, employment, communication, healthcare, and daily life. AT ensures that individuals with disabilities can access and utilize ICT resources on an equal basis with others, promoting inclusivity and eliminating barriers to participation in the digital world.

Equal Access to Information: Access to information is a fundamental right, yet individuals with disabilities may face challenges in accessing digital content due to barriers such as inaccessible websites, untagged images, or videos without captions. AT tools like screen readers, text-to-speech software, and captioning solutions make digital information accessible to users with visual, auditory, or cognitive impairments, ensuring equal access to educational materials, online resources, and communication platforms.

Communication Accessibility: ICT plays a crucial role in facilitating communication, but individuals with speech or language disabilities may encounter difficulties in expressing themselves or accessing communication platforms. AT solutions such as speech-generating devices, AAC software, and alternative keyboards enable individuals with communication disabilities to communicate effectively, participate in conversations, and engage in digital communication channels.

Digital Inclusion in Education: Inclusive education aims to provide equitable learning opportunities for all students, including those with disabilities. AT in ICT enables students with disabilities to access digital learning materials, participate in online courses, and utilize educational technology tools tailored to their needs. By promoting accessibility and accommodation in educational ICT environments, AT fosters equal opportunities for academic success and lifelong learning.

Employment Opportunities: In the workplace, ICT skills are increasingly essential for accessing job opportunities, performing tasks, and communicating with colleagues and clients. AT assists individuals with disabilities in overcoming barriers to employment by providing accessible software, adaptive hardware, and assistive communication tools that enable them to effectively perform job tasks, access digital work platforms, and communicate with coworkers.

Compliance with Accessibility Standards: Governments and organizations worldwide have adopted accessibility standards and regulations, such as the Web Content Accessibility Guidelines (WCAG), to ensure that digital content and ICT systems are accessible to individuals with disabilities. AT solutions help organizations achieve compliance with these standards by implementing accessible design practices, incorporating assistive features, and conducting accessibility testing to ensure that digital products and services are usable by all users.

Enhancing User Experience: Accessibility benefits not only individuals with disabilities but also the general population by improving the usability and user experience of digital products and services. AT features such as keyboard shortcuts, voice commands, and customizable display settings provide options for users to personalize their interactions with ICT devices and software, enhancing usability, productivity, and satisfaction for all users.

Overall, the integration of Assistive Technologies in ICT is essential for promoting digital inclusion, accessibility, and equitable access to information and communication resources for individuals with disabilities. By addressing barriers and providing accommodations, AT empowers individuals to fully participate in the digital society, benefit from technological advancements, and contribute to social, economic, and cultural activities on an equal basis with others.

b) Types of Assistive Technology

Assistive technology (AT) is any device, software, or equipment that helps people with disabilities perform tasks they might have difficulty with otherwise. There are many different types of assistive technology, designed to meet the needs of people with a wide range of disabilities. Broadly assistive technology may be divided in to following three categories such as personal assistive devices, adaptive assistive devices and cognitive assistive devices.

Personal assistive devices are tools or equipment designed to assist individuals in their daily activities, mobility, communication, and overall independence. These devices are tailored to meet the specific needs of the user and can greatly enhance their quality of life. Here are some examples of personal assistive devices.

i. Wheelchairs: It is a vital type of assistive technology for people with mobility limitations. They come in two main categories Manual or powered chairs used by individuals with mobility impairments to move around independently.

ii. Manual wheelchairs: These are propelled by the user themself, using their hands on the hand rims. Manual wheelchairs come in a variety of styles, weights, and features to suit different needs and preferences. Figure 1.4 shows manual wheel chair.

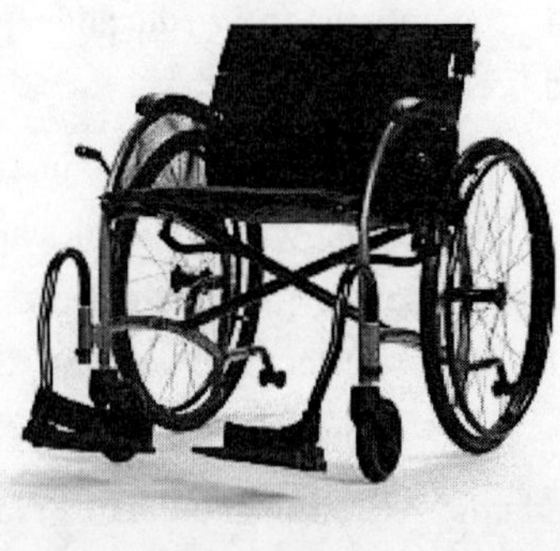

Figure 1.4: Manual wheel chair as an assistive technology

iii. Powered wheelchairs: Also known as electric wheelchairs, these are battery-operated and controlled by a joystick or other control device. Powered wheelchairs can be a good option for people who don't have the upper body strength to propel a manual wheelchair, or for those who need to travel long distances. Figure 1.5 shows the powered wheel chair for assistive technology

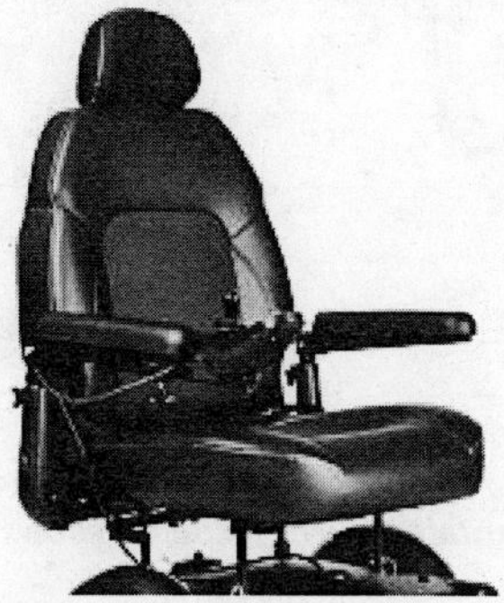

Figure 1.5: Powered wheel chair as an assistive technology

iv. Canes and Crutches: Assistive devices for individuals with mobility issues, providing support and stability while walking.

- *Canes and Crutches:* Assistive devices for individuals with mobility issues, providing support and stability while walking.
- *Hearing Aids:* Small electronic devices worn in or behind the ear to amplify sound for individuals with hearing impairments.
- *Visual Aids:* Devices such as magnifiers, electronic reading machines, and Braille displays used by individuals with visual impairments to read and access information.
- *Communication Aids:* Speech-generating devices (SGDs), text-to-speech software, communication boards, and other tools to assist individuals with speech or language difficulties.
- *Prosthetics:* Artificial limbs designed to replace missing body parts and restore mobility and function. Figure 1.6 show the upper limb prosthetics which replace arms and hands. They can range from simple devices that help with gripping objects to complex myoelectric prosthetics that can be controlled by muscle signals.

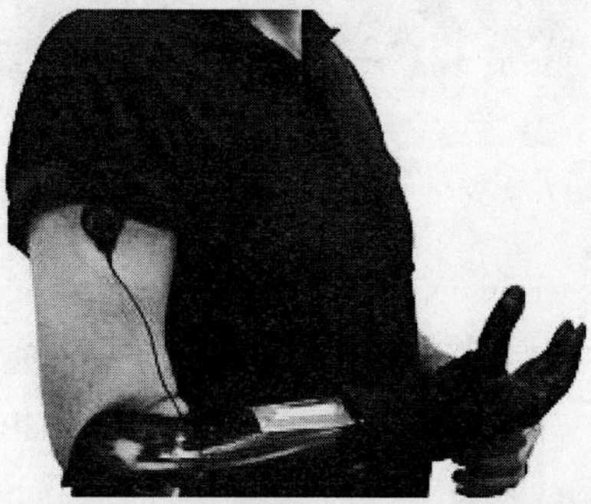

Figure 1.6: shows the Upper limb prosthetics

- *Medical Alert Systems:* Wearable devices or home-based systems that enable individuals to call for help in case of emergencies and shown in figure 1.7 (a) and (b).

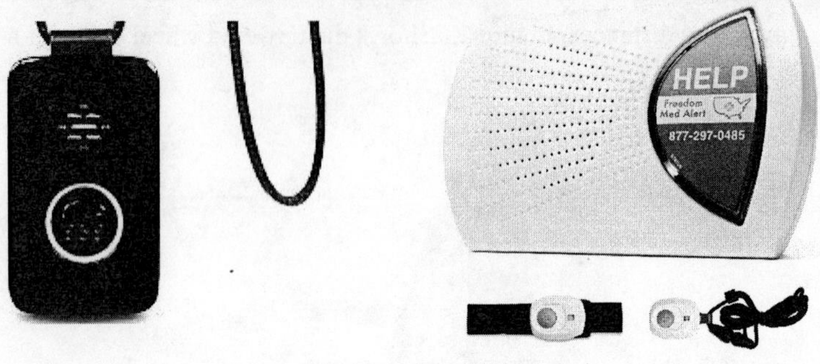

(a) (b)

Figure 1.7: (a) shows the wearable devices while (b) shows the home-based system

- *Medication Management Devices:* Pill organizers, automatic pill dispensers, and reminder systems to help individuals manage their medications independently.

v. Adaptive assistive devices: are specialized tools or equipment designed to accommodate the unique needs of individuals with disabilities or limitations. These devices are tailored to provide assistance, support, or accessibility in various aspects of daily living. Here are some examples of adaptive assistive devices.

- Screen Recorder: A computer screen reader is a type of assistive technology that allows blind or visually impaired people to interact with computers. It functions by reading aloud the text on the screen, as well as describing any images or graphical elements. Screen readers shown in figure 1.8 also allow users to navigate through menus and dialogs, and to fill out forms.

Figure 1.8: Screen recorder as an assistive technology

- *Adaptive Seating:* Chairs, cushions, and seating systems designed to provide comfort and support for individuals with mobility impairments or postural challenges.

- *Adaptive Utensils and Eating Aids:* Modified eating utensils, plate guards, adaptive cups, and specialized dining equipment to assist individuals with limited hand dexterity or mobility in feeding themselves.

- *Adaptive Clothing:* Clothing with features such as Velcro closures, magnetic fasteners, elastic waistbands, and adaptive designs to make dressing easier for individuals with mobility or dexterity limitations.
- *Adaptive Bathroom Equipment:* Grab bars, shower chairs, raised toilet seats, and other bathroom aids to enhance safety and accessibility for individuals with mobility challenges.
- *Adaptive Computer Accessories:* Ergonomic keyboards, alternative mouse devices, voice recognition software, and other computer peripherals designed to accommodate individuals with mobility, vision, or cognitive impairments.
- *Adaptive Sports and Recreation Equipment:* Wheelchair basketball chairs, adaptive bicycles, specialized prosthetics for sports, and other equipment tailored to enable individuals with disabilities to participate in various recreational activities.
- *Adaptive Driving Controls:* Hand controls, pedal extensions, steering wheel knobs, and other vehicle modifications to make driving accessible for individuals with physical disabilities.
- *Adaptive Gardening Tools:* Ergonomic garden tools, raised garden beds, and adaptive equipment designed to facilitate gardening for individuals with mobility or strength limitations.
- *Adaptive Mobility Aids:* Customized walkers, rollators, canes, and mobility scooters designed to meet the specific needs and preferences of individuals with mobility impairments.
- *Adaptive Learning Tools:* Tactile learning materials, large-print textbooks, audio books, and other adaptive educational resources for individuals with visual, hearing, or learning disabilities.

vi. Another example of assistive device: is glasses with technology-enabled cameras. These are electronic glasses or smart glasses specifically designed to assist people with visual impairments. They incorporate small cameras within the frame that capture the user's surroundings. Paired with advanced software and sometimes other sensors, these glasses offer various functionalities to enhance the user's experience. Figure 1.9 shows the smart goggle with technology enabled camera system.

Figure 1.9: Smart goggle with technology enabled camera

Additionally, there are numerous visually challenged mobile apps that are easily accessible on a mobile device. For example, Color identification applications are indeed a valuable form of assistive technology, particularly for individuals who are blind or have visual impairments. These apps leverage the camera functionality of mobile devices to detect and identify colors in the user's environment, providing auditory or tactile feedback to convey this information.

These are just a few examples of adaptive assistive devices, and there are many more available to address a wide range of needs and preferences among individuals with disabilities. The goal of adaptive technology is to promote independence, accessibility, and inclusion for people of all abilities.

The third types of assistive devices are cognitive assistive technologies (CATs) tools that help people with cognitive disabilities manage daily tasks and activities. These disabilities can affect memory, attention, planning, problem-solving, and other thinking skills. Here are some examples of CATs.

- *Memory aid based Digital Calendars and Reminders*: These can be set on smartphones, computers, or tablets to provide visual and auditory alerts for appointments, medications, or to-do lists. Figure 1.10 shows computer based digital calendar.

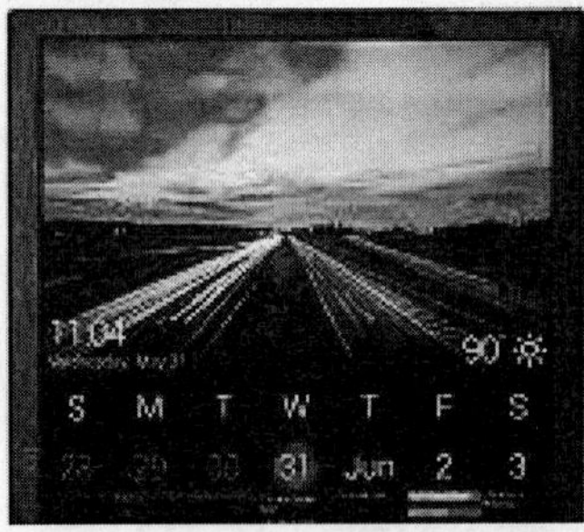

Figure 1.10 shows digital calendar

- *Daily Planners and Checklists:* Paper-based or digital planners with checklists can help users break down tasks into smaller steps, prioritize activities, and track progress. Figure 1.11 shows the daily planners and checklists tool.

Figure 1.11 Daily planners and checklists

- *Picture Communication Boards:* These boards contain pictures or symbols that allow users to point to express their needs and wants. They can be especially helpful for people with limited verbal communication skills. Figure 1.12 shows the picture communication board.

Figure 1.12 Picture communication board used to express their needs.

- *Word Prediction Software:* This software suggests words as the user starts typing, reducing errors and improving efficiency for those with slower typing speeds or difficulty spelling. Figure 1.13 shows the word prediction software used on computer screen.

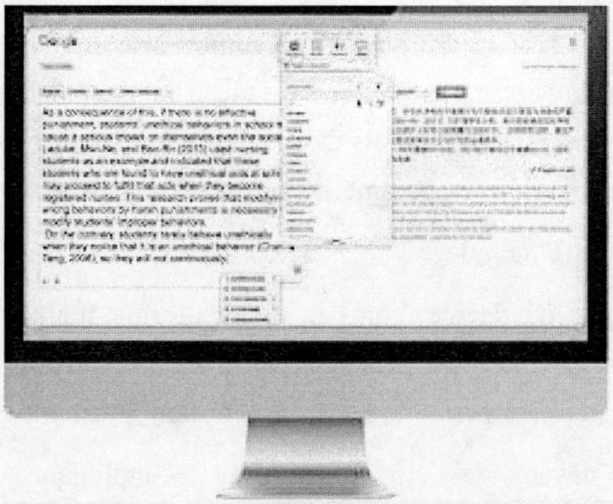

Figure 1.13 Word prediction software used on computer screen

- *Text-to-speech Software:* This software reads aloud the text on a computer screen, which can be beneficial for people with reading difficulties or learning disabilities such as dyslexia. Figure 1.14 show the text to speech software as an assistive tool for disable persons.

Figure 1.14 Text to speech software on computer screen

- *Noise-Cancelling Headphones:* These headphones block out background noise and distractions, improving focus in noisy environments. Figure 1.15 shows the noise cancelling headphone

Figure 1.15 Noise cancelling headphone device

1.1.4 Internet of Things (IOT)

The Internet of Things (IoT) refers to a network of interconnected devices embedded with sensors, software, and other technologies that enable them to collect and exchange data with each other and with central systems over the internet. In simpler terms, IoT encompasses any device or object that can connect to the internet and communicate with other devices or systems.

The concept of IoT revolves around the idea of creating a seamlessly interconnected network of physical objects, ranging from everyday consumer devices to industrial machinery, vehicles, and infrastructure. These objects are equipped with sensors and actuators that allow them to gather data from their environment, analyze it, and take actions based on predefined parameters or user commands.

a) Key components of IoT include:

i. Devices and Sensors: IoT devices come in various forms, including smartphones, wearable gadgets, smart home appliances, industrial sensors, and many more. These devices are equipped with sensors that collect data such as temperature, humidity, motion, location,

ii. Connectivity: IoT devices rely on connectivity technologies such as Wi-Fi, Bluetooth, cellular networks, Zigbee, and RFID (Radio-Frequency Identification) to transmit data to other devices or centralized systems over the internet.

iii. Data Processing and Analytics: The vast amounts of data generated by IoT devices need to be processed, analyzed, and interpreted to extract meaningful insights. Cloud computing platforms, edge computing solutions, and analytics algorithms play a crucial role in handling IoT data and deriving actionable intelligence from it.

iv. Communication Protocols: IoT systems use various communication protocols to facilitate data exchange and interoperability between devices and networks. Common protocols include MQTT (Message Queuing Telemetry Transport), CoAP (Constrained Application Protocol), and HTTP (Hypertext Transfer Protocol).

v. Security and Privacy: Ensuring the security and privacy of IoT devices and data is a critical consideration. Measures such as encryption, authentication, access control, and regular software updates help mitigate security risks and protect against unauthorized access or data breaches.

Indeed, the strong growth observed in IoT applications can be attributed to several major underlying trends that are now coming to execution. These trends are driving the widespread adoption of IoT technologies across various industries and use cases.

Some of the key trends contributing to the growth of IoT applications include.

i. Advancements in Connectivity Technologies: The evolution of wireless communication technologies such as 5G, LPWAN (Low-Power Wide-Area Network), and NB-IoT (Narrowband IoT) has significantly expanded the capabilities and reach of IoT devices. These technologies offer higher bandwidth, lower latency, and improved coverage, enabling more reliable and scalable IoT deployments.

ii. Miniaturization and Cost Reduction of Hardware: Advances in semiconductor technology have led to the development of smaller, more power-efficient, and cost-effective IoT hardware components, including sensors, microcontrollers, and communication modules. This trend has made it easier and more affordable to deploy IoT solutions across a wide range of devices and applications.

iii. Proliferation of Connected Devices: The increasing availability and affordability of connected devices, including smartphones, wearables, smart home appliances, and industrial sensors, have led to a growing ecosystem of interconnected devices. This proliferation of devices creates opportunities for data collection, analysis, and interaction, driving innovation and new IoT applications.

iv. Cloud Computing and Edge Computing: The rise of cloud computing platforms and edge computing technologies has enabled scalable storage, processing, and analysis of IoT data. Cloud-based IoT platforms offer centralized management, real-time analytics, and integration with other enterprise systems, while edge computing brings computing resources closer to IoT devices, reducing latency and enabling faster response times.

v. Data Analytics and Artificial Intelligence (AI): Advances in data analytics and AI technologies have enhanced the capabilities of IoT systems to derive actionable insights from large volumes of data. Machine learning algorithms can analyze IoT data to identify patterns, predict outcomes, and optimize decision-making, enabling more intelligent and autonomous IoT applications.

vi. Industry Standards and Interoperability: The development of industry standards and protocols for IoT connectivity, security, and interoperability has helped drive adoption and innovation in the IoT ecosystem. Standard organizations and industry consortia are working to establish common frameworks and guidelines to ensure compatibility and seamless integration between different IoT devices and platforms.

vii. Growing Awareness of Benefits and Use Cases: As organizations and individuals become more aware of the potential benefits of IoT technologies, including improved efficiency, productivity, safety, and sustainability, there is growing interest and investment in IoT solutions across diverse industries and sectors. Use cases such as smart cities, connected healthcare, industrial automation, and precision agriculture demonstrate the transformative impact of IoT applications.

Overall, these underlying trends are driving the rapid growth and adoption of IoT applications, paving the way for a more connected, intelligent, and efficient future. As technology continues to evolve and new innovations emerge, the potential of IoT to revolutionize industries and enhance quality of life for individuals around the world will continue to expand.

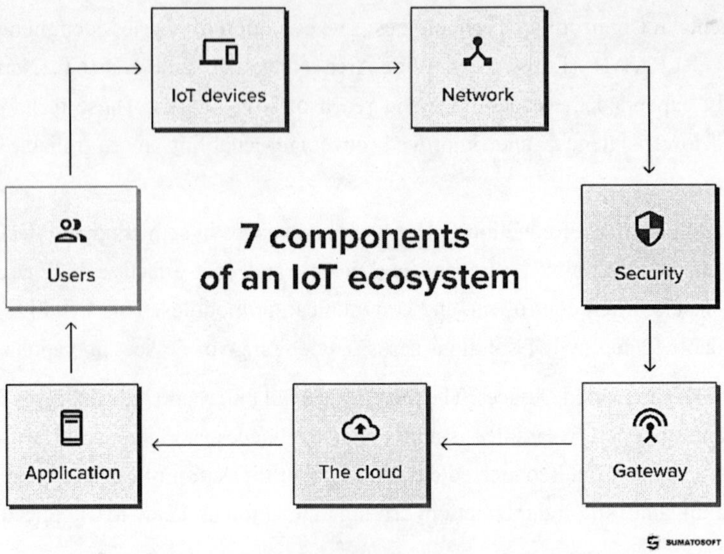

Figure 1.16: Functional components of an IoT system

b) Functional Component of IOT

An IoT system functions through a network of interconnected devices collecting, transmitting, and utilizing data. This network can be broken down into several key functional components, as illustrated in above figure 1.16.

i. Sensors and Actuators (IoT Devices): Sensors are devices that collect data from the physical environment, such as temperature, humidity, light, motion, or location. Actuators, on the other hand, are devices that can perform actions or control physical processes based on input from sensors. These components are the backbone of an IoT system as they gather real-world data and initiate actions.

ii. Network and Communication: Communication refers to the means by which IoT devices interact with each other and with backend systems over the internet. This can include various wireless and wired communication technologies such as Wi-Fi, Bluetooth, cellular networks, Zigbee, LoRaWAN, or Ethernet.

iii. Data Processing and Storage: Once data is collected from sensors, it needs to be processed, analyzed, and stored. This can be done locally on the device itself (edge computing) or in centralized cloud platforms. Data processing involves filtering, aggregating, and transforming raw sensor data into meaningful insights, while data storage involves storing the processed data for future reference or analysis.

iv. IoT Gateway: The IoT gateway serves as a bridge between IoT devices and the cloud or central backend system. It aggregates data from multiple devices, performs data preprocessing tasks, and securely transmits the data to the cloud. The gateway may also provide local processing capabilities and connectivity to legacy or proprietary systems.

v. Cloud Platform: The cloud platform serves as the backend infrastructure for an IoT system, providing storage, computing resources, and analytics capabilities. It receives data from IoT devices via the gateway, stores the data in databases or data lakes, and performs advanced analytics to derive insights and make decisions.

vi. Application Layer: The application layer encompasses the user-facing applications and interfaces that enable users to interact with the IoT system. This can include web-based dashboards, mobile apps, or desktop applications that allow users to monitor, control, and analyze IoT devices and data. Application layer also involves APIs (Application Programming Interfaces) for integration with other systems or services.

c) Applications domains of IoT system includes

i. Smart Home: IoT technologies enable the creation of smart homes equipped with interconnected devices that can be controlled remotely. This includes smart thermostats, lighting systems, security cameras, door locks appliances, and voice assistants. Smart home solutions enhance convenience, energy efficiency, and security for homeowners. Figure 1.17 represents some of the applications areas of IoT.

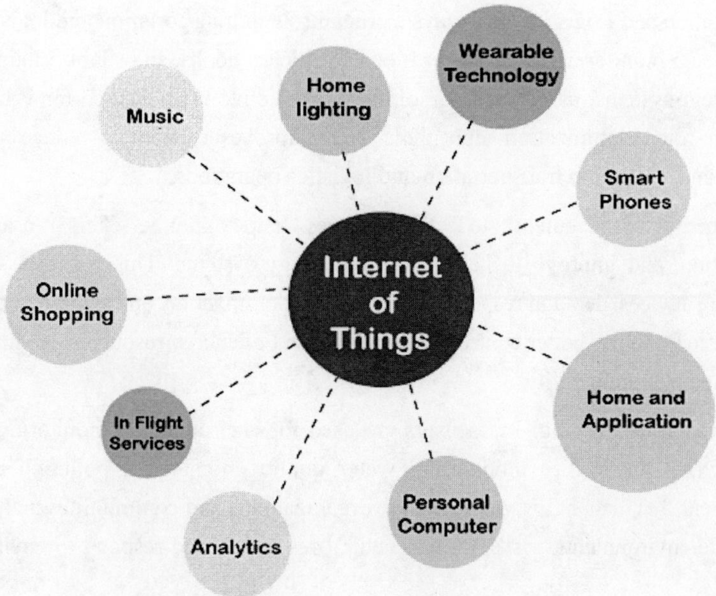

Figure 1.17 Applications areas of internet of things.

ii. Healthcare: IoT has numerous applications in healthcare, including remote patient monitoring, telemedicine, wearable health trackers, and smart medical devices. IoT devices can collect real-time health data, track medication adherence, monitor chronic conditions, and enable early detection of health issues, leading to improved patient outcomes and reduced healthcare costs.

iii. Smart Cities: IoT solutions are used to create smart cities by integrating sensors, networks, and data analytics to optimize urban infrastructure and services. This includes smart transportation systems, intelligent traffic management, waste management, environmental monitoring, energy management, public safety, and citizen engagement initiatives. Smart cities aim to improve quality of life, sustainability, and efficiency for urban residents.

iv. Industrial IoT (IIoT): IIoT applies IoT technologies to industrial settings to enhance efficiency, productivity, and safety. This includes predictive maintenance, remote monitoring of equipment and machinery, asset tracking, supply chain optimization, process automation, and condition monitoring. IIoT solutions enable data-driven decision-making, reduce downtime, and increase operational efficiency in manufacturing, logistics, energy, and other industries.

v. Agriculture: IoT is transforming agriculture with applications such as precision farming, smart irrigation systems, crop monitoring, livestock tracking, and agricultural drones. IoT sensors and data analytics help farmers optimize crop yields, conserve water and resources, monitor soil health, and manage livestock more effectively, leading to increased productivity and sustainability in agriculture.

vi. Retail: In retail, IoT technologies are used for inventory management, supply chain optimization, customer engagement, and personalized shopping experiences. This includes RFID tags for tracking merchandise, smart shelves that monitor product levels, beacon technology for location-based marketing, and personalized recommendations based on customer data.

vii. Transportation and Logistics: IoT plays a crucial role in transportation and logistics by enabling real-time tracking, monitoring, and optimization of vehicles, goods, and supply chains. This includes fleet management systems, asset tracking solutions, predictive maintenance for vehicles, smart logistics hubs, and route optimization algorithms. IoT improves efficiency, reduces costs, and enhances visibility and security in transportation and logistics operations.

viii. Energy Management: IoT technologies help optimize energy usage, monitor energy consumption, and improve the efficiency of energy systems. This includes smart meters, energy monitoring devices, demand response systems, grid optimization, and smart home energy management solutions. IoT enables better control and management of energy resources, leading to cost savings and environmental sustainability.

ix. Environmental Monitoring: IoT sensors are used for environmental monitoring and management in areas such as air quality monitoring, water quality monitoring, pollution control, and disaster management. IoT data helps governments, organizations, and communities make informed decisions to mitigate environmental risks, protect natural resources, and respond to environmental challenges effectively.

x. Education: IoT is increasingly being applied in education to create interactive learning environments, personalize learning experiences, and enhance student engagement. This includes IoT-enabled classrooms with smart boards, wearable devices for student tracking and safety, and adaptive learning platforms that use data analytics to tailor instruction to individual students' needs.

The Internet of Things continues to evolve and expand, driving innovation, efficiency, and connectivity across various domains, with the potential to transform how we live, work, and interact with the world around us. However, challenges such as interoperability, security, data privacy, and scalability must be addressed to fully realize the potential benefits of IoT.

d) Challenges in IoT implementation

The Internet of Things (IoT) offers a world of possibilities, but it also comes with its own set of challenges. Here are some of the various challenges that need to be addressed for widespread IoT adoption:

i. Security and Privacy: Security is a major concern in IoT due to the large number of interconnected devices and the potential vulnerabilities in IoT ecosystems. IoT devices often lack built-in security features, making them susceptible to cyberattacks, data breaches, and unauthorized access. Additionally, IoT devices may collect sensitive personal data, raising privacy concerns regarding data protection, consent, and transparency.

ii. Interoperability: The lack of interoperability standards and compatibility between different IoT devices, platforms, and protocols hinders seamless communication and integration within IoT ecosystems. This fragmentation complicates IoT deployment and scalability, leading to interoperability issues, vendor lock-in, and integration challenges.

iii. Scalability and Complexity: IoT deployments often involve a large number of heterogeneous devices, networks, and data sources, resulting in complex and distributed systems. Managing and scaling IoT deployments across diverse environments, devices, and applications can be challenging, requiring robust infrastructure, management tools, and expertise.

iv. Reliability and Resilience: IoT systems need to be reliable and resilient to ensure continuous operation and minimize downtime, especially in critical applications such as healthcare, transportation, and industrial automation. Factors such as network connectivity, device reliability, power management, and environmental conditions can affect the reliability of IoT deployments.

v. Data Management and Analytics: Managing the vast amounts of data generated by IoT devices, and extracting actionable insights from this data presents challenges in terms of data storage, processing, analysis, and interpretation. IoT data may be heterogeneous, real-time, and streaming in nature, requiring scalable data management and analytics solutions to derive meaningful insights and value.

vi. Regulatory and Compliance: IoT deployments must comply with regulatory requirements and standards governing data privacy, security, interoperability, and environmental sustainability. Compliance with regulations such as GDPR (General Data Protection Regulation), HIPAA (Health Insurance Portability and Accountability Act), and industry-specific standards can be complex and costly for IoT stakeholders.

vii. Energy Efficiency and Sustainability: IoT devices often operate on limited battery power or energy sources, making energy efficiency and sustainability important considerations. Optimizing power consumption, implementing energy-efficient designs, and exploring renewable energy solutions are essential for prolonging battery life, reducing environmental impact, and ensuring the sustainability of IoT deployments.

viii. Ethical and Societal Implications: The widespread adoption of IoT raises ethical and societal concerns related to privacy invasion, surveillance, data ownership, algorithmic bias, and automation-induced job displacement. Addressing these concerns requires careful consideration of ethical principles, regulatory frameworks, and stakeholder engagement to ensure responsible and equitable deployment of IoT technologies.

Addressing these challenges requires collaborative efforts from industry stakeholders, policymakers, regulators, researchers, and technology providers to develop standards, best practices, and solutions that promote security, interoperability, reliability, privacy, and sustainability in IoT ecosystems.

1.1.5 5th Generation Mobile Networks

Fifth Generation Mobile Networks, commonly referred to as 5G, represent the latest evolution in mobile telecommunications technology. 5G networks promise to deliver unprecedented levels of speed, capacity, reliability, and connectivity compared to previous generations, enabling transformative applications and services across various industries.

a) Key features of 5G networks

i. Ultra-fast speeds: 5G boasts theoretical peak speeds exceeding 20 Gbps, which is significantly faster than 4G's maximum speeds of around 1 Gbps. This translates to much faster download and upload times for data, enabling activities like:

- Downloading large files (movies, games) in seconds.
- Real-time streaming of high-resolution video content without buffering.
- Enhanced mobile gaming experiences with faster response times.

ii. Low latency: Latency refers to the time it takes for data to travel between two points. 5G offers significantly lower latency compared to 4G. This minimizes delays in data transmission, making it ideal for applications that require real-time responsiveness, such as:

- Remote surgery or other telemedicine procedures.
- Autonomous vehicles and connected car technology.
- Online gaming with minimal lag or disconnections.
- Industrial automation and control processes requiring real-time data exchange.

iii. Massive network capacity: 5G can handle a much larger number of connected devices compared to 4G. This is crucial for the growing number of Internet of Things (IoT) devices that require constant connectivity. Imagine a smart city with millions of sensors collecting data, or a connected factory with countless machines communicating with each other - 5G provides the capacity to accommodate such large-scale deployments.

b) Criteria to Qualify for 5G

There isn't a single set of criteria that a user or device necessarily needs to qualify for 5G access. Qualifying for 5G typically involves meeting certain criteria set by network operators or regulatory bodies. While specific criteria may vary depending on the region and the requirements of individual operators, some common factors that determine eligibility for 5G includes Network Infrastructure in which Network operators must deploy the necessary infrastructure to support 5G technology, including base stations, antennas, backhaul connections, and core network upgrades. The deployment of 5G infrastructure may require significant investments in hardware, software, and network planning.

Access to suitable radio frequency spectrum is essential for deploying 5G networks. Network operators need to acquire licenses for 5G spectrum bands allocated by regulatory authorities. These spectrum bands may include sub-6 GHz frequencies, mid-band frequencies, and high-frequency millimeter-wave (mmWave) bands, each offering different characteristics in terms of coverage, capacity, and propagation characteristics. Devices accessing 5G networks must be compatible with the required 5G standards and specifications. This includes smartphones, tablets, IoT devices, and other consumer electronics equipped with 5G-capable modems and antennas. Additionally, network infrastructure and equipment must comply with 5G standards to ensure interoperability and compatibility.

Network operators may have specific coverage requirements that must be met to qualify for 5G deployment. This includes providing adequate coverage in urban, suburban, and rural areas, as well as ensuring seamless handover and roaming between 5G and legacy networks. Coverage maps and service availability are often used to assess compliance with coverage requirements.

Qualifying for 5G may also involve meeting certain performance metrics, such as data speeds, latency, reliability, and throughput. Network operators may conduct performance testing and optimization to ensure that 5G networks meet or exceed specified performance benchmarks under various usage scenarios and network conditions. Moreover, operators must comply with regulatory requirements and standards governing 5G deployment, including spectrum licensing, network security, environmental regulations, health and safety guidelines. Regulatory authorities may impose specific conditions and obligations to ensure the responsible and lawful deployment of 5G technology.

Finally, the demand for 5G services and applications from customers and businesses plays a significant role in qualifying for 5G deployment. Network operators assess market demand, consumer preferences, and industry trends to determine the timing and scope of 5G rollouts, prioritizing areas with high demand and potential for growth. Overall, qualifying for 5G deployment involves a combination of technical, regulatory, and market considerations, with network operators striving to meet the requirements for delivering high-performance, reliable, and scalable 5G services to their customers.

c) 5G opportunities and standards

5G technology presents a multitude of opportunities across various industries and applications, driven by its high data speeds, low latency, massive connectivity, and reliability. Some of the key opportunities offered by 5G include:

i. Enhanced Mobile Broadband (eMBB): 5G enables significantly faster data speeds and higher capacity compared to previous generations, allowing for seamless streaming of ultra-high-definition video, immersive gaming experiences, and faster downloads/uploads on mobile devices. This unlocks new opportunities for mobile entertainment, media consumption, and productivity applications.

ii. Internet of Things (IoT) and Industrial IoT (IIoT): 5G's massive connectivity capabilities support a vast number of IoT devices and sensors, enabling the deployment of large-scale IoT networks for smart cities, smart homes, industrial automation, healthcare monitoring, asset tracking, and many more. 5G's low latency and high reliability are particularly beneficial for mission-critical IoT applications, such as autonomous vehicles, remote surgery, and industrial control systems.

iii. Augmented Reality (AR) and Virtual Reality (VR): 5G's high data speeds and low latency enable immersive AR and VR experiences with real-time rendering and interaction. This opens up opportunities for applications in gaming, entertainment, education, training, remote collaboration, and virtual tourism, transforming how users interact with digital content and environments.

iv. Autonomous Vehicles and Smart Transportation: 5G networks facilitate real-time communication and data exchange between vehicles, infrastructure, and traffic management systems, enabling safer and more efficient transportation systems. 5G's low latency is critical for supporting autonomous driving technologies, vehicle-to-vehicle (V2V) communication, and advanced driver assistance systems (ADAS).

v. Telemedicine and Remote Healthcare: 5G's high-speed, low-latency connectivity enables telemedicine applications such as remote consultations, medical imaging, surgical procedures, and patient monitoring. 5G networks support the transmission of large medical datasets in real-time, enabling healthcare professionals to deliver timely and efficient care, especially in remote or underserved areas.

vi. Smart Cities and Infrastructure: 5G enables the development of smart city solutions for optimizing urban infrastructure, energy management, public safety, transportation, and environmental monitoring. Smart city applications leverage 5G's connectivity, data analytics, and IoT capabilities to improve efficiency, sustainability, and quality of life for residents.

vii. Edge Computing and Cloud Gaming: 5G networks leverage edge computing capabilities to process data closer to the user, reducing latency and improving responsiveness for cloud-based applications and services. This enables cloud gaming platforms to deliver high-quality gaming experiences on mobile devices without the need for high-end hardware, opening up new opportunities for the gaming industry.

In terms of standards, the development and deployment of 5G technology are governed by various international standards organizations and industry consortia, including:

i. 3rd Generation Partnership Project (3GPP): 3GPP develops technical specifications for mobile telecommunications standards, including 5G NR (New Radio) standards. 3GPP's work on 5G standards ensures interoperability and compatibility between different vendors' equipment and networks.

ii. International Telecommunication Union (ITU): ITU establishes global standards and guidelines for telecommunications technologies, including 5G. ITU's efforts focus on spectrum allocation, radio interface specifications, and performance requirements for 5G networks and services.

iii. Institute of Electrical and Electronics Engineers (IEEE): IEEE develops standards for wireless communications, networking, and related technologies. IEEE's work on 5G standards covers areas such as wireless LAN, mobile broadband, and network architecture.

iv. European Telecommunications Standards Institute (ETSI): ETSI develops standards for telecommunications technologies, including 5G network architecture, security, and protocols. ETSI's work ensures interoperability and compliance with regulatory requirements for 5G deployments in Europe and beyond.

Overall, the development and adoption of 5G standards are essential for driving innovation, interoperability, and global deployment of 5G technology, unlocking the full potential of 5G-enabled applications and services across industries and regions.

d) Applications of 5G

5G's superior speed, low latency, and massive network capacity open doors for a wide range of applications, transforming various aspects of our lives. Here's a breakdown of some key applications across different domains:

i. Enhanced Mobile Broadband (eMBB):

- Superior Mobile Experience: Enjoy faster downloads and uploads, enabling activities like: downloading large files (movies, games) in seconds.
- Real-time streaming of high-definition and even ultra-high-definition video content without buffering.
- Lag-free video conferencing and enhanced mobile gaming experiences.

ii. Ultra-Reliable Low-Latency Communication (uRLLC):

- *Revolutionizing Critical Infrastructure:* Applications demanding minimal delays benefit from uRLLC, including:
- *Remote surgery and other telemedicine procedures:* Enabling real-time data transmission for more precise and efficient medical interventions.
- *Autonomous vehicles and connected car technology:* Supporting reliable data exchange for vehicle-to-infrastructure (V2X) communication, enhancing safety and traffic management.
- *Industrial automation and control processes:* Facilitating real-time communication between machines and control systems, optimizing production and maintenance in factories.

iii. Massive Machine-Type Communication (mMTC):

- *Internet of Things (IoT) Explosion:* The massive network capacity empowers a vast number of connected devices, fostering:
- *Smart cities:* Deploying millions of sensors to collect data for traffic management, environmental monitoring, and resource optimization, leading to more efficient and sustainable urban environments.
- *Connected factories:* Machines seamlessly communicate, enabling real-time monitoring, predictive maintenance, and intelligent automation for optimized production processes.
- *Wearable technology and remote patient monitoring:* Continuous health data collection from wearables allows for better healthcare management and preventive measures.

Beyond these core categories, 5G has the potential to disrupt and enhance various other sectors:

- *Education:* Immersive learning experiences through virtual reality (VR) and augmented reality (AR) applications.
- *Entertainment:* High-fidelity live streaming of events, concerts, and sporting activities.
- *Retail:* Enhanced customer experiences with personalized recommendations and interactive product displays.
- *Agriculture:* Precision agriculture for optimized crop yields and resource management through real-time data collection from sensors.
- *Public Safety:* Improved emergency response times and better coordination through faster data sharing between first responders.

These are just a few examples, and as 5G technology continues to evolve, we can expect even more innovative applications to emerge, transforming how we live, work, and interact with the world around us. The possibilities are truly limitless.

1.1.6 Artificial Intelligence and Machine Learning

Artificial intelligence (AI) and machine learning (ML) are two closely related fields that are often used interchangeably. However, there is a key distinction between the two.

Artificial intelligence is a broad field of computer science that deals with the creation of intelligent agents, which are systems that can reason, learn, and act autonomously. AI research has been highly successful in developing effective techniques for solving a wide range of problems, from game playing to medical diagnosis.

Machine learning is a subfield of AI that is concerned with the development of algorithms that can learn from data. Machine learning algorithms are trained on large amounts of data, and they are able to improve their performance over time as they are exposed to more data. Machine learning is used in a wide variety of applications, including spam filtering, fraud detection, and product recommendations. Table 1.2 gives the differences between AI and ML.

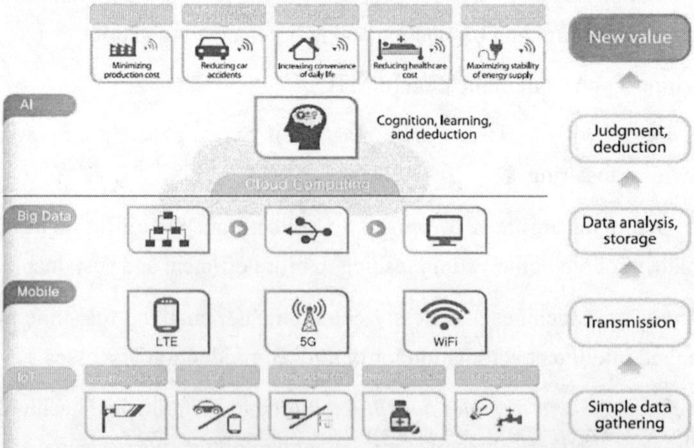

Figure 1.18 shows the AI and the emerging technologies

Table 1.2 summarize the key differences between AI and ML

Feature	Artificial Intelligence (AI)	Machine Learning (ML)
Definition	A broad field of computer science that deals with the creation of intelligent agents	A subfield of AI that is concerned with the development of algorithms that can learn from data.
Goel	To create intelligent machines that can think and act like humans.	To develop algorithms that can learn from data and improve their performance over time.
Method	Can include rule-based system, expert systems, and machine learning algorithm.	Focuses on training algorithms on data to produce models that can perform specific tasks.

Typical applications of AI and ML are as follows:

Artificial Intelligence (AI) and Machine Learning (ML) have a wide range of applications across various industries. Here are some typical applications. Above figure 1.18 represents the potential application domains of AI and ML along with their associations to other ICTs are given.

a) Predictive Analytics: ML algorithms are used for predictive analytics in industries such as finance, marketing, healthcare, and manufacturing. They analyze historical data to identify patterns and trends, making predictions about future outcomes.

b) Recommendation Systems: AI-powered recommendation systems are used by e-commerce platforms, streaming services, social media platforms, and content websites to suggest products, movies, music, articles, or connections based on user preferences and behavior.

c) Natural Language Processing (NLP): NLP techniques are used for tasks such as sentiment analysis, text classification, named entity recognition, language translation, chatbots, virtual assistants, and text summarization.

d) Computer Vision: Computer vision algorithms are used for image and video analysis in applications such as object detection, facial recognition, image classification, medical image analysis, autonomous vehicles, surveillance, and augmented reality.

e) Healthcare: ML is used in healthcare for medical image analysis (e.g., detecting tumors in radiology images), personalized medicine, drug discovery, patient monitoring, virtual health assistants, and predictive analytics for disease diagnosis and prognosis.

f) Finance: ML algorithms are employed in finance for fraud detection, algorithmic trading, credit scoring, risk assessment, customer service automation, portfolio management, and personalized financial advice.

g) Autonomous Systems: AI technologies, including computer vision, sensor fusion, and ML, are used in autonomous systems such as self-driving cars, drones, and robots for navigation, object detection, path planning, and decision-making.

h) Manufacturing and Robotics: AI-powered robotics systems are used in manufacturing for tasks such as assembly, quality control, predictive maintenance, and warehouse automation.

i) Energy Management: ML algorithms are used for optimizing energy consumption, predictive maintenance of energy infrastructure, and energy demand forecasting.

j) Customer Service: AI-powered chatbots and virtual assistants are used for customer service automation, handling inquiries, providing support, and improving customer experience.

k) Supply Chain Management: ML techniques are applied in supply chain management for demand forecasting, inventory optimization, logistics planning, and predictive maintenance of equipment.

l) Education: AI technologies are used in education for personalized learning, adaptive learning platforms, intelligent tutoring systems, automated grading, and educational content recommendation.

These are just a few examples, and the applications of AI and ML continue to expand across industries as the technology advances and new use cases emerge.

AI is divided into numerous subfields, each of which has important relationships and characteristics with the others that together form the ecosystem. Figure 1.19 displays the ones that are currently in use.

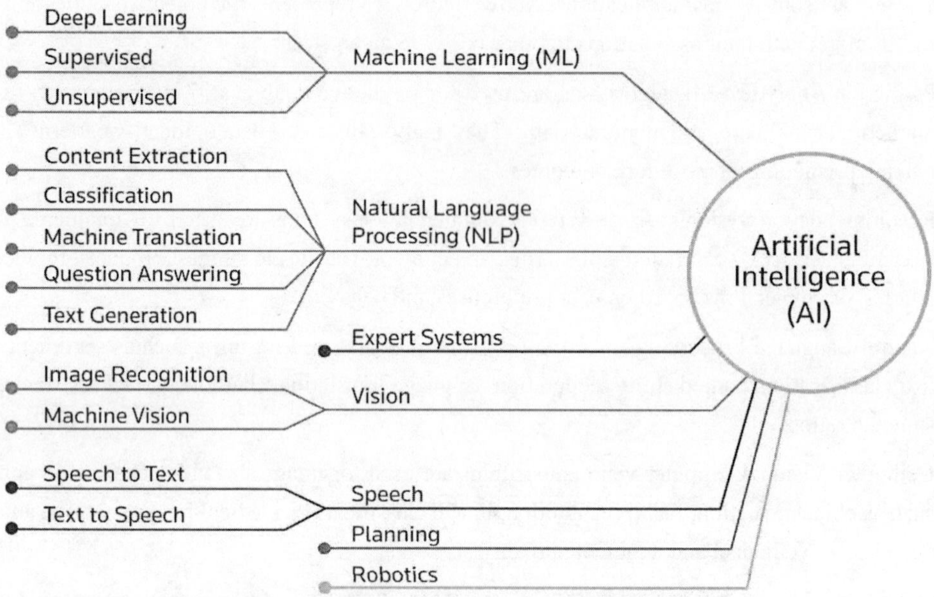

Figure 1.19 show the different branches of AI and ML

1.1.7 Blockchain and Shared Ledger

In 2008, the concept of blockchain was introduced by Satoshi Nakamoto, the pseudonymous creator of Bitcoin, published a white paper describing a blockchain as the public ledger for Bitcoin transactions. This marked the first real-world application of blockchain technology. However, bitcoin and blockchain both are not the same. In 2009, Nakamoto launched Bitcoin, bringing the blockchain concept to life and demonstrating its potential for secure, decentralized digital transactions. Since then, blockchain technology has continued to evolve and find applications beyond cryptocurrencies. Now, blockchain technology has many applications in various domains such as supply chain management, healthcare and finance sectors and may also be used in supply chain tracking and peer to peer to transactions.

A block is a collection of transactions on a blockchain, which is a record of transactions. When combined, they create an architecture known as a blockchain. These transactions may include the transfer of funds as well as goods, amenities, and data. A national identity number being assigned or making a digital payment via an application for banking are two examples. Figure 1.20 show a record of blockchain transaction.

Figure 1.20 Record transaction in blockchain

Blockchain is a distributed network of computers that each have a replica of the database. By agreeing on a common accord based on mathematical reasoning, the network of computers can modify the database's state

Blockchain is a specific type of distributed ledger technology (DLT) that stores data in blocks chained together in a chronological sequence. Each block contains a list of transactions and a reference to the previous block, creating a chain of blocks. It relies on consensus mechanisms such as Proof of Work (PoW), Proof of Stake (PoS), or other methods to validate and add new blocks to the chain. Blockchain is decentralized, meaning there is no central authority controlling the network, and transactions are validated by a network of participants.

The data on a blockchain is immutable, meaning once recorded, it is difficult to alter without consensus from the network. Blockchain gained prominence as the underlying technology behind cryptocurrencies like Bitcoin, but its applications extend beyond finance to supply chain management, healthcare, voting systems, and more.

a) Role of Ledger

A shared ledger is a general term for a database that is distributed across a network of computers. Each participant in the network has a copy of the ledger, and updates are synchronized across all copies. This eliminates the need for a central authority to maintain the ledger, which can improve security and transparency.

In summary, while blockchain is a specific type of shared ledger that offers immutability, decentralization, and transparency through a chain of blocks, shared ledgers encompass a broader range of technologies and architectures that enable multiple parties to share and synchronize data or transactions. In essence, all blockchains are shared ledgers, but not all shared ledgers are blockchains. Blockchains offer a higher level of security and immutability than traditional shared ledgers.

b) Applications of Blockchain Technology

Blockchain technology has a wide range of applications across various industries due to its unique properties such as decentralization, immutability, transparency, and security. Some prominent applications include.

i. Financial Services

- *Streamlined Transactions:* Blockchain can significantly reduce settlement times and transaction costs for international payments and trade finance.
- *New Financial Instruments:* The technology can facilitate the creation of new financial products like security tokens representing ownership in real-world assets.

ii. Supply Chain Management

- *Enhanced Tracking:* Blockchain can track the movement of goods from origin to destination, ensuring product authenticity, identifying inefficiencies, and improving overall supply chain visibility.
- *Food Safety:* By recording critical data points (e.g., temperature, location) throughout the food supply chain, blockchain can enhance food safety and traceability.

iii. Voting Systems

- *Increased Security:* Blockchain can create secure and transparent voting systems, reducing the risk of fraud and manipulation.
- *Improved Accessibility:* The technology can potentially enable secure remote voting, increasing voter participation.

iv. Identity Management

- *Secure Storage:* Individuals can store and manage their digital identities on a blockchain, giving them more control over their personal data.
- *Simplified Access:* This secure identity verification can streamline access to various services, like healthcare or financial institutions.

v. Other Potential Applications

- *Intellectual Property Management:* Blockchain can securely track ownership and rights associated with intellectual property like copyrights and patents.
- *Recordkeeping:* The technology can be used for secure and tamper-proof recordkeeping in various sectors like healthcare and government.
- *Data Sharing:* Blockchain can facilitate secure and controlled data sharing between different organizations.

These are just a few examples of how blockchain technology is being applied across various sectors to drive innovation, enhance efficiency, and promote transparency and trust in digital transactions.

c) Here are some specific applications of shared ledgers:

i. Supply Chain Management: Shared ledgers can be used to track the movement of goods from origin to destination. This can improve visibility within the supply chain, identify bottlenecks, and ensure the authenticity of products.

ii. Financial Services: Shared ledgers can be used to streamline cross-border payments, improve trade finance, and create new financial instruments.

iii. Voting Systems: Shared ledgers can be used to create secure and transparent voting systems, reducing the risk of fraud and increasing voter confidence.

iv. Identity Management: Shared ledgers can be used to store and manage digital identities securely. This can give individuals more control over their personal data and make it easier to access services.

Overall, shared ledgers have the potential to revolutionize the way we conduct business and interact with each other. Their ability to provide secure, transparent, and efficient record-keeping makes them a powerful tool for a variety of applications.

1.1.8 3D Printing

3D printing, also known as additive manufacturing, is a process of creating three-dimensional objects from a digital file. Unlike traditional manufacturing methods that involve subtracting material from a solid block, 3D printing builds objects layer by layer using a variety of materials.

a) Breakdown of how 3D printing works

   i. Digital Design: The first step involves creating a 3D model of the object using computer-aided design (CAD) software or 3D scanning technology.

   ii. Slicing the Model: The 3D model is then sliced into thin horizontal layers by slicing software. Imagine a loaf of bread being cut into thin slices.

   iii. Material Deposition: The 3D printer reads the sliced data and deposits material layer by layer to build the object. The way the material is deposited depends on the specific 3D printing technology being used.

   iv. Solidification: The deposited material hardens or fuses together to form the desired shape.

b) Some common 3D printing technologies

   i. Fused Deposition Modeling (FDM): This is the most popular form of 3D printing, commonly used for prototyping and hobbyist applications. It works by extruding molten plastic filament through a heated nozzle, building the object layer by layer.

   ii. Stereolithography (SLA): This technology uses a vat of liquid resin and a laser to cure the resin layer by layer, creating a high-resolution object.

   iii. Selective Laser Sintering (SLS): This process uses a laser to sinter (fuse) powdered plastic, metal, or ceramic particles together. SLS is known for its ability to produce strong and functional parts.

c) Applications of 3D Printing: 3D printing has a wide range of applications across various industries, including:

   i. Prototyping: 3D printing allows for rapid creation of prototypes for design verification and testing before mass production.

   ii. Manufacturing: Complex and customized parts can be 3D printed for various applications in aerospace, automotive, and medical industries.

iii. Healthcare: Custom implants, prosthetics, and even bioprinting of tissues and organs are potential applications of 3D printing in healthcare.

iv. Consumer Goods: 3D printing is increasingly used for creating customized consumer products like jewelry, eyewear, or even footwear.

d) Benefits of 3D Printing:

i. Design Flexibility: 3D printing allows for the creation of complex geometries that are difficult or impossible with traditional manufacturing methods.

ii. Rapid Prototyping: It enables faster and more cost-effective prototyping compared to traditional methods.

iii. Customization: Products can be customized and personalized to individual needs.

iv. Reduced Waste: 3D printing often uses less material compared to traditional subtractive manufacturing methods.

As 3D printing technology continues to evolve, we can expect even more innovative applications and advancements in this exciting field.

1.1.9 Big Data Analytics

Big data analytics refers to the process of examining large and varied data sets to uncover hidden patterns, correlations, trends, and other valuable insights. It involves the use of advanced analytical techniques and technologies to process and analyze massive volumes of data, which traditional data processing applications cannot handle effectively. Big data analytics enables organizations to derive actionable insights from their data, leading to informed decision-making, improved operational efficiency, and competitive advantages.

a) Key components of big data analytics include

i. Data Collection: Big data analytics begins with the collection of data from various sources, including structured data from databases, unstructured data from text documents, social media, sensors, and multimedia files, as well as semi-structured data like XML or JSON files.

ii. Data Storage and Management: Given the large volume, velocity, and variety of data involved, organizations often use distributed storage systems such as Hadoop Distributed File System (HDFS) or cloud-based storage solutions to store and manage big data effectively.

iii. Data Processing: Big data analytics platforms employ parallel processing techniques to analyze data in parallel across distributed computing clusters. Technologies such as Apache Spark, Apache Flink, and Hadoop MapReduce enable scalable and efficient data processing.

iv. Data Analysis: Various analytical techniques are applied to big data sets to extract meaningful insights. This includes descriptive analytics to summarize and aggregate data, predictive analytics to forecast future trends or outcomes, and prescriptive analytics to recommend actions based on analysis results.

v. Data Visualization: Data visualization plays a crucial role in big data analytics by presenting complex data sets in an intuitive and easily understandable format. Visualization tools like Tableau,

Power BI, and D3.js enable users to create interactive charts, graphs, and dashboards to visualize insights and trends.

vi. Machine Learning and AI: Machine learning algorithms are increasingly used in big data analytics to automate the process of deriving insights from data. These algorithms can identify patterns, classify data, make predictions, and optimize processes based on historical data.

b) Applications of big data analytics span across various industries and domains, including:

i. Retail: Analyzing customer purchase history and behavior to personalize marketing campaigns, optimize pricing strategies, and improve inventory management.

ii. Healthcare: Leveraging patient data to enhance clinical decision-making, predict disease outbreaks, and improve patient outcomes.

iii. Finance: Detecting fraudulent activities, assessing credit risk, and optimizing investment portfolios using big data analytics.

iv. Manufacturing: Monitoring and analyzing sensor data from equipment to predict maintenance needs, minimize downtime, and optimize production processes.

v. Marketing and Advertising: Analyzing social media data and customer interactions to target advertising campaigns, measure campaign effectiveness, and enhance customer engagement.

Overall, big data analytics has become a critical tool for organizations looking to unlock the value hidden within their data and gain a competitive edge in today's data-driven world.

c) Big data process

Big data analytics is the process of collecting, organizing, and analyzing massive amounts of data to extract valuable insights, inform decisions, and improve business operations. Here's a breakdown of the big data analytics process given in figure 1.21.

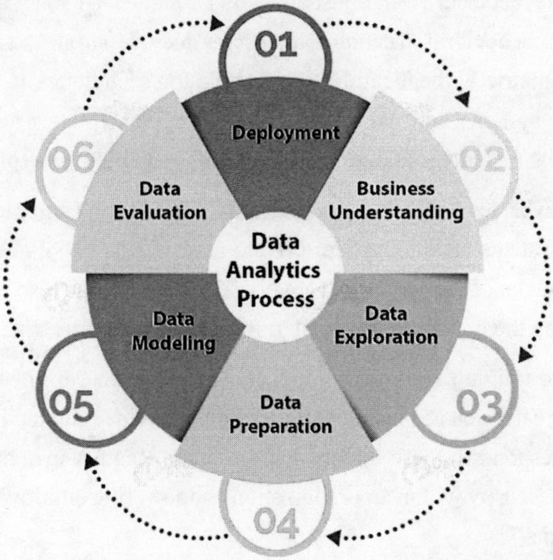

Figure 1.21 Process of big data analytics.

i. Define the Business Problem or Opportunity: The first step is to identify the specific business question or opportunity you're trying to address with big data analytics. This could be anything from understanding customer behavior to improving operational efficiency.

ii. Data Identification and Acquisition: Once you know what you're looking for, you need to identify the data sources that will help you answer your question. This data can come from a variety of sources, including internal databases, social media, customer relationship management (CRM) systems, sensor data, and public data sets.

iii. Data Extraction, Transformation, and Loading (ETL): The data collected will likely be in a variety of formats and from different sources. It includes Data Extraction, Data Transformation and Data Loading.

iv. Data Storage: Big data is often stored in data warehouses. Data warehouses are designed for storing structured data that has already been processed and organized.

v. Data Exploration and Analysis: Once your data is stored and cleaned, then it may begin to explore and analyze it. This may involve using a variety of techniques, such as statistical analysis, machine learning, and data visualization.

vi. Data Visualization: Data visualization is the process of creating visual representations of data.

vii. Actionable Insights & Decision Making: The goal of big data analytics is to extract actionable insights from the data that can be used to improve business decisions.

1.1.10 Cryptographic measures

Cybersecurity measures are essential components of any organization's strategy to protect their digital assets, data, and infrastructure from malicious actors. These measures encompass a wide range of practices, technologies, and policies aimed at preventing unauthorized access, data breaches, and other cyber threats.

One fundamental aspect of cybersecurity is robust authentication mechanisms. There are two main categories of measures: technical and behavioral. Technical measures include strong password policies, multi-factor authentication (MFA), biometric authentication, and encryption techniques to ensure that only authorized users can access sensitive systems and data. Additionally, regular updates and patches for software and operating systems are crucial to address known vulnerabilities that could be exploited by cyber attackers.

Another critical aspect of cybersecurity is network security. This involves implementing firewalls, intrusion detection and prevention systems (IDPS), virtual private networks (VPNs), and other tools to monitor and control traffic flowing in and out of the network. Network segmentation can also help limit the potential impact of a cyber-attack by dividing the network into smaller, more manageable segments with restricted access.

Furthermore, education and training are vital components of cybersecurity measures. Employees should be aware of common cyber threats such as phishing attacks, social engineering tactics, and malware, and trained on how to recognize and respond to these threats appropriately. Regular cybersecurity awareness programs can help foster a culture of security within an organization, empowering employees to become the first line of defense against cyber-attacks.

Behavioral measures focus on how you interact with the online world. This includes being cautious about suspicious emails and links, avoiding public Wi-Fi for sensitive activities, and having a healthy dose of skepticism towards online offers. Educating yourself and others about common cyber threats is crucial, as is backing up your data regularly in case of an attack.

Below are some key cybersecurity measures such as:

- Firewalls and Intrusion Detection Systems (IDS)/Intrusion Prevention Systems (IPS)
- Encryption
- Access Control Mechanisms
- Regular Software Updates and Patch Management
- Security Awareness Training
- Data Backup and Disaster Recovery Planning
- Endpoint Security

In conclusion, by implementing a combination of technical and behavioral measures, it can significantly reduce the risk of falling victim to cyberattacks and keep the information safe. Also, effective cybersecurity measures require a multi-layered approach that combines technological solutions, policies, and employee awareness. By implementing robust authentication mechanisms, network security protocols, and ongoing education initiatives, organizations can significantly reduce their risk exposure to cyber threats and safeguard their digital assets and sensitive information.

1.2 Understanding of design and implementation of e-Government Projects

The evolution of e-governance in India has been a transformative journey marked by significant technological advancements, policy reforms, and the government's commitment to leveraging digital innovations for improved governance and citizen services. The initial steps towards digital governance in India can be traced back to the establishment of the National Informatics Centre (NIC) in 1976, which laid the foundation for computerization of government processes and services. However, it was in the late 1990s and early 2000s that e-Governance in India began to gain momentum with the introduction of various standalone projects aimed at automating administrative tasks and improving service delivery.

One of the most significant milestones in the evolution of e-governance in India was the launch of the Unique Identification Authority of India (UIDAI) and the Aadhaar program in 2009. Aadhaar, a biometric-based identification system, aimed to provide every resident of India with a unique identity number. Aadhaar has since become the cornerstone of various e-Governance initiatives, enabling efficient delivery of welfare schemes, subsidies, and financial services while promoting transparency and accountability in governance.

The Digital India initiative, launched in 2015, further accelerated the pace of e-governance transformation in India. Digital India aimed to bridge the digital divide by promoting digital literacy, expanding broadband connectivity, and enhancing access to digital services across rural and urban areas. Key components of Digital India include the BharatNet project for rural broadband connectivity, e-healthcare, e-education, and e-governance services.

In recent years, there has been a growing emphasis on harnessing emerging technologies such as artificial intelligence (AI), blockchain, and Internet of Things (IoT) to further enhance the efficiency and effectiveness of e-Governance services. Initiatives like the National Artificial Intelligence Mission (N-AIM) and the National Blockchain Strategy aim to leverage these technologies for improving governance, service delivery, and fostering innovation-led growth.

Overall, the evolution of e-governance in India reflects a progressive shift towards digital governance models that prioritize citizen-centricity, transparency, and efficiency. While significant strides have been made, there are ongoing efforts to address challenges such as digital divide, cybersecurity threats, and data privacy concerns to realize the full potential of e-governance in India's socio-economic development journey.

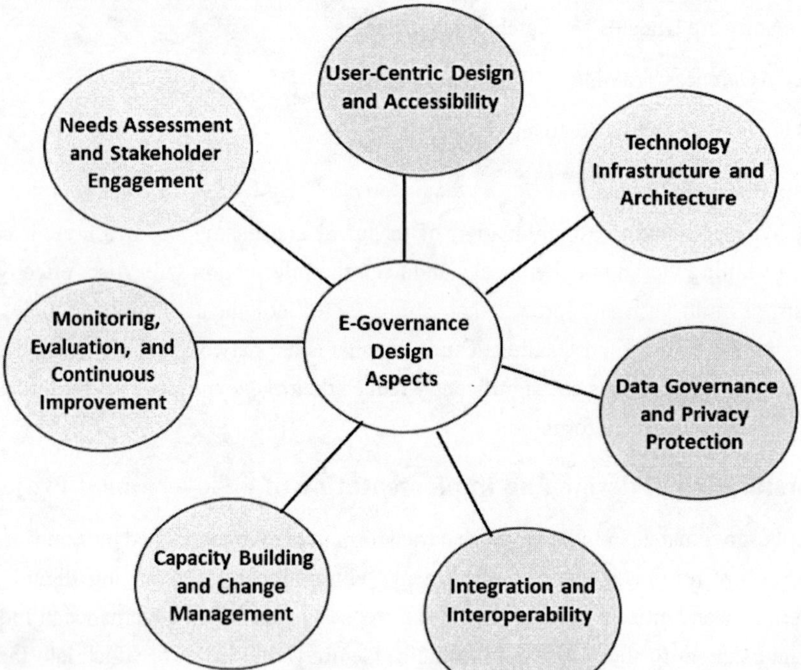

Figure 1.22 E-Governance design process

Designing e-governance projects involves a comprehensive approach that integrates technological solutions with administrative processes to enhance government services and interactions with citizens. At its core, the design of e-governance projects aims to leverage digital tools and platforms to improve accessibility, efficiency, transparency, and accountability within the public sector.

Firstly, the process begins with a thorough understanding of the needs, challenges, and aspirations of both the government and the citizens it serves. This entails conducting extensive research, stakeholder consultations, and needs assessments to identify key areas where digital interventions can make a meaningful impact. Understanding the diverse needs and preferences of citizens is paramount in shaping user-centric e-governance solutions that prioritize accessibility and usability.

Secondly, the design of e-governance projects involves the careful selection of appropriate technologies and architectures to support the delivery of digital services. This includes considerations such as scalability, interoperability, security, and compliance with regulatory frameworks. By choosing the right technology stack and architectural framework, governments can build robust and resilient digital platforms that can adapt to evolving needs and integrate seamlessly with existing systems and data sources.

Furthermore, e-governance project design emphasizes the importance of data governance and privacy protection. Given the sensitive nature of government data, it is imperative to implement robust data governance policies, security controls, and privacy safeguards to protect citizens' personal information and ensure compliance with data protection regulations. This involves establishing clear guidelines for data collection, processing, storage, and sharing, as well as implementing encryption, access controls, and audit trails to safeguard against unauthorized access and data breaches.

Additionally, e-governance projects prioritize inclusivity and accessibility to ensure that digital services are accessible to all citizens, including those with disabilities or limited access to technology. This requires adherence to web accessibility standards, the provision of alternative channels for accessing services, and the design of user interfaces that are intuitive and easy to navigate for users with diverse needs and abilities.

Overall, the design of e-governance projects is a multidisciplinary endeavor that requires collaboration between government agencies, technology experts, civil society organizations, and citizens themselves. By adopting a holistic approach that integrates technological innovation with administrative reform, governments can build e-governance solutions that empower citizens, enhance government efficiency, and foster greater trust and transparency in public institutions. The pictorial representation of complete e-governance design process is show in the figure 1.22. Below are some key aspects of e-governance project design phases.

1. Needs Assessment and Stakeholder Engagement

   - Conduct research and consultations to understand government and citizen needs.

   - Identify pain points, challenges, and opportunities for improvement.

2. User-Centric Design and Accessibility

   - Prioritize user experience (UX) and design intuitive, accessible interfaces.

   - Ensure inclusivity for all citizens, including those with disabilities.

3. Technology Infrastructure and Architecture

   - Select appropriate technologies and frameworks for scalability and security.

   - Ensure interoperability with existing systems and data sources.

4. Data Governance and Privacy Protection

   - Implement robust data governance policies and security controls.

   - Safeguard citizens' personal information and comply with privacy regulations.

5. Integration and Interoperability

   - Seamlessly integrate e-governance systems with existing government infrastructure.

   - Establish interoperability standards and APIs for data exchange.

6. Capacity Building and Change Management

   - Provide training and support for government staff to adapt to digital tools.

   - Drive organizational change and foster a culture of innovation.

7. Monitoring, Evaluation, and Continuous Improvement

- Implement mechanisms for monitoring project performance and user satisfaction.

- Collect feedback and data to inform iterative improvements and optimizations.

1.2.1 Leading e-Governance projects initiatives

India has seen a remarkable evolution in e-governance initiatives over the years, each contributing to enhancing citizen services, administrative efficiency, and transparency in governance. A variety of initiatives have been taken in this area by the Union and the State Governments. Here are some pioneering initiatives:

a) Bhoomi Project (Karnataka) : Online Delivery of Land Records

The Bhoomi Project in Karnataka stands as a remarkable endeavor in the domain of e-governance, particularly in the management and delivery of land records. Initiated in 2000, Bhoomi aimed to digitize land records and establish an online platform for their efficient management and delivery across the state.

At its core, the Bhoomi Project sought to streamline the process of accessing land records, which traditionally involved complex and time-consuming procedures. By digitizing land records, including ownership details, survey numbers, and transaction history, Bhoomi facilitated their online availability to citizens and government officials alike.

The implementation of Bhoomi brought significant advantages. It replaced the manual, paper-based system with a digital database, reducing errors and enhancing transparency in land administration. Citizens gained the convenience of accessing their land records remotely, eliminating the need for physical visits to government offices. Furthermore, Bhoomi contributed to the reduction of corruption and malpractices in land transactions by providing real-time access to accurate and up-to-date records. It also expedited the processing of land-related transactions, such as mutations and transfers, leading to improved efficiency and responsiveness in land administration.

Some key learnings from Bhoomi Project are as follows:

i. Digitization Enhances Accessibility and Transparency: Bhoomi demonstrated that digitizing land records significantly enhances accessibility and transparency. By making land records available online, citizens could access them conveniently from anywhere, reducing the need for physical visits to government offices and promoting transparency in land administration.

ii. Real-Time Updates Improve Data Integrity: The project highlighted the importance of real-time updates in maintaining the integrity of land records. By enabling instant updates to land records, Bhoomi minimized discrepancies and errors, ensuring that the information available to citizens and government officials was accurate and up-to-date.

iii. Community Engagement is Vital: Bhoomi underscored the importance of community engagement and participation in e-governance initiatives. Stakeholder involvement, including citizens, government officials, and other relevant parties, was crucial for the success of the project. Engaging with stakeholders helped in identifying their needs, addressing concerns, and fostering ownership of the initiative.

iv. Capacity Building is Essential: Bhoomi emphasized the importance of capacity building and training for government officials and stakeholders involved in land administration. Providing training and support to users of the Bhoomi portal ensured that they were equipped with the necessary skills and knowledge to effectively utilize the system and implement land-related processes digitally.

v. Robust Security Measures are Critical: The project highlighted the need for robust security measures to safeguard land records against unauthorized access and tampering. Bhoomi implemented advanced encryption techniques, access controls, and audit trails to ensure the security and integrity of land data, underscoring the importance of data protection in e-governance initiatives.

vi. Continuous Monitoring and Evaluation are Key: Bhoomi demonstrated the importance of continuous monitoring and evaluation to assess the progress and effectiveness of e-governance initiatives. Regular monitoring helped in identifying challenges, addressing issues, and making necessary improvements to ensure the success and sustainability of the project.

vii. Scalability and Interoperability are Crucial: Bhoomi highlighted the importance of scalability and interoperability in e-governance projects. Designing systems that can accommodate growing volumes of data and integrate with existing infrastructure and systems ensures that initiatives can scale effectively and collaborate seamlessly with other government departments and agencies.

b) eSeva (Andhra Pradesh): Front-end Citizen Service Delivery

The eSeva project in Andhra Pradesh stands as a landmark initiative aimed at revolutionizing front-end citizen service delivery through a network of service centers. Launched in 1999, eSeva epitomized a citizen-centric approach, redefining the interaction between citizens and government services. At the heart of eSeva's success was its commitment to providing citizens with convenient access to a wide array of government services, all consolidated under one roof.

By establishing one-stop service centers strategically across urban and rural areas, eSeva ensured that government services were within easy reach of citizens. This move not only enhanced accessibility but also transformed the perception of government services, making them more approachable and user-friendly. Citizens no longer had to navigate through multiple government offices; instead, they could access various services seamlessly at eSeva centers, saving time and effort. The eSeva project leveraged technology to streamline service delivery, marking a departure from traditional bureaucratic processes. Through the use of computerized systems and internet connectivity, eSeva centers digitized service requests, reducing paperwork and administrative bottlenecks. This technological integration not only improved efficiency but also determined the way for enhanced transparency and accountability in service delivery.

Crucially, eSeva embraced a public-private partnership model, collaborating with the private sector to establish and operate service centers. This partnership allowed for the harnessing of private sector expertise and resources, ensuring the scalability and sustainability of the project while maintaining government oversight and accountability. Additionally, eSeva prioritized capacity building, investing in training programs for government officials and service center operators to ensure the seamless implementation and operation of the project.

Feedback mechanisms were integral part to eSeva's success, enabling continuous monitoring and evaluation of service delivery processes. By soliciting feedback from citizens and stakeholders, eSeva identified areas for improvement, iteratively refining its operations to better meet citizens' evolving needs. This emphasis on responsiveness and adaptability ensured that eSeva remained at the forefront of citizen service delivery, setting a precedent for similar initiatives nationwide.

In essence, the eSeva project in Andhra Pradesh epitomized the transformative potential of citizen-centric e-governance initiatives. By prioritizing convenience, accessibility, technology adoption, public-private collaboration, capacity building, and feedback mechanisms, eSeva redefined the landscape of government service delivery, empowering citizens and fostering a culture of efficiency, transparency, and accountability in governance.

Here is some key learning from the eSeva project are:

i. Real-Time Online Transactions: eSeva facilitated real-time online transactions, allowing citizens to access services efficiently and promptly.

ii. Service Variety: The project provided various services, including Payment of electricity bills, Telephone bill payments and Booking of services.

iii. One-Stop Shop: Citizens could avail themselves of these services conveniently from a single location, streamlining their interactions with the government.

c) KHAJANE (Karnataka): End-to-end automation of Government Treasury System

It is marked a major shift from traditional manual processes, introducing a new era of efficiency, transparency, and accountability in financial management. Its primary goal was to fully digitize treasury operations, covering areas like fund allocation, expenditure tracking, and financial reporting. By centralizing and automating these essential tasks, KHAJANE aimed to simplify operations, reduce administrative workload, and minimize the risk of errors or discrepancies.

Central to KHAJANE's success was its emphasis on online fund management systems, enabling government departments to access funds electronically. This shift from paper-based transactions to electronic fund transfers facilitated faster, more transparent, and secure transactions, enhancing overall efficiency in financial operations. Moreover, KHAJANE's integration with banking systems allowed for seamless transactions between the treasury and bank accounts, further reducing manual intervention and enhancing operational efficiency. The project also introduced real-time monitoring mechanisms, providing government officials with access to up-to-date financial data and reports. This real-time visibility into fund utilization and expenditures empowered decision-makers to make informed choices, optimize resource allocation, and ensure fiscal discipline. Additionally, KHAJANE prioritized user-friendly interfaces, designed to simplify tasks such as fund allocation, budget tracking, and financial reporting. Intuitive dashboards and tools made it easier for treasury staff and government officials to navigate the system, promoting widespread adoption and utilization.

KHAJANE placed a strong emphasis on data security and compliance, implementing robust measures to safeguard sensitive financial information. Encryption, access controls, and audit trails were deployed to protect against unauthorized access and ensure compliance with regulatory requirements. Furthermore, the project included comprehensive capacity-building initiatives to train government officials and treasury staff on the effective use of the KHAJANE system. These training programs were essential in facilitating the smooth transition to the new automated processes and technologies. Here is some key learning from KHAJANE project are as follows:

i. Khajane demonstrated that end-to-end automation of treasury operations significantly enhances efficiency by streamlining processes, reducing paperwork, and minimizing manual intervention.

ii. The project underscored the importance of transparency and accountability in financial management.

iii. Khajane's integration with banking systems proved crucial in facilitating seamless electronic transactions between the treasury and bank accounts.

iv. User-friendly interfaces were involved in promoting the adoption and utilization of the Khajane system among treasury staff and government officials.

v. The project highlighted the importance of robust data security measures to safeguard sensitive financial information.

vi. Capacity-building initiatives played a crucial role in facilitating the successful implementation and adoption of the Khajane system. Training programs ensured that government officials and treasury staff were equipped with the necessary skills and knowledge to effectively use the system, maximizing its benefits and impact.

vii. Khajane emphasized the importance of stakeholder engagement throughout the project lifecycle. Collaboration with government departments, treasury staff, and other stakeholders was essential in garnering support, gathering feedback, and ensuring that the system met the diverse needs of its users.

Throughout its implementation, KHAJANE prioritized stakeholder engagement, collaborating closely with government departments, treasury staff, and other stakeholders. This engagement ensured that the system met the diverse needs of its users and garnered support and feedback throughout the implementation process. Ultimately, KHAJANE's end-to-end automation of the government treasury system represented a paradigm shift in financial management practices in Karnataka, setting a new standard for efficiency, transparency, and accountability in public finance management.

d) Aadhar (India) e-Governance project

Aadhaar, India's ambitious e-governance project, represents one of the world's largest biometric identification systems launched in 2009 by the Unique Identification Authority of India (UIDAI). Aadhaar aims to provide every resident of India with a unique, digitally verifiable identity number. The Aadhaar number, a 12-digit unique identifier, is linked to biometric and demographic information, including fingerprints and iris scans, making it one of the most comprehensive identity systems globally.

At its core, Aadhaar seeks to streamline the delivery of government services and subsidies by eliminating duplicate and fake identities, reducing leakages, and enhancing transparency and efficiency in governance. By providing a universal and portable identity platform, Aadhaar enables individuals to access a wide range of government services and benefits, including social welfare schemes, financial services, healthcare, and education, with greater ease and convenience.

The Aadhaar authentication system allows individuals to verify their identity securely and instantly using biometric or demographic information. This authentication process has transformed the way government services are delivered, enabling seamless and paperless transactions across various sectors. Whether it's opening a bank account, applying for a passport, or receiving government subsidies, Aadhaar authentication has simplified processes and reduced the burden of paperwork for citizens.

Moreover, Aadhaar has played a crucial role in promoting financial inclusion and digital payments by enabling the linkage of Aadhaar numbers with bank accounts and mobile numbers. This linkage has facilitated direct benefit transfers (DBT), enabling the government to transfer subsidies and welfare payments directly to beneficiaries' bank accounts, thereby reducing leakage and ensuring targeted delivery of benefits.

Despite its transformative potential, Aadhaar has faced scrutiny and debate over privacy and security concerns, particularly regarding the collection and storage of biometric data. The project has been subject to legal challenges, with the Supreme Court of India ruling in 2018 that Aadhaar is constitutionally valid but imposing restrictions on its use and mandating stringent privacy safeguards.

In conclusion, Aadhaar represents a paradigm shift in India's approach to identity management and service delivery, leveraging technology to empower citizens and enhance governance. While it has faced challenges and controversies, Aadhaar continues to evolve as a cornerstone of India's digital infrastructure, driving financial inclusion, improving service delivery, and empowering millions of citizens across the country.

Below are some key learnings from Aadhar e-Governance project:

i. Scalability: Aadhaar demonstrated the importance of scalability in designing and implementing e-governance projects. With over a billion Aadhaar numbers issued to date, the project showcases the ability to scale up to serve a vast population efficiently.

ii. Interoperability: Aadhaar emphasized the need for interoperability between different government systems and databases. The Aadhaar authentication system seamlessly integrates with various government services, enabling citizens to access multiple services using a single identification number.

iii. Inclusive Design: Aadhaar's inclusive design approach ensured accessibility for all citizens, including those in rural and remote areas. The project leveraged biometric technology to provide a robust identity solution that is inclusive and accessible to individuals across diverse socioeconomic backgrounds.

iv. Data Security and Privacy: Aadhaar highlighted the importance of robust data security and privacy measures in e-governance projects. The project implemented stringent security protocols to protect biometric and demographic data, addressing concerns related to privacy and data breaches.

v. User-Centric Design: Aadhaar's user-centric design focused on simplifying processes and enhancing user experience. The Aadhaar authentication system streamlined service delivery by enabling citizens to verify their identity securely and instantly, reducing the need for manual paperwork and authentication processes.

vi. Partnerships and Collaboration: Aadhaar's success relied on partnerships and collaboration between government agencies, private sector partners, and other stakeholders. The project demonstrated the importance of collaboration in implementing complex e-governance initiatives and leveraging the expertise and resources of multiple stakeholders.

vii. Continuous Innovation: Aadhaar emphasized the need for continuous innovation and adaptation to evolving technologies and user needs. The project has continually evolved, introducing new features and functionalities to enhance security, improve user experience, and address emerging challenges.

viii. Legal and Regulatory Framework: Aadhaar underscored the importance of establishing a robust legal and regulatory framework to govern e-governance projects. The project navigated legal challenges and regulatory requirements, leading to landmark Supreme Court rulings that affirmed the project's validity while imposing safeguards to protect citizens' privacy and rights.

Overall, Aadhaar's e-governance project offers valuable insights into the design, implementation, and management of large-scale identity and service delivery initiatives. Its success underscores the importance of scalability, interoperability, inclusive design, data security, user-centricity, collaboration, innovation, and a robust legal and regulatory framework in driving transformative change through e-governance.

e) MyGov: Government of India's citizen engagement portal

MyGov is an innovative e-governance initiative launched by the Government of India in 2014. It serves as a unique platform for citizen engagement, enabling citizens to participate in governance, contribute ideas, and collaborate with government departments on various initiatives and policies. MyGov aims to foster a culture of participatory governance and harness the collective wisdom and creativity of citizens in shaping the country's development agenda.

At its core, MyGov functions as an online portal where citizens can register and become members of various thematic groups and communities based on their interests and expertise. These groups cover diverse topics such as education, health, urban development, environment, and technology, allowing citizens to engage with government officials and other stakeholders on issues of national importance.

One of the key features of MyGov is its crowdsourcing platform, which enables citizens to share ideas, suggestions, and feedback on government policies and programs. Government departments can launch challenges and campaigns on the platform, seeking innovative solutions to specific problems or initiatives. Citizens can participate by submitting their ideas, which are then evaluated by experts and policymakers for potential implementation. Moreover, MyGov serves as a communication channel between the government and citizens, providing regular updates on government initiatives, policies, and campaigns. Through the platform, citizens can stay informed about government activities and contribute to discussions on various topics. Additionally, MyGov facilitates two-way communication, allowing government officials to seek input and feedback from citizens on policy formulation and implementation.

MyGov has emerged as a powerful tool for promoting transparency, accountability, and citizen participation in governance. It has facilitated meaningful engagement between citizens and government departments, leading to the co-creation of policies and programs that address the needs and priorities of the people. By leveraging technology to bridge the gap between the government and citizens, MyGov is empowering individuals to play an active role in shaping the future of the country.

Below are some key learnings from MyGov e-governance project:

i. MyGov highlighted the importance of citizen engagement in governance.

ii. The project showcased the power of crowdsourcing in generating innovative ideas and solutions to complex challenges.

iii. MyGov leveraged technology to overcome barriers to citizen participation in governance.

iv. MyGov emphasized the importance of two-way communication between the government and citizens. The platform facilitated dialogue and exchange of ideas between policymakers and citizens, enabling government officials to seek input and feedback on policy formulation and implementation.

v. MyGov promoted transparency and accountability in governance by providing regular updates on government initiatives and campaigns.

vi. The project demonstrated the benefits of collaboration across government departments and agencies. MyGov brought together stakeholders from diverse sectors and facilitated collaboration on common goals, leading to more coordinated and effective governance.

In conclusion, MyGov represents a paradigm shift in governance, moving towards a more inclusive and participatory model of decision-making. By harnessing the collective intelligence and creativity of citizens, MyGov is driving positive change and fostering a sense of ownership and responsibility among the people. As India continues its journey towards digital transformation, MyGov stands as a shining example of the potential of e-governance to empower citizens and build a more democratic and responsive government.

1.3 e-Governance Projects lifecycle

The e-governance project development lifecycle encompasses a series of structured phases aimed at conceptualizing, designing, implementing, and maintaining digital initiatives within government frameworks. The pictorial representation of e-governance project lifecycle is given in figure 1.23.

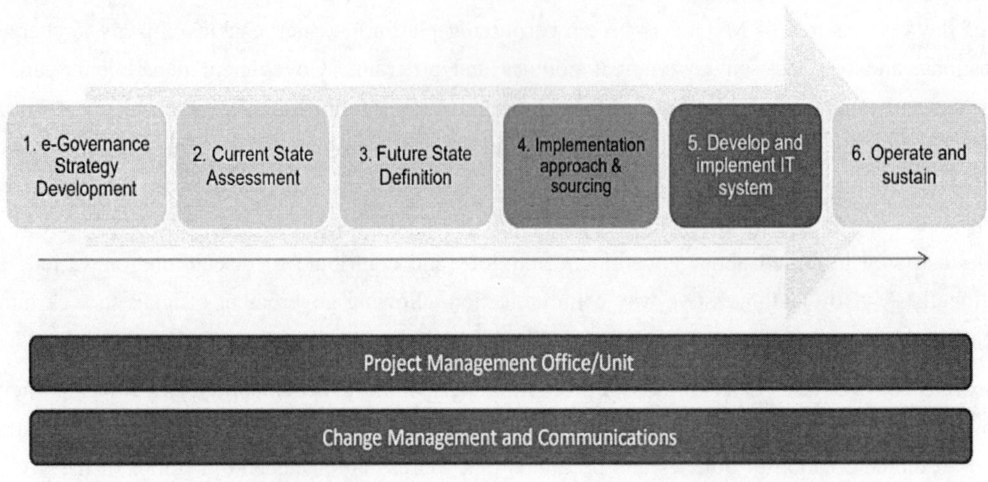

Figure 1.23 Life cycle of e-governance project development

- e-Government Strategy Development
- Current State Assessment
- Future State Definition
- Implementation approach & sourcing
- Develop and implement IT System
- Operate and Sustain.

Below are the e-governance project life-cycle stages. The different processes under each stage are shown in the figure 1.24.

a) e-Government Strategy Development: This phase encompasses several essential tasks, including assessing needs, establishing a clear vision and objectives, prioritizing services and projects, integrating insights from both domestic and international contexts, identifying organizational structures and capacities for implementation, outlining funding needs, and establishing a monitoring and evaluation framework.

   The outcomes of this phase include the formulation of an e-governance vision, the description of e-governance objectives, and the development of an e-governance strategy.

   This phase encompasses a variety of tasks, including conducting a thorough assessment of business functions and services targeted for inclusion in the e-governance project.

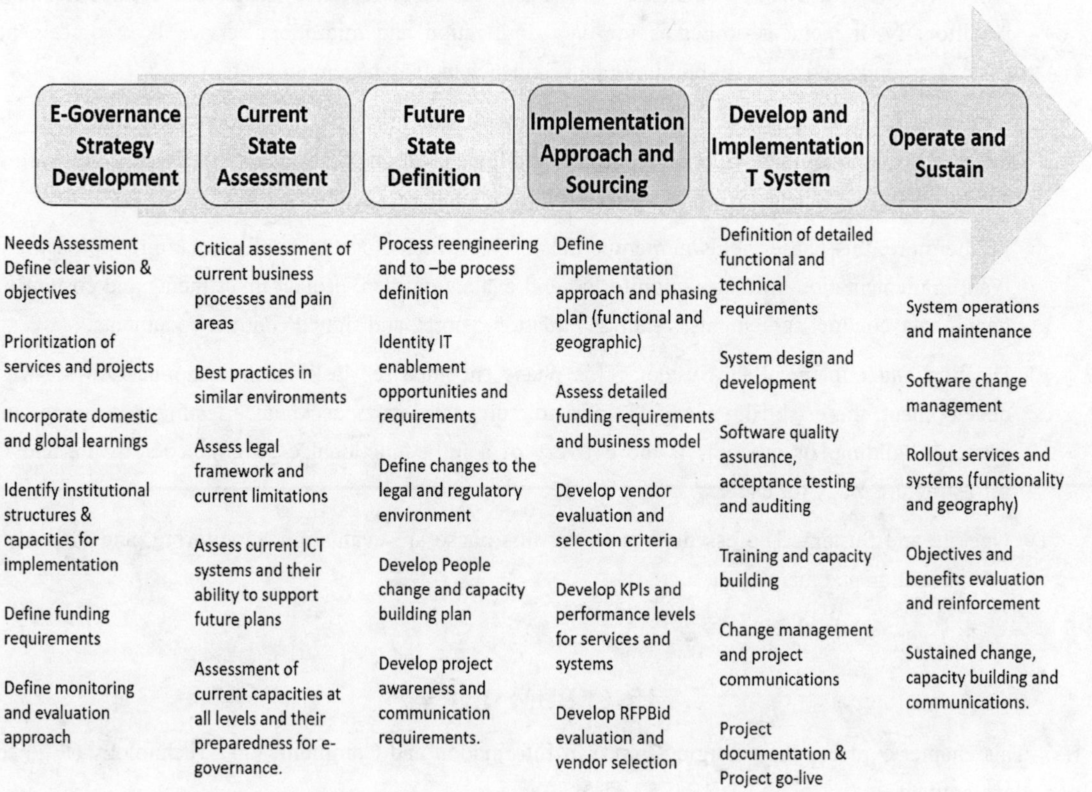

Figure 1.24 Various processes under each e-governance project life-cycle

b) Current State Assessment

   Understand the current approach to performing business functions and service delivery.
   Identify key challenges and areas for improvement.

   i. Capture stakeholder needs and expectations.

   ii. Evaluate existing IT systems within the department, including their coverage and any gaps.

   iii. Assess organizational structures and the capacities of personnel.

The outcomes of this phase include the creation of process maps, identification of initial improvement areas, understanding stakeholder needs, assessment of IT systems, determination of scope and functionality, evaluation of IT infrastructure (network, security, data center), examination of organizational structures, clarification of roles and responsibilities, and assessment of capacities and skill sets.

c) Future State Definition: This phase entails several activities, including specifying how the identified business functions and services will be carried out, compiling IT solutions and services for automating new business processes, and delineating change management, capacity-building, and communication needs for project execution.

   The deliverables for this phase encompass several components, such as newly defined business processes with associated metrics, functional architecture, and requirement specifications. Additionally, it includes strategies for data digitization and migration, service level agreements (SLAs), training and capacity-building plans, and a change management strategy.

d) Implementation approach & sourcing: This phase comprises a range of tasks, including the development of an Implementation Approach and Plan, creation of a Business Model, and the drafting and evaluation of Requests for Proposals (RFPs) for vendor selection.

   Furthermore, this phase yields numerous deliverables, including the Implementation Approach and Plan, implementation timelines, monitoring and evaluation plan, project investments and costs, RFP documents, contract agreements, vendor evaluation reports, and signed contract documents.

e) Develop and implement IT System: This phase encompasses tasks such as application software development, the establishment of IT infrastructure, third-party acceptance testing & training, and capacity building. Its outcome is the delivery of a fully functional e-governance software and IT infrastructure ready for use.

f) Operate and Sustain: The essential tasks for this phase are evaluation, monitoring, and IT system administration and maintenance.

UNIT SUMMARY

1. This chapter explored the emerging trends in Information and Communication Technology (ICT) for development.
2. In this chapter it is discussed how digital healthcare is enhancing medical services through telemedicine and electronic health records.
3. Mobile payment systems are transforming financial transactions, boosting financial inclusion.
4. Assistive technologies are empowering individuals with disabilities, fostering greater independence.
5. The Internet of Things (IoT) connects everyday objects to the internet, enabling smarter systems.
6. 5th Generation Mobile Networks (5G) offer high-speed, low-latency communication for advanced applications.

7. Artificial Intelligence (AI) and Machine Learning (ML) provide data-driven insights and process automation.
8. Blockchain technology ensures secure and transparent transactions with tamper-proof records.
9. 3D printing facilitates rapid prototyping and production, reducing costs and waste.
10. Big Data Analytics uncovers patterns and trends, aiding in decision-making and policy formulation.
11. Cryptographic measures protect data integrity, confidentiality, and authentication.
12. After ICT trends the design and implementation of e-Government projects has been discussed to improve public services.
13. Leading e-governance initiatives set benchmarks in transparency, efficiency, and service delivery.
14. The e-governance lifecycle covers the process from conceptualization to maintenance of digital systems.
15. Understanding these technologies is crucial for developing effective and sustainable e-government solutions.
16. By integrating these innovations, governments can enhance service delivery and citizen engagement.
17. Ultimately, these advancements drive sustainable development and improve the quality of life for all citizens.

EXERCISES

Q1. Which of the following is a key emerging trend in ICT for development?

A. Analog technology
B. Cloud computing
C. Dial-up internet
D. Floppy disks

Q2 How does mobile technology contribute to development in rural areas?

A. By increasing physical postal services
B. By providing access to banking and financial services
C. By reducing the need for internet access
D. By promoting traditional farming methods

Q3 What role does big data play in ICT for development?

A. It helps in decision-making by providing large-scale data analysis.
B. It replaces the need for internet infrastructure
C. It hinders the collection of information
D. It reduces the importance of digital literacy

Q4 What is the primary goal of e-Government projects?

A. To increase bureaucracy

B. To improve government services through digital means

C. To reduce government transparency

D. To limit public access to information

Q5. Which phase involves the identification of stakeholder needs in e-Government project design?

A. Implementation phase B. Evaluation phase

B. Planning phase D. Closure phase

Q6. In e-Government project implementation, what is critical for ensuring user adoption?

A. High project costs B. User training and support

C. Complexity of the system D. Limited accessibility

Q7. Which is the first step in the e-Governance project lifecycle?

A. Evaluation B. Implementation

C. Initiation D. Closure

Q8. What is a common challenge in leading e-Governance projects?

A. Excessive funding B. Lack of stakeholder engagement

C. Over-simplification of processes D. High public trust

Q9. Why is continuous monitoring important in the governance lifecycle?

A. To reduce transparency

B. To ensure ongoing improvement and effectiveness

C. To limit public feedback

D. To avoid project updates

Q10. Which strategy can help in the successful implementation of e-governance projects ?

A. Ignoring stakeholder feedback B. Ensuring data security and privacy

C. Reduced digital literacy programs D. Limited access to digital services

Answers

Q.N.	1	2	3	4	5	6	7	8	9	10
Option	B	B	A	B	C	B	C	B	B	B

Short Answer Type Questions

1. Why is it essential to learn current ICT trends?

2. What are the emerging trends in information technology?
3. What new technologies does the healthcare sector use?
4. What is the role of ICT in achieving sustainable development goals (SDGs)?
5. Explain the concept of digital divide.
6. How can ICT improve education in developing countries?
7. Describe how mobile technology can enhance healthcare services.
8. What is the impact of e-governance on public service delivery?
9. How can big data analytics be used to address social issues?
10. Explain the significance of blockchain technology in development projects.
11. What are the challenges of implementing ICT solutions in rural areas?
12. Discuss the role of artificial intelligence in economic development.
13. What are the benefits of using the Internet of Things (IoT) in smart city initiatives?
14. What is the importance of cybersecurity in ICT for development?
15. What is the importance of artificial intelligence and machine learning in ICT for development?

Long Answer Types Questions

1. Explain how Artificial Intelligence (AI) and Machine Learning (ML) are transforming development initiatives. Provide examples of specific applications and their impacts on various sectors such as healthcare, agriculture, and education.
2. Discuss the role of the Internet of Things (IoT) in sustainable development. How can IoT solutions contribute to achieving the United Nations Sustainable Development Goals (SDGs)?
3. Analyze the potential benefits and challenges of using blockchain technology in development projects. How can blockchain ensure transparency, security, and efficiency in sectors like finance, supply chain management, and public services?
4. Evaluate the impact of mobile technology on socio-economic development in developing countries. What are the key factors that drive mobile technology adoption, and what challenges need to be addressed to maximize its benefits?
5. Explore the significance of Big Data analytics in formulating development policies. How can data-driven decision-making enhance the effectiveness of development programs? Provide examples of successful implementations.
6. Describe the key principles and frameworks involved in designing and implementing an e-Government system. How do these principles ensure efficient and effective public service delivery?
7. Discuss the critical success factors for implementing e-Government initiatives. What are the common challenges faced during the implementation phase, and how can they be mitigated?

8. Analyze the role of public-private partnerships (PPPs) in the development and implementation of e-Government services. Provide examples of successful PPPs.

9. Evaluate the importance of user-centric design in e-Government systems. How can governments ensure that their digital services are accessible, inclusive, and user-friendly for all citizens?

10. Examine the security and privacy concerns associated with e-Government systems. What measures can be implemented to protect citizens' data and ensure trust in digital government services?

11. Outline the stages of the e-Government governance lifecycle. How does each stage contribute to the successful implementation and sustainability of e-Government projects?

12. Discuss the role of stakeholder engagement in the e-Government governance lifecycle. How can effective communication and collaboration with stakeholders improve project outcomes?

13. Analyze the impact of policy and regulatory frameworks on e-Government projects. How can governments create an enabling environment for the successful deployment of e-Government services?

14. Examine the importance of continuous monitoring and evaluation in the e-Government governance lifecycle. What tools and methodologies can be used to assess the performance and impact of e-Government initiatives?

15. Evaluate the role of capacity building and training in the sustainability of e-Government projects. How can governments ensure that their workforce is equipped with the necessary skills to manage e-Government systems?

Dynamic QR code for further reading

REFERENCES AND SUGGESTED READINGS

1. Bhatnagar, S. C. (2009). Unlocking E-Government Potential: Concepts, Cases, and Practical Insights. SAGE Publications India.

2. Ayyangar, S. K. (2012). E-Governance in India: Its Impacts on Relations among Stakeholders and Popular Perception. VDM Verlag.

3. Monga, A. (2008). E-Government in India: Opportunities and Challenges. Journal of Administration & Governance, 3(2), 52-61.

4. Singh, P. J., & Bhattacharya, J. (2011). Indian E-Government 2020: Roadmap for Innovative, Inclusive and Open Governance. Rupa Publications.

5. Gupta, M. P., Kumar, P., & Bhattacharya, J. (Eds.). (2008). Government Online: Opportunities and Challenges. Tata McGraw Hill.

6. Prasad, K. (Ed.). (2013). E-Governance and Development: Issues and Impacts. ICFAI University Press.

7. Kumar, R. (2004). E-Governance and ICT for Sustainable Development. Authors Press.

8. Pathak, R. D., & Prasad, R. S. (2006). E-Governance in India: A Blueprint for the Future. SAGE Publications India.

9. India Telecom Regulatory Authority. (2017). ICT and E-Governance in India: A Status Report.

10. National e-Governance Plan (NeGP). (2006). National e-Governance Plan: Approach and Key Components. Government of India.

2 Government Process Re-engineering

UNIT SPECIFIES

Through this unit we discuss the following aspects:

- *Need for Government Process Re-engineering (GPR)*
- *National e-Governance Plan(NeGP) for India*
- *SMART Governments & Thumb Rules*

RATIONALE

This unit begins with need for Government Process Re-engineering (GPR) stems from the necessity to enhance efficiency, transparency, and responsiveness in governmental operations. Then, the national e-Governance Plan (NeGP) of India is discussed aims to leverage Information and Communication Technology (ICT) to transform public service delivery, making it more accessible and reliable for citizens. After that the principles of SMART governments was introduced which is, measurable, achievable, relevant, and time-bound objectives—ensures that government initiatives are well-defined, trackable, feasible, aligned with public needs, and timely. At last the thumb rules provide best practices and heuristic guidelines that simplify decision-making and enhance operational consistency. Together, these initiatives foster a citizen-centric, accountable, and sustainable governance model, improving the overall quality of life and driving the nation towards a digitally empowered society.

PRE-REQUESITE

- *Contents of unit-1*
- *Fundamentals of e-governance*
- *Basics of Business Process Re-engineering*

UNIT OUTCOMES

After completion of this unit the learner will be able to:

U2-O1: Understand the government process re-engineering (GPR)

U2-O2: Differentiate between government process and business process re-engineering

U2-O3: Understand national e-governance Plan(NeGP) component and framework

U2-O4: Understand SMART government and thumb rule

Unit-2 Outcomes	Expected Mapping with Programme Outcomes (1- Weak Correlation; 2- Medium correlation; 3- Strong Correlation)					
	CO-1	CO-2	CO-3	CO-4	CO-5	CO-6
U2-O1	1	3	1	1	1	0
U2-O2	1	3	1	1	1	0
U2-O3	1	2	2	1	1	1
U2-O4	1	1	1	2	2	0

2.1 Need for Government Process Re-engineering

Government process re-engineering refers to the systematic redesign and improvement of governmental processes to enhance efficiency, effectiveness, and service delivery. It involves the comprehensive review, analysis, and restructuring of existing workflows, procedures, and policies with the goal of achieving significant improvements in performance, productivity, and outcomes. This approach often incorporates the adoption of innovative technologies, streamlining of bureaucratic procedures, elimination of redundant tasks, and the reorganization of administrative structures to better align with the needs of citizens and stakeholders. Government process re-engineering aims to optimize resource utilization, minimize delays, reduce costs, and enhance the overall quality of public services, thereby contributing to the modernization and transformation of government operations.

2.1.1 e-Governance vs. conventional e-governance approach

In recent years, there has been a significant transformation in the concepts of government and governance. This shift is driven not only by rising pressures and expectations for governments to operate with greater efficiency and effectiveness, often referred to as the imperative to 'do more with less' annually, but also by the growing demand for government transparency and accountability to democratic principles.

There is a growing focus on leveraging ICT for the delivery of public services with greater efficiency and effectiveness. However, the adoption of new technologies extends beyond mere efficiency gains. These technologies are beginning to reshape the government landscape by redefining relationships, particularly in terms of power and responsibility, among various stakeholders. This includes interactions between service providers and industry, among the public, private, and third-party sectors, and between government and citizens. Therefore, ICT has the potential to drive *transformative change* in government, enabling the cultivation and preservation of the capacity and capability to innovate and effectively utilize technology as it evolves.

Undertaking process redesign, which involves critically analyzing and radically redesigning workflows and processes within and across government departments, is crucial for achieving significant improvements in performance.

Therefore, the essence of successful Business Process Reengineering (BPR) lies in redefining processes to enhance the convenience of citizens.

Innovativeness: The system should embrace innovation, offering solutions that go beyond replicating manual processes.

Transformational: It should drive significant enhancements in the quality of services delivered.

Rationalization of Application Form and Data Requirements: Frequently, application forms request information that is either seldom utilized or already within government records. A robust BPR approach would challenge the necessity of all requested information.

Efficient Utilization of Government Data: Frequently, information requested is already within the Government's domain. For instance, the date of birth, commonly sought, typically requires a duly attested certificate as proof. However, this redundant practice could be eliminated as the Government already possesses this information through individual date of birth records. Therefore, requesting a birth certificate becomes unnecessary.

Clarification of Government Rules versus Procedures: Often, there's confusion between a government rule and its corresponding procedure. At an operational level, procedures are sometimes mistaken for rules. For instance, while the rule might state that pensions are granted to individuals above the age of 65, the procedure for verifying age could vary, including options such as a class 10th pass certificate, birth certificate, or passport. It's essential to distinguish between these rules and procedures to ensure accurate implementation. Figure 2.1 shows the difference between the government rule and procedures.

In Business Process Reengineering (BPR), it's essential to distinguish between government rules and procedures which is . Frequently, procedures can undergo significant transformation through the application of IT. In the scenario mentioned above, the necessity for such documents can be eliminated if officials have access to birth data, rendering the requirement for proof unnecessary.

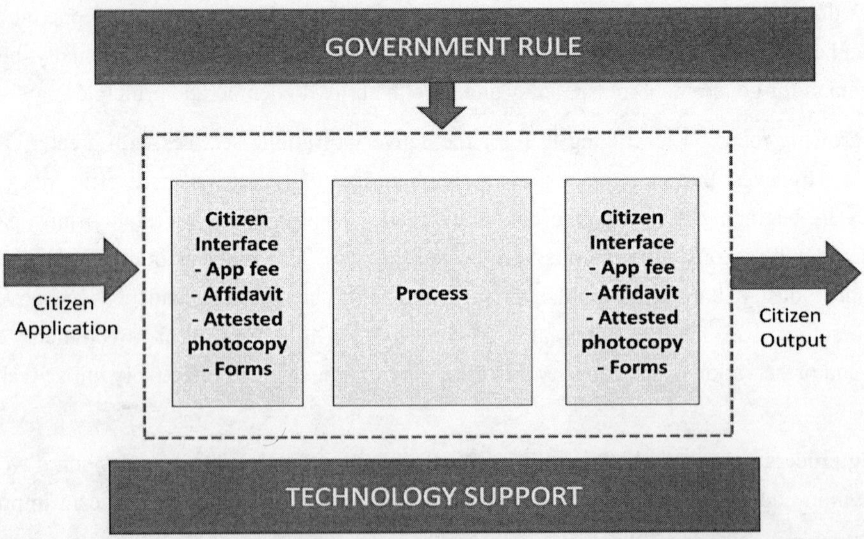

Figure 2.1 Difference between government rule and procedures.

2.1.2 Government Process Re-engineering

The re-engineering of governmental processes is imperative for realizing the benefits of e-Governance. Emphasizing the importance of process redesign to facilitate and uphold best practices in e-Governance is crucial. Process redesign must entail critical analysis and radical restructuring of workflows and processes within and across governmental departments to achieve significant improvements in performance. While deploying IT solutions enhances operational efficiency, optimal results are not guaranteed unless processes are reconfigured to suit specific circumstances. Alternatively, there is a constant risk that substituting manual processes with machine-based ones will simply result in "automated" inefficiencies. Process re-engineering guarantees that processes are revamped to maximize effectiveness and provide optimal value to the government, its employees, and most importantly, the citizens.

The experiences of several governments indicate that the true essence of convergent or integrated delivery of public and private services resides in the re-engineering of government and business processes (40%) and effective change management (45%), rather than solely relying on technology, including hardware and software (15%).

"Re-engineering is the fundamental rethinking and radical redesign of business processes to achieve dramatic improvements in critical, contemporary measures of performance, such as cost, quality, service, and speed."
—Hammer and Champy, 1993.

In many cases, starting from scratch to redesign a business or process is not feasible. Six Sigma's DMAIC (Define, Measure, Analyze, Improve and Control) methodology provides a framework for elevating existing processes to higher levels of performance, which may involve some degree of redesign.

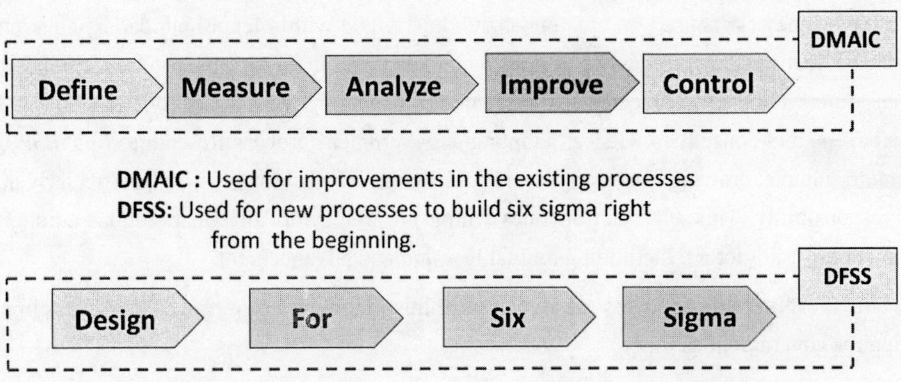

Figure 2.2 shows two techniques DMAIC and DFSS for enhancing processes using Six Sigma methodologies.

Alternatively, Design for Six Sigma (DFSS) presents a methodology tailored for developing new processes and offerings. SIX-SIGMA, conversely, constitutes a structured approach aimed at enhancing service quality and performance. By utilizing Six Sigma methodologies to gauge the actual performance level of any service, we can subsequently elevate that performance level. The following figure 2.2 provide detailed information on two commonly employed techniques for enhancing processes using Six Sigma methodologies.

Six Sigma contributes to Business Process Reengineering (BPR) by incorporating the following components:

- Established array of statistical tools and techniques for reducing variation.

- Data-driven approach to design or enhance processes.
- Utilization of scorecards, dashboards, metrics, and baselines.
- Stage gating to verify initial assumptions' validity while remaining alert to changes.
- Reduction of waste in time, effort, or resources.
- Alignment of all endeavors with the 'Voice of the Customer', business strategy, and objectives.

2.1.3 Business Process Re-engineering (BPR)

Re-engineering aligns with the evolving governance paradigm of the Information Age, emphasizing mission-driven, results-focused initiatives. Despite this shift, certain aspects of the public sector pose persistent challenges for those implementing re-engineering strategies. Notably, governmental agencies operate under heightened political executive oversight, influenced by electoral cycles and administrative turnovers. Unlike their private sector counterparts, governments are constrained by immutable missions and operations. Factors such as legislation, taxpayer scrutiny, resource competition, ongoing change, and collaborations with international, state, and local entities further complicate re-engineering efforts. A fundamental obstacle facing governments is their inherent aversion to risk-taking, historically ingrained within their culture. To succeed in re-engineering, governments must embrace change and navigate risks judiciously.

Although there is a lot of experience with business Process Re-engineering (BPR), it's essential to recognize that government operations differ significantly from those of businesses. While businesses undertake BPR to overhaul legacy systems and encounter similar challenges, equating government to a large business simplifies the complexity of the issue. Governments face unique contextual drivers and obstacles absent in the business realm. Unlike businesses focused on creating shareholder value within legal boundaries, governments must fulfill diverse objectives. Government operations remain distinct due to various factors, including the inability to select customers and the multifaceted roles assumed by users of government services, who also function as voters, taxpayers, and consumers. Hence, adopting a 'government process Re-engineering' (GPR) approach could be more suitable, drawing lessons from and contributing to business practices, particularly in areas such as social responsibility. This approach operates within the framework of collaborations among the public, private, and non-profit sectors, facilitating mutual learning and advancement.

According to the National Academy of Public Administration in USA re-defined the definition of re-engineering for government as follows.

"Government business process re-engineering represents a transformative methodology that thoroughly assesses, reimagines, and reconstructs mission-critical product and service processes within the confines of a political landscape. It delivers substantial enhancements in mission performance, catering to the diverse needs of customers and stakeholders. Integral to an overarching process management strategy for maximizing efficiency, it entails ongoing evaluation, adjustment, or elimination of processes to ensure optimal performance". – NAPA, 1995.

It is clear that Government Process Re-engineering (GPR) is crucial for developing transparency in government operations, minimizing bureaucratic constraints, enhancing efficiency and productivity, and lowering the costs of service provision. An effective GPR strategy should be rooted in a forward-thinking and enlightened vision. This vision entails a realignment of resources and workforce training from a leaner and more effective administrative setup towards direct citizen engagement and service delivery, as part of a systematic and deliberate policy shift aimed at rebalancing the 'front' and 'back' offices shown in the figure 2.3.

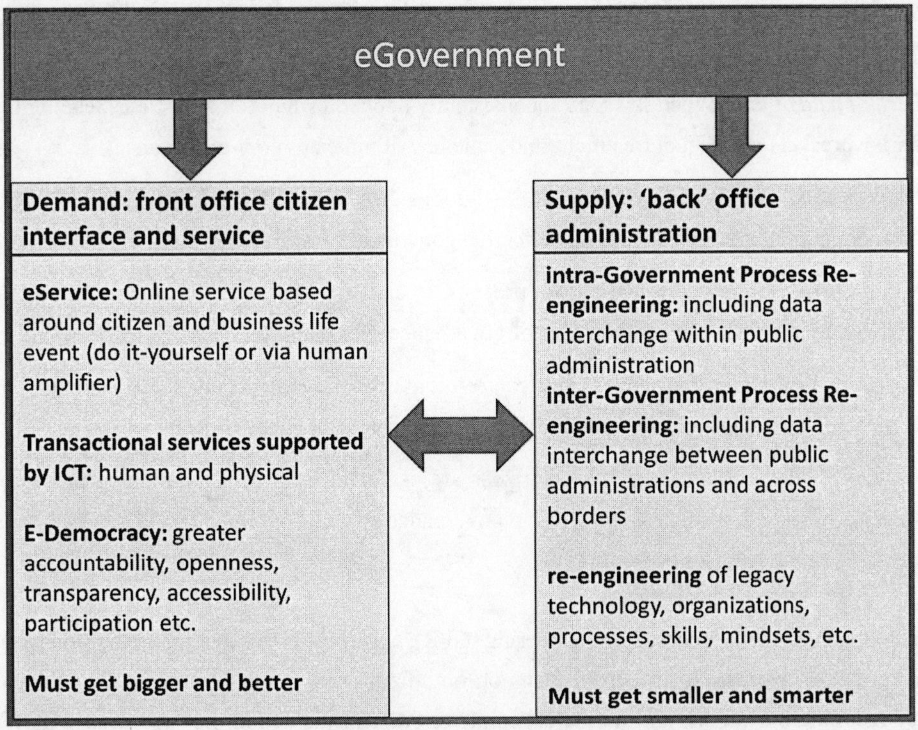

Figure 2.3 Re-balancing e-Government

Information and Communication Technology (ICT) plays a vital role in augmenting the quality of traditional government services, including those in healthcare, education, and social care. It is crucial that technology doesn't displace frontline personnel, as this could result in a less personal and lower quality service. Instead, ICT should directly support frontline staff by enhancing the quality of services they provide and by rendering them more responsive to the needs of citizens. Rather than adopting a technology-centric approach, it's essential to leverage the strengths of both people and technology. As Alan Mather, from the UK's eEnvoy Office, once remarked, "e-Government isn't fundamentally different from traditional government; it simply has the potential to make it better, and sooner."

Sign of Poor governance and may be identified by various signs, including:

- *Lack of transparency:* When decision-making processes are opaque and information is not readily accessible to the public, it indicates poor governance.
- *Corruption:* The presence of bribery, embezzlement, nepotism, or other forms of corruption within government institutions suggests weak governance.

- *Ineffective leadership:* When leaders fail to provide clear direction, accountability, or fail to address the needs of their constituents, it reflects poorly on governance.
- *Abuse of power:* When those in positions of authority misuse their power for personal gain or to suppress dissent, it signals governance deficiencies.
- *Inefficient service delivery:* When government services are consistently delayed, inadequate, or fail to meet the needs of the population, it points to governance failures.
- *Lack of rule of law:* When laws are inconsistently applied or ignored altogether, leading to impunity for lawbreakers or unequal treatment under the law, it indicates poor governance.
- *Weak institutions:* When government institutions lack independence, capacity, or fail to uphold democratic principles, it undermines effective governance.
- *Social unrest:* Prolonged social unrest, protests, or civil disobedience often stem from dissatisfaction with governance and can be indicative of governance shortcomings.
- *Economic instability:* Poor governance can result in economic mismanagement, leading to high levels of inequality, unemployment, inflation, or unsustainable debt burdens.
- *Lack of public participation:* When citizens are excluded from decision-making processes or their voices are ignored, it suggests a deficit in governance.

2.1.4 Understand Service Quality

In the realm of Government Process Re-engineering (GPR), ensuring service quality is paramount for effective and efficient governance. GPR initiatives focus on optimizing governmental processes to enhance service delivery, streamline operations, and ultimately improve citizen satisfaction. Service quality plays a pivotal role in this context as it directly impacts the overall effectiveness and success of GPR efforts.

Firstly, maintaining high service quality in GPR initiatives fosters trust and confidence among citizens in the government's ability to meet their needs. By prioritizing service quality, governments can ensure that citizens receive reliable, timely, and satisfactory services. This not only enhances citizen satisfaction but also reinforces the legitimacy and credibility of the government.

Secondly, emphasizing service quality in GPR initiatives contributes to the achievement of broader policy objectives, such as fostering economic growth, social inclusion, and sustainable development. By optimizing processes and delivering high-quality services, governments can stimulate economic activity, attract investment, and promote social cohesion. Moreover, a focus on service quality enables governments to identify areas for improvement, implement best practices, and adapt to changing citizen expectations and technological advancements.

In conclusion, service quality is a fundamental consideration in GPR initiatives as it underpins citizen satisfaction, government effectiveness, and the attainment of policy objectives. By prioritizing service quality, governments can enhance trust, improve efficiency, and ultimately drive positive societal outcomes.

2.1.5 Business Process Re-engineering (BPR) and GPR

An extensively acknowledged characterization of Business Process Re-engineering (BPR) is that it entails a profound reimagining and revolutionary redesign of business processes to attain significant enhancements in key, modern indicators of performance, including cost, quality, service, and speed.

The evolution of Government Process Re-engineering (GPR) stems from the adaptation of business process re-engineering (BPR) principles to government services. GPR encompasses the potential to target either all or specific service quality attributes outlined for governmental services.

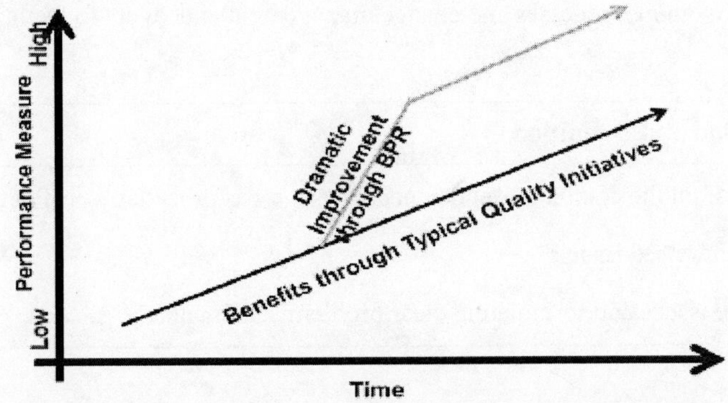

Figure 2.4 Performance improvement after integrating BPR

Government Process Re-engineering (GPR) empowers governments to realize significant enhancements in performance, and integrating IT into re-engineered processes promises superior outcomes for stakeholders, as illustrated in the figure 2.4.

To fully capitalize on the benefits of the GPR endeavor, it's essential to implement appropriate IT enablement for the re-engineered processes.

2.1.6 Steps involved in GPR

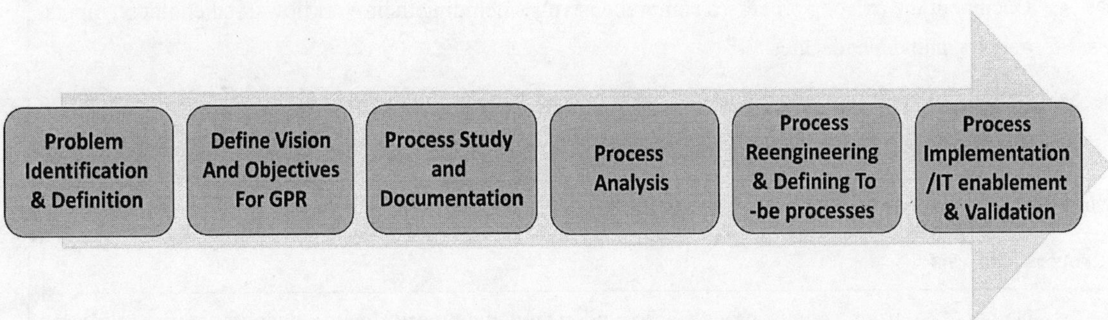

Figure 2.5 Various steps involved in GPR

The different stages of GPR initiatives are shown in the figure 2.5. The initial phase involves identifying and articulating the problem within the current process scenario. Subsequently, the vision and objectives of GPR are defined. Prior to embarking on process re-engineering, existing processes are studied and documented.

This phase also entails gathering data from various processes to gain a comprehensive understanding and establish baseline metrics.

The documented processes undergo analysis utilizing diverse tools and methodologies to find opportunities for enhancement. This includes identifying value-adding/non-value-adding activities, assessing process complexity, and establishing process metrics.

In the re-engineering phase, new processes are crafted in alignment with the drivers of process redesign. This could necessitate reworking, redesigning, outsourcing, or replacing processes/sub-processes. The newly defined processes are then implemented, often with IT enablement. Implementation may entail adjustments to the legal framework governing processes and change management endeavors to facilitate a smooth rollout.

Stage 1:

Problem Identification and Definition
• Examination of public complaints and concerns as well as proactive voice of the customer surveys • Investigation of raised issues. • Identifying the issues and formulating clear problem statements

Stage 2:

Define vision and objectives for GPR
• Examine the portfolio of services and carry out a service prioritizing process. • Define GPR's vision based on challenges found and service priorities. • Establish quantifiable goals for the GPR exercise.

Stage 3:

Process Study and Documentation
• Document the existing processes comprehensively, including their workflows, stakeholders, inputs, outputs, and dependencies. • keeping track of time and additional data at every stage of the procedure • Validation of departmental process document

Stage 4:

Process Analysis
• Gather data from various processes to understand their performance, identify bottlenecks, and establish baseline metrics. • Analyze this data using appropriate tools and methodologies to identify improvement opportunities.

Stage 5:

Process Reengineering
• Design new processes based on the findings from the analysis phase and in alignment with the defined objectives. • This may involve reworking, redesigning, outsourcing, or replacing processes and sub-processes.

Stage 6:

Process Implementation
• Develop a plan for implementing the newly designed processes, considering factors such as IT enablement, changes to the legal framework, and change management efforts. • Execute the plan to implement the new processes, often with the integration of IT solutions to enhance efficiency and effectiveness. • Continuously monitor the performance of the re-engineered processes against established metrics. • Evaluate the outcomes to assess the success of the GPR initiative and identify further areas for improvement.

2.2 National e-Governance Plan(NeGP) for India

In the 1980s and early 1990s, the first steps towards e-Governance primarily concentrated on networking government departments and creating in-house government applications. These applications were developed in areas such as defense, economic monitoring, planning, and IT deployment for managing data-intensive functions like elections, census, and tax administration. However, the focus of these applications was mainly on automating internal government processes rather than enhancing service delivery to citizens.

Emphasizing this issue, Dr. APJ Abdul Kalam, former President of India and a pioneer in the area of e-Governance, outlined the fundamental challenge facing the country during his inaugural address at IIT Delhi during the International Conference on e-Governance on December 18, 2003.

E-Governance must prioritize citizen-friendliness. Serving the public is considered one of the government's primary responsibilities. With more than a billion people living in a democratic country like India, e-Government must to make it easier for people to obtain information and move it between the federal framework's state and federal government systems. *No country has yet effectively deployed an e-Government system for a population of this size. It shows a serious obstacle for us*.

In recent times, across various platforms, the Government of India has expressed its dedication to delivering efficient and transparent governance to all segments of society. E-Governance is increasingly recognized as a pivotal component of the nation's governance and administrative reform agenda. The Government of India aims to offer following efficient and transparent services.

- A government that is comprehensible and answerable to its citizens, must be open to democratic participation and scrutiny (an open and transparent government).

- A citizen-centric government that encompasses all its services and acknowledges everyone as individuals by offering personalized services.
- An efficient government that ensures the highest value for taxpayers' money.

Therefore, the Government of India perceives e-Governance as a means to initiate and uphold reforms by concentrating on three main domains: Public services, Management, and Governance.

The current Union Government's National Common Minimum Programme also prioritizes enhancing the quality of fundamental governance. In this regard, it suggests promoting e-Governance extensively in areas relevant to the general public.

The country's e-Government policy has been greatly impacted by the lessons learned from both successful and unsuccessful endeavors. Consequently, there arose a necessity to adopt a comprehensive perspective encompassing multiple e-Governance initiatives nationwide. It became increasingly evident that expediting e-Governance across various governmental branches and levels would require a programmatic approach guided by a clear vision, strategy, and methodology. Such an approach would offer the additional benefit of substantial cost savings by sharing core and support infrastructure, facilitating interoperability through standards, and ultimately providing citizens with a seamless experience of government services.

The turning point came with the launch of the National e-Governance Plan (NeGP) in 2006, which marked a strategic shift towards more integrated and citizen-centric digital initiatives. NeGP envisioned the establishment of a common IT infrastructure and framework for delivering e-Governance services across central, state, and local governments. Under NeGP, several Mission Mode Projects (MMPs) were launched to automate key government services such as land records management, tax filing, and public distribution systems.

NeGP aimed to provide citizens with convenient and efficient access to government services while enhancing transparency and accountability in administration. NeGP recognized the potential of digital technologies in improving service delivery and sought to leverage them for the benefit of citizens across the country.

At its core, NeGP focused on building a robust digital infrastructure to support the delivery of various government services electronically. This infrastructure included the establishment of common service centers (CSCs) at the village level to ensure last-mile connectivity, as well as the development of core platforms such as the State Data Centers (SDCs) and the State Wide Area Networks (SWANs) to facilitate seamless information exchange between different government departments.

One of the key objectives of NeGP was to streamline and simplify government processes through the implementation of electronic governance (e-governance) initiatives. This involved digitizing government records, automating workflows, and introducing online portals for service delivery. By eliminating bureaucratic hurdles and reducing paperwork, NeGP aimed to make government services more accessible and efficient for citizens.

Furthermore, NeGP emphasized the importance of capacity building and institutional reforms to enable the successful implementation of e-governance initiatives. It focused on training government officials in the use of information and communication technologies (ICTs) and promoting a culture of innovation and collaboration within government departments.

Over the years, NeGP has evolved to keep pace with advancements in technology and changing citizen expectations. It has witnessed the launch of several mission mode projects (MMPs) targeting specific sectors such as healthcare, education, and agriculture to address sector-specific challenges through digital interventions.

The emergence of the National e-Governance Plan marked a significant milestone in India's journey towards leveraging technology for inclusive and transparent governance. By laying the groundwork for a digital government infrastructure and promoting the adoption of e-governance initiatives, NeGP has played a pivotal role in driving administrative reforms and improving service delivery mechanisms across the country.

The Department of Information Technology (DIT) and the Department of Administrative Reforms & Public Grievances (DAR&PG) have developed the National e-Governance Plan (NeGP). On May 18, 2006, the Union Government authorized the National e-Governance Plan (NeGP), which had eight components and 27 Mission Mode Projects (MMPs).

The government has authorized the strategy, vision, key elements and implementation structure for the NeGP.

2.2.1 Vision of NeGP

The vision of the National e-Governance Plan (NeGP) is to make all government services accessible to the common man in his locality through common service delivery outlets and ensure efficiency, transparency, and reliability of such services at affordable costs to realize the basic needs of the common man. NeGP envisions the following key aspects:

a) Accessibility: NeGP aims to make government services accessible to every citizen, irrespective of their geographical location or socio-economic status. This accessibility is facilitated through the establishment of common service centers (CSCs) at the village level, ensuring that even citizens in rural areas can avail themselves of government services conveniently.

b) Efficiency: NeGP focuses on streamlining government processes and procedures to make service delivery more efficient. By digitizing records, automating workflows, and introducing online portals, NeGP aims to reduce bureaucratic delays and improve the speed and responsiveness of government services.

c) Transparency: A key aspect of NeGP's vision is to enhance transparency in governance. By digitizing government records and making information readily available to citizens, NeGP seeks to promote accountability and reduce corruption in the administration.

d) Reliability: NeGP strives to ensure the reliability and quality of government services. By leveraging information technology, NeGP aims to standardize service delivery processes and minimize errors and discrepancies in service provision.

e) Affordability: NeGP is committed to providing government services at affordable costs to citizens. By optimizing resources and leveraging economies of scale through digital platforms, NeGP aims to reduce the financial burden on citizens while maintaining the quality and accessibility of services.

Overall, the vision of NeGP is to harness the power of information technology to transform governance, making it more citizen centric, efficient, transparent, and affordable. By leveraging digital innovations, NeGP aims to bridge the gap between the government and citizens, ensuring that every individual can access and avail themselves of their entitled services easily and effectively.

2.2.2 NeGP Stakeholders

To ensure alignment and coherence among the numerous projects undertaken by Union and State Government departments, the National e-Governance Plan (NeGP) devised a robust institutional framework. Given the intricate nature of e-Governance implementation and the necessity for widespread adoption, effective monitoring and control mechanisms are imperative. Thus, establishing an empowered institutional setup becomes crucial for overseeing, driving, and managing implementation processes. While specific arrangements may vary across different levels, key roles such as formulating and enforcing uniform policies and standards, addressing implementation challenges, and monitoring progress remain consistent. At the national level, NeGP has instituted a well-defined institutional structure to fulfill these functions. The below figure 2.6 shows the well-defined institutional structure of NeGP.

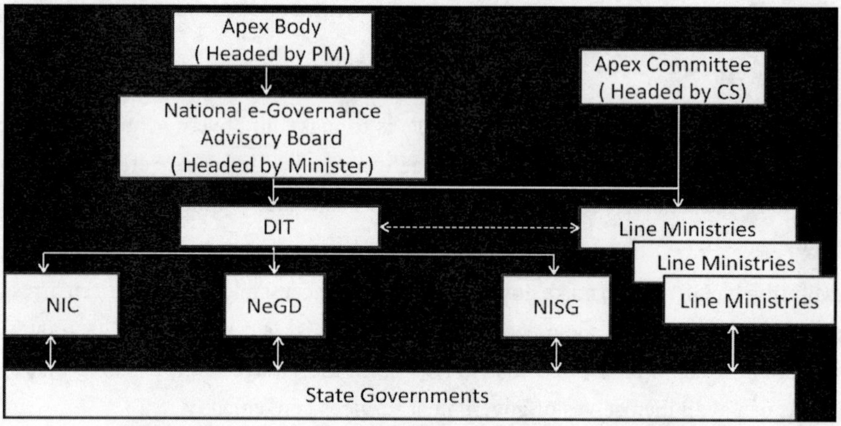

Figure 2.6 Well-defined institutional structure of NeGP

The major responsibilities of each stockholders associated in the implementation of NeGP are as follows:

- *The apex body* in the National e-Governance Plan (NeGP) is the National e-Governance Apex Committee (NeGAC). This committee serves as the highest decision-making authority and provides strategic direction for the implementation of e-Governance initiatives across the country. Chaired by the Cabinet Secretary at the national level, NeGAC comprises senior officials from various central government ministries and departments, as well as representatives from state governments and the private sectors.
- *The National e-Governance Advisory Board (NeGAB)* is an important component of the National e-Governance Plan (NeGP). It serves as a consultative body, providing strategic guidance and advice on e-Governance policies and initiatives. Comprising eminent experts from various fields including academia, industry, civil society, and government, NeGAB plays a crucial role in shaping the direction of e-Governance efforts in India.
- *The Apex Committee* within the framework of the National e-Governance Plan (NeGP) is chaired by the Cabinet Secretary, with the Secretary of the Department of Information Technology (DIT) serving

as its member convener. This committee has been established to supervise the NeGP program, offering policy guidance and strategic direction for its execution. It also addresses inter-ministerial challenges, facilitates and leads service enhancements, process re-engineering efforts, and ensures service levels are maintained for each Mission Mode Project (MMP) as necessary.

- *Line Ministries and Departments* play a crucial role in the implementation of the National e-Governance Plan (NeGP). These ministries and departments are responsible for executing e-Governance initiatives within their respective domains and sectors. They collaborate with the Department of Information Technology (DIT) and other relevant authorities to ensure the successful rollout of e-Governance projects. Each Line Ministry or Department focuses on digitizing and modernizing government services and processes related to its specific area of responsibility.
- *State Governments and Union Territory (UT) Administrations* are vital stakeholders in the implementation of the National e-Governance Plan (NeGP) in India. They play a significant role in executing e-Governance initiatives at the regional level, ensuring the delivery of digital services to citizens within their respective jurisdictions.
- *The Department of Information Technology (DIT),* which is now known as the Ministry of Electronics and Information Technology (MeitY), along with the National Informatics Centre (NIC), plays a central role in the National e-Governance Plan (NeGP) in India. DIT/MeitY serves as the nodal agency responsible for coordinating and overseeing the implementation of e-Governance initiatives across the country. It formulates policies, guidelines, and standards for e-Governance projects, ensuring consistency and interoperability among different systems and platforms.

2.2.3 e-Governance Implementation Strategy

Implementing e-Governance is a bit difficult process involving hardware, software, networking, process re-engineering, and change management. Earlier, numerous e-Governance projects have been pursued through individual initiatives, yielding varying degrees of success. Some have met their objectives, while others were unable to produce desired outcome over time. Hence, a judicious approach is proposed for the National e-Governance Plan (NeGP), informed by lessons learnt from past endeavors and successful e-Governance implementations both domestically and globally. The approach and methodology outlined for NeGP comprise the following components.

a) Common Support Infrastructure: Under the NeGP implementation, establishing common and supportive IT infrastructure is imperative. This includes the setup of State Wide Area Networks (SWANs), State Data Centres (SDCs), Common Services Centres (CSCs), and Electronic Service Delivery Gateways.

b) Governance: Necessary mechanisms for monitoring and coordinating NeGP implementation, under the guidance of competent authorities, have been established. The program also encompasses the development or establishment of standards and policy guidelines, the provision of technical support, capacity building initiatives, research and development, and similar endeavors. DIT enhances its capabilities, along with various institutions such as NIC, STQC, CDAC, NISG, etc., to effectively fulfill these roles.

c) Centralized Initiative, Decentralized Implementation: The promotion of e-Governance occurs through a centralized initiative, to the extent required to ensure a citizen-centric approach, achieve interoperability among various e-Governance applications, and optimize the utilization of ICT infrastructure and resources, while accommodating a decentralized implementation model.

d) The Public-Private Partnerships (PPP) model will be embraced wherever possible to expand the resource pool while maintaining security standards.

e) Integrative Elements: Encouraging the adoption of unique identification codes for citizens, businesses, and property is advocated to facilitate integration and prevent ambiguity.

f) Programmatic Approach at National and State Levels: The implementation of the NeGP includes multiple union ministries/departments and state governments. For various agencies involved and the necessity for comprehensive aggregation and integration at the national level, the NeGP is being executed as a program, with clearly defined roles and responsibilities for each involved agency. To facilitate this, appropriate program management structures have been established.

g) Defining the role of DIT: DIT serves as the facilitator and catalyst for NeGP implementation by various ministries and state governments, providing technical assistance as needed. It acts as a secretariat to the Apex Committee, aiding in program management. Additionally, DIT oversees the implementation of pilot, infrastructure, technical, and special projects, along with support components. DAR&PG is responsible for Government Process Re-engineering and Change Management across all government departments. The Planning Commission and Ministry of Finance allocate funds for NeGP through plan and non-plan budgetary provisions, establishing relevant procedures accordingly.

h) Ownership of Ministries: Within the NeGP framework, various Mission Mode Projects (MMPs) are managed and led by the respective line ministries. If there are any existing projects falling under the MMP category, they will be appropriately augmented to align with NeGP objectives. Line ministries overseeing major projects such as Bharat Nirman and Rural Employment Guarantee Schemes are encouraged to incorporate e-Governance and automation techniques from the project's inception. States have the autonomy to identify additional state-specific projects conducive to the state's economic development.

2.2.4 Mission Mode Projects (MMP)

Below is the list of Mission Mode Projects (MMPs) at the central, state, and integrated levels. While certain MMPs are at advanced stages of implementation, others are still in the conceptualization phase.

Table 2.1 Various mission mode projects at central and state level.

S N	Projects	Line Ministry/ Deptt. responsible	Project Summary
Mission Mode Projects govern by Central Government			
1	Passport	Ministry of External Affairs/	The Passport Seva Project was initiated by the Ministry of External Affairs to provide passport

		Ministry of Home Affairs	services to citizens in a convenient, accessible, and reliable manner. The MMP offers various e-services, including the issuance/re-issuance of passports, issuance of duplicate Passports, issuance of tatkal passports, changes in name, address, ECNR/ECR suspensions, and passport status inquiries.
2	Visa and Immigration	Ministry of External Affairs/ Ministry of Home Affairs	To update and enhance immigration services, "Immigration, Visa, and Foreigners Registration & Tracking (IVFRT)" has been designated as one of the MMPs to be undertaken by the Ministry of Home Affairs as part of the National e-Governance Plan (NeGP). The primary aim of this project is to establish and execute a secure and integrated service delivery framework that facilitates legitimate travelers while making security measures stronger.
3	MCA21	Ministry of Corporate Affairs	The MCA21 project is a significant initiative undertaken by the Ministry of Corporate Affairs (MCA) in India. It aims to modernize and streamline the processes related to the administration of corporate affairs in the country. The "MCA21" stands for "Ministry of Corporate Affairs 21st Century," reflecting its goal of bringing corporate governance practices into the digital age.
4	Insurance	Department of Banking	MMP aims at facilitating customer services, automating grievance redressal mechanism and, creating a holistic database of insurance users.
5	Income Tax	Ministry of Finance/Central Board of Direct Taxes	Overall, Income Tax projects play a crucial role in modernizing tax administration, enhancing taxpayer services, and strengthening revenue collection efforts. By the use of computer technology and data-driven approaches, tax authorities can achieve greater efficiency and effectiveness in managing income tax systems while promoting fairness and equity in tax compliance.
6	National Citizen Database/UID	Ministry of Home Affairs/Registrar General of India	The UID project, also known as Aadhaar, is a pioneering initiative by the Government of India aimed at providing a unique identification number to residents of India. Launched by the Unique

			Identification Authority of India (UIDAI) in 2009, Aadhaar seeks to provide every individual with a unique 12-digit identification number linked to biometric and demographic data.
7	Central Excise	Department of Revenue/Central Board of Excise & Customs	The Central Excise project by the Government of India primarily revolves around the digitization and modernization of the central excise tax system to enhance efficiency, transparency, and compliance. This project aims to streamline the process of levying and collecting excise duties on goods manufactured or produced in India.
8	Pensions	Department of Pensions & Pensioners Welfare and Department of Expenditure	This Mission Mode Project (MMP) offers updated information on government pension rules and regulations, facilitates the registration of pensioners' grievances, monitors the timely sanction of pension/gratuity, maintains a database of pensioners, and provides links to the websites of the Directorates of Pensions and the Accountant Generals (AGs) of various states.
9	Banking	Department of Banking	Its purpose is to channelize different e-services start-ups implemented by individual banks.
10	e-office	Department of Administrative Reforms & Public Grievances	The e-Office project is a transformative initiative aimed at digitizing and modernizing office processes across various government departments and ministries. Launched to enhance efficiency, transparency, and accountability in government functioning, the e-Office project seeks to replace traditional paper-based office processes with electronic workflows and document management systems.
Mission Mode Projects by State Sectors			
1	Land Record	Ministry of Rural Development	The Land Record project generally refers to efforts by government to digitize and modernize land records management systems. Traditional land records often involve paper-based documents that can be cumbersome to manage, prone to errors, and difficult to access. By digitizing land records, governments aim to create a more efficient,

			transparent, and accessible system for managing land ownership, transactions, and related information.
2	Road Transport	Ministry of Road Transport & Highways	A Road Transport project typically refers to initiatives undertaken by governments to improve transportation infrastructure, enhance road safety, and streamline the management of road networks. These projects aim to address various challenges associated with road transportation, such as congestion, road accidents, inefficient logistics, and inadequate infrastructure.
3	Agriculture	Department of Agriculture & Cooperation	Agriculture projects encompass a wide range of initiatives aimed at improving various aspects of agricultural practices, productivity, sustainability, and socio-economic conditions for farmers and rural communities. These projects can be implemented by governments, non-governmental organizations (NGOs), international agencies, research institutions, or private sector entities.
4	Treasuries	Ministry of Finance	This program (or initiative) focuses on modernizing treasuries through computerization. It establishes a uniform set of guidelines to ensure smooth integration between all participating government agencies.
5	Municipalities	Ministry of Urban Employment and Poverty Alleviation	A Municipalities project initiated by a state government typically focuses on improving the functioning, infrastructure, and services provided by municipal bodies within the state. These projects aim to enhance urban governance, promote sustainable development, and improve the quality of life for residents in urban areas.
6	Gram Panchayats	Ministry of Panchayati Raj	A Gram Panchayats project initiated by a state government typically focuses on empowering and strengthening the functioning of rural local self-government bodies known as Gram Panchayats. These projects aim to improve governance, promote sustainable development, and enhance the quality of life for residents in rural areas.

7	Commercial Taxes	Ministry of Finance	A Commercial Taxes project initiated by a state government typically focuses on modernizing and streamlining the administration of commercial taxes within the state. These projects aim to improve tax collection efficiency, enhance compliance, reduce tax evasion, and create a business-friendly environment.
8	Police (CCTNS)	Ministry of Home Affairs	The Police (CCTNS) project, initiated by state governments, stands for Crime and Criminal Tracking Network & Systems. It's a comprehensive and integrated system aimed at modernizing the functioning of police forces across the country.
9	Employment Exchanges	Ministry of Labour & Employment	Employment Exchanges projects initiated by state governments are aimed at facilitating the employment process for job seekers and employers within their respective states.
10	E-District	Department of Information Technology (DIT)	The e-District project initiated by state governments aims to deliver various government services to citizens through digital channels, thereby enhancing accessibility, transparency, and efficiency in service delivery.
		Mission Mode Projects – Integrated Category	
1	EDI (e-Commerce)	Ministry of Commerce & Industry/ Department of Commerce	An EDI (Electronic Data Interchange) project in e-commerce aims to streamline communication between businesses by automating the exchange of information in a standardized electronic format.
2	e-Biz	Department of Industrial Policy & Promotion / Department of Information Technology	The e-Biz project is an initiative aimed at simplifying the process of starting and operating businesses in India through electronic means. It's a government-driven project focused on providing a single-window platform for businesses to interact with various regulatory authorities and obtain necessary approvals, licenses, and permits.
3	Common Services Centers	Department of Information Technology	The Common Services Centers (CSC) project is an initiative by the Government of India aimed at providing various government and non-government services to citizens in rural and remote areas through

			a network of digitally equipped service delivery points.
4	India Portal	India Portal Department of Information Technology and Department of Administrative Reforms & Public Grievances	The India Portal project is a centralized web platform launched by the Government of India with the aim of providing citizens, businesses, and government officials easy access to various government services, information, and resources.
5	National Service Delivery Gateway (NSDG)	Department of Information Technology	The National Service Delivery Gateway (NSDG) project is an initiative by the Government of India aimed at providing a unified platform for the delivery of government services to citizens and businesses through digital channels.
6	e-Courts	Department of Justice, Ministry of Home Affairs	The e-Courts project is an ambitious initiative undertaken by the Government of India with the aim of digitizing the functioning of the Indian judiciary system
7	e-Procurement	Ministry of Commerce & Industry/ DGS&D	The e-Procurement MMP (Mission Mode Project) is an initiative aimed at modernizing and streamlining the procurement processes of government departments through the use of Information Technology (IT) solutions.

2.2.5 NeGP Components

The Department of Information Technology (DIT) is leading the implementation of NeGP (National e-Governance Plan). To achieve this, they're building essential infrastructure like national and state-wide networks, data centers, and citizen service gateways. They're also setting up monitoring and coordination systems to ensure smooth implementation under government guidance.

Table 2.2 Essential infrastructure components of NeGP

S. No.	Support Components	Line Ministry/ Department Responsible
1	Core Polices	DIT
2	Core Infrastructure (SWAN, NICNET, SDCs, etc.)	DIT
3	Support Infrastructure (CSCs, etc.)	DIT
4	Technical Assistance	DIT

S. No.	Support Components	Line Ministry/ Department Responsible
5	R&D	DIT
6	Human Resource Development & Training	DIT and DAR&PG
7	Awareness & Assessment	DIT and DAR&PG
8	Organization structures	DIT and DAR&PG

2.2.6 NeGP Framework

The e-Governance framework consists of back-ends, which consist of databases from various government sectors, service providers, state governments, etc. middleware and front-end delivery channels, such as home PCs, mobile phones, and integrated citizen service centers, are provided for businesses and citizens. The middleware includes communication and security infrastructure, gateways, and integrated services which makes it easier to combine interdepartmental services. The NeGP framework is depicted in the following figure 2.7.

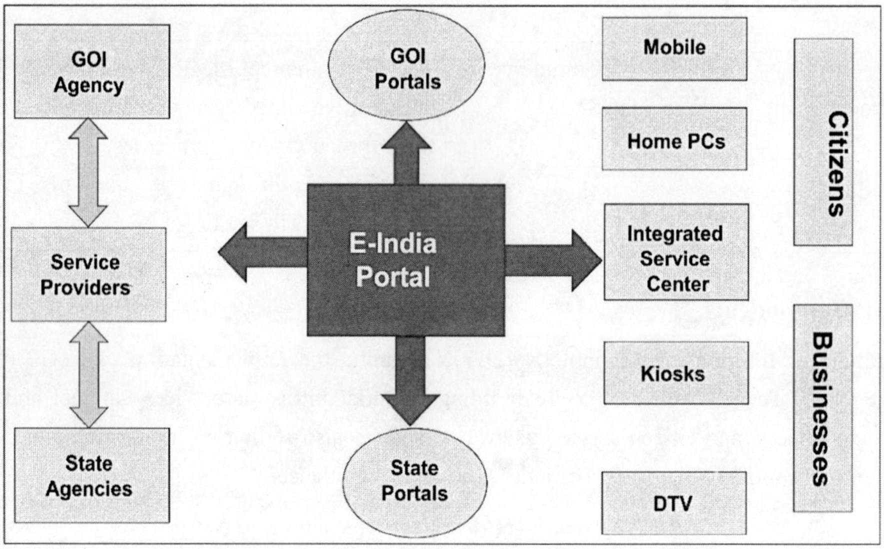

Figure 2.7 NeGP program framework

2.2.7 Required Infrastructure Support

NeGP relies on three infrastructure pillars for efficient delivery of government services. These pillars ensure that citizens can access information and services anytime, anywhere through the web. Here are the three main pillars of e-Governance infrastructure that NeGP envisions.

a) State Wide Area Network (SWAN)

b) National Data Bank/State Data Centers (SDC)

c) Common Services Centers (CSC)

a) State Wide Area Network (SWAN)

The State Wide Area Network (SWAN) is a crucial component of the National e-Governance Plan (NeGP). It serves as a backbone network infrastructure that connects various government offices, departments, and service delivery points within a state. SWAN facilitates the exchange of data, information, and digital services among different government entities, enabling seamless communication and collaboration. The three-tier architecture of state wide area network (SWAN) is shown in the figure 2.8.

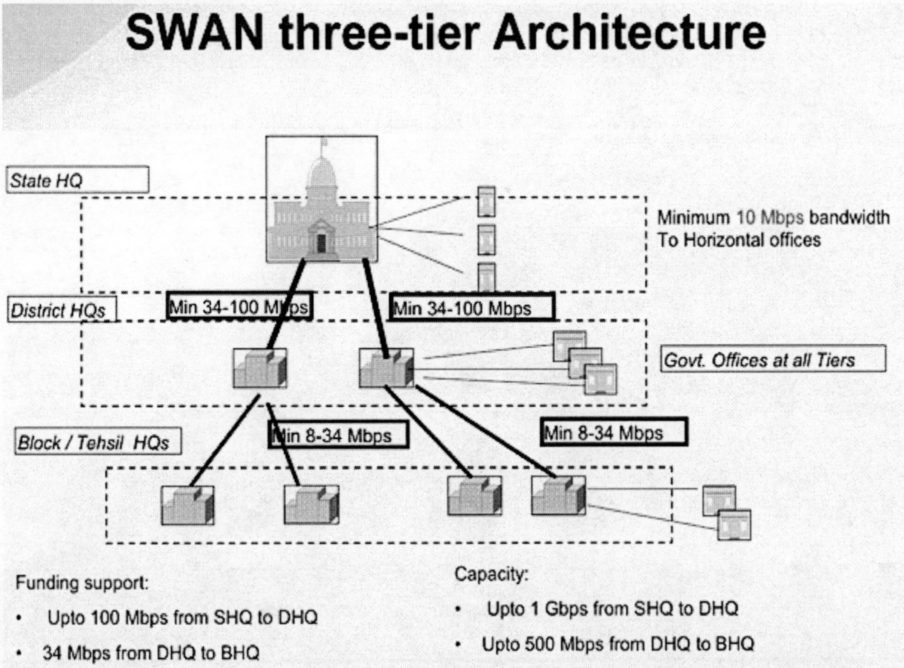

Figure 2.8 Three-tier architecture of state wide area network (SWAN).

SWAN aims to create a reliable, high-speed, and secure network infrastructure that supports the efficient delivery of e-Governance services to citizens, businesses, and government agencies across the state. It provides connectivity to district headquarters, block offices, tehsils, and other administrative units, ensuring that government services are accessible even in remote and rural areas.

The key objectives of SWAN within NeGP include:

- *Connectivity:* Establishing a robust network infrastructure that interconnects all government offices and service delivery points within the state, ensuring seamless connectivity and communication.
- *Accessibility:* Ensuring that e-Governance services are accessible to citizens and businesses across the state, irrespective of their geographical location.
- *Reliability:* Providing a reliable and resilient network infrastructure that can withstand disruptions and ensure uninterrupted access to critical government services.
- *Security:* Implementing robust security measures to protect sensitive government data and ensure the integrity and confidentiality of information exchanged over the network.

- *Scalability:* Designing the network infrastructure to accommodate future growth and expansion of e-Governance services and applications, ensuring scalability and flexibility to meet evolving needs.

Overall, SWAN plays a vital role in the successful implementation of NeGP by providing the necessary connectivity and infrastructure to support the delivery of e-Governance services and promote digital inclusion and empowerment across the state.

b) National Data Bank/State Data Centers (SDC)

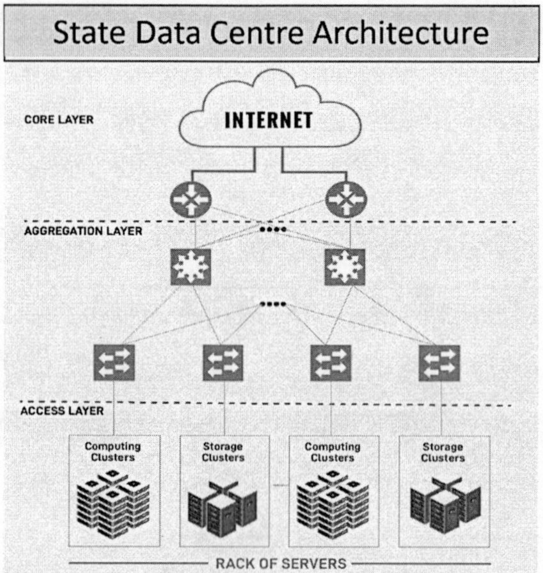

Figure 2.9 Architecture of state data center

The National Data Bank, also known as the State Data Centers (SDCs), is a critical component of the National e-Governance Plan (NeGP). These centers serve as centralized repositories for hosting and managing government data and applications at the national and state levels, respectively. Here's an overview of their role and significance within NeGP:

- *Data Storage and Management:* The National Data Bank and State Data Centers are responsible for storing, managing, and safeguarding government data and information. They serve as secure and reliable repositories for storing various types of data, including citizen records, administrative data, statistical information, and government applications. The figure 2.9 shows the architecture of state data center.

- *Centralized Hosting:* These centers provide centralized services for hosting government applications and services. By consolidating hosting services in a centralized data center environment, they enable efficient resource utilization, cost savings, and better management of IT infrastructure.

- *Data Security and Compliance:* National Data Bank and State Data Centers implement robust security measures to protect sensitive government data and ensure compliance with data protection and privacy regulations. They employ advanced security technologies, such as encryption, access controls, and intrusion detection systems, to safeguard data against unauthorized access, breaches, and cyber threats.

- *Disaster Recovery and Business Continuity:* These centers establish disaster recovery and business continuity mechanisms to ensure the availability and integrity of government data and services in the event of natural disasters, system failures, or other disruptions. They implement backup and recovery solutions, redundant infrastructure, and contingency plans to minimize downtime and maintain service continuity.
- *Interoperability and Integration:* National Data Bank and State Data Centers facilitate interoperability and integration among different government systems and databases. They provide standardized interfaces, data exchange protocols, and middleware services to enable seamless integration of disparate systems and promote data sharing and collaboration among government departments and agencies.
- *Capacity Building and Support:* These centers offer capacity building and technical support services to government departments and agencies in managing and leveraging data effectively. They provide training, guidance, and technical assistance to government officials and IT staff in data management best practices, application hosting, and utilization of data analytics tools and technologies.

Overall, the National Data Bank/State Data Centers play a crucial role in supporting the digital transformation of government operations, enhancing service delivery, and promoting data-driven decision-making within the framework of the National e-Governance Plan.

c) Common services Centers (CSC)

Common Services Centers (CSCs) play a vital role in the implementation of the National e-Governance Plan (NeGP). These centers act as service delivery points located at the grassroots level, providing a range of digital services to citizens, particularly in rural and remote areas. The figure 2.10 given below shows the common service center ecosystem.

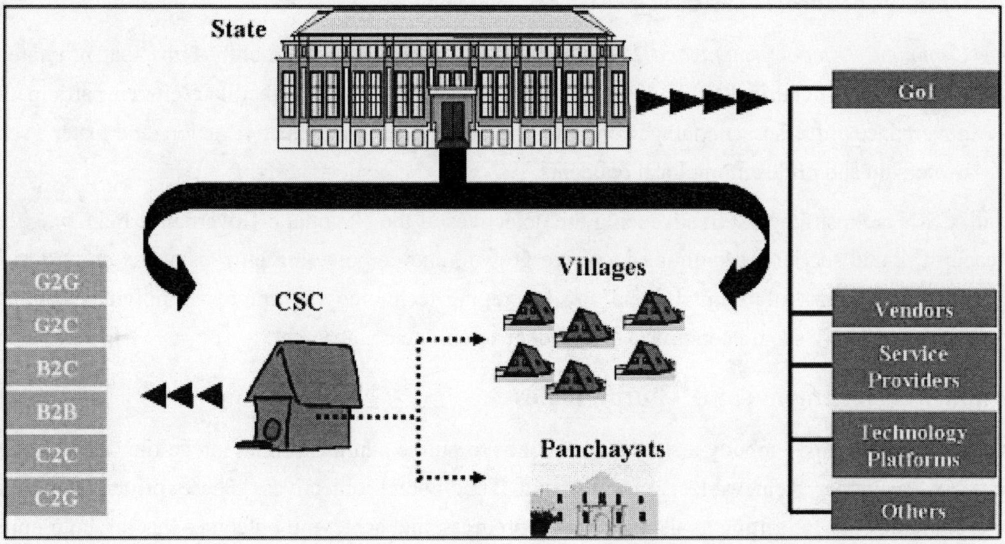

Figure 2.10 Common Service Centers Ecosystem

Here's an overview of CSCs and their significance within NeGP:

- *Last-Mile Connectivity:* CSCs bridge the digital divide by extending e-Governance services to citizens in remote and rural areas where internet connectivity and access to digital infrastructure are limited. They serve as the last-mile connectivity points, ensuring that government services reach even the most underserved populations.
- *One-Stop Service Delivery:* CSCs offer a wide range of government and private sector services under one roof, making it convenient for citizens to access various services at a single location. These services may include utility bill payments, banking services, insurance services, healthcare consultations, educational services, agricultural information, and digital literacy programs.
- *Entrepreneurship and Livelihood Generation:* CSCs are operated by local entrepreneurs known as Village Level Entrepreneurs (VLEs). By empowering VLEs to operate CSCs, NeGP promotes entrepreneurship and livelihood generation opportunities in rural areas. VLEs act as agents of change, facilitating the delivery of digital services while also creating employment and income opportunities for themselves.
- *Digital Literacy and Skill Development:* CSCs play a crucial role in promoting digital literacy and skill development among citizens, particularly in rural areas where awareness and access to digital technologies may be limited. They offer training programs and workshops on basic digital skills, internet usage, and online service access, empowering citizens to leverage digital tools for their personal and professional development.
- *Facilitation of Government Services:* CSCs facilitate access to a wide range of government services and schemes, including application submission, document verification, and service delivery. Citizens can visit CSCs to avail themselves of government services, apply for certificates and licenses, submit forms and documents, and track the status of their applications.
- *Community Empowerment and Participation:* CSCs serve as community hubs that promote civic engagement, social inclusion, and community development. They facilitate citizen participation in governance processes, encourage community collaboration and collective action, and foster a sense of ownership and pride among local residents.

Overall, CSCs are instrumental in advancing the objectives of the National e-Governance Plan by extending the reach of digital services, promoting inclusive growth, and empowering citizens at the grassroots level. They embody the spirit of "Digital India" by leveraging technology to empower individuals, transform communities, and drive socio-economic development across the country.

2.3 Smart Governments and Thumb Rules

"***SMART Governments***" embody a strategic approach to public administration, integrating the principles of Specific, Measurable, Achievable, Relevant, and Time-bound objectives. These principles provide a structured framework for setting goals, monitoring progress, and achieving outcomes that are both impactful and sustainable. By adhering to SMART criteria, governments can enhance their efficiency, effectiveness, and responsiveness in delivering services and addressing societal challenges.

At the core of SMART Governments lies specificity, ensuring that objectives are clearly defined, leaving no room for ambiguity or misinterpretation. Specific goals provide focus and direction, guiding policymakers and administrators in allocating resources and designing interventions that address identified needs and priorities. Measurability complements specificity by enabling progress towards goals to be quantified and tracked using relevant indicators or metrics. Measurable targets facilitate evidence-based decision-making, allowing policymakers to assess performance, identify areas for improvement, and allocate resources strategically.

Achievability emphasizes the importance of setting realistic and attainable goals within the constraints of available resources, time, and capacity. Achievable objectives inspire confidence and motivation among stakeholders, fostering a culture of success and enabling incremental progress towards larger objectives. Relevance ensures that goals are aligned with broader strategic priorities and societal needs, promoting meaningful outcomes and generating tangible benefits for citizens. Time-bound targets establish deadlines and milestones for achieving results, creating a sense of urgency and promoting accountability among stakeholders.

Implementing SMART principles in governance requires a comprehensive and integrated approach that encompasses policy formulation, program design, resource allocation, performance monitoring, and stakeholder engagement.

2.3.1 Significance of smart government in context of Indian bureaucracy

In the context of Indian bureaucracy, the significance of SMART Government principles cannot be overstated. India's bureaucratic machinery, often criticized for its inefficiencies, bureaucratic red tape, and lack of responsiveness, stands to benefit immensely from the adoption of SMART principles. These principles, focusing on Specific, Measurable, Achievable, Relevant, and Time-bound objectives, offer a structured framework for improving governance outcomes, streamlining administrative processes, and enhancing service delivery to citizens.

One of the most pressing challenges facing Indian bureaucracy is the need for greater efficiency and effectiveness in delivering public services. SMART Government emphasizes setting clear and specific objectives, enabling bureaucrats to prioritize tasks and allocate resources judiciously. By defining measurable targets and outcomes, bureaucrats can monitor progress, identify bottlenecks, and take corrective actions to ensure that objectives are achieved within stipulated timelines. This results in a more streamlined and accountable bureaucratic machinery that is better equipped to meet the needs and expectations of citizens.

Transparency and accountability are foundational principles of SMART Government, addressing long-standing concerns about corruption and lack of transparency in Indian bureaucracy. By promoting openness, accessibility, and accountability in decision-making and service delivery, SMART principles help build public trust and confidence in government institutions. Clear goals, measurable indicators, and transparent processes enable citizens to hold bureaucrats accountable for their actions, fostering a culture of accountability and integrity within the bureaucracy.

Moreover, SMART Government emphasizes a citizen-centric approach to service delivery, aligning bureaucratic processes and initiatives with the needs and priorities of citizens. By setting achievable and relevant objectives that directly impact citizens' lives, Indian bureaucracy can enhance the quality, accessibility, and responsiveness of public services. Measurable targets enable bureaucrats to monitor service delivery outcomes, identify areas for improvement, and make data-driven decisions to enhance citizen satisfaction and well-being.

Innovation and adaptability are also key tenets of SMART Government, encouraging bureaucrats to embrace new technologies, methodologies, and best practices to address emerging challenges and changing needs. By investing in digital transformation, data analytics, and agile governance practices, Indian bureaucracy can enhance its capacity to respond to complex governance challenges and deliver services more efficiently and effectively. Innovation-driven initiatives enable bureaucrats to stay ahead of the curve, driving continuous improvement and innovation in public administration.

Ultimately, the adoption of SMART Government principles offers a transformative opportunity for Indian bureaucracy to overcome bureaucratic inertia, foster a culture of innovation and accountability, and deliver better outcomes for citizens. By embracing SMART principles, Indian bureaucracy can enhance its efficiency, effectiveness, and responsiveness, ultimately contributing to the country's socio-economic development and well-being.

2.3.2 Principles of SMART Government or thumb rules

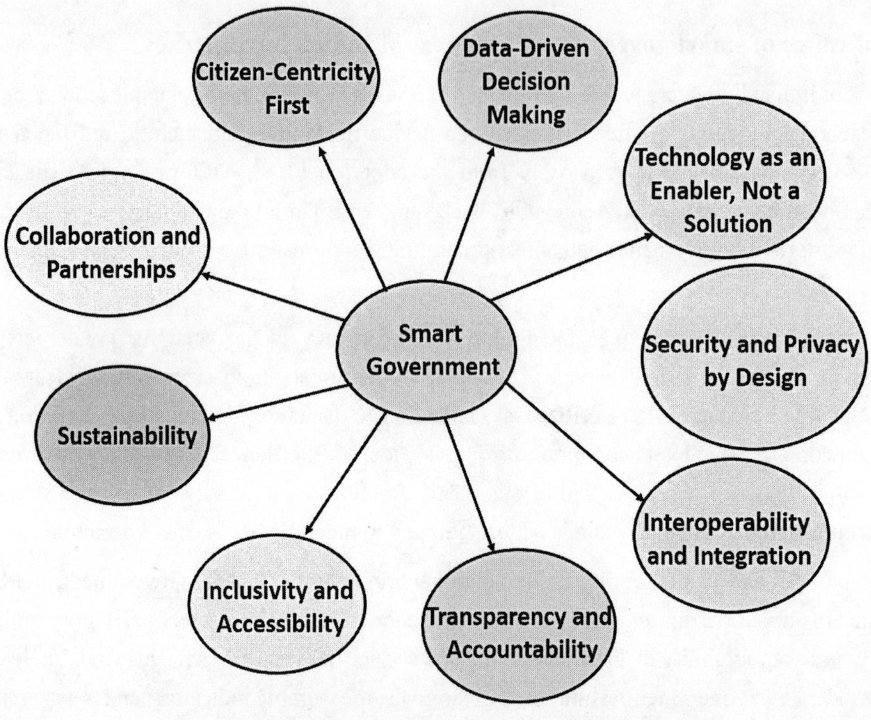

Figure 2.11 Principles of Smart Government or thumb rules.

The concept of SMART government or thumb rules refers to a model of governance that leverages technology, data, and innovation to improve efficiency, transparency, and citizen engagement. The major components of principles of SMART government are mentioned in the figure 2.11 and typically include:

A "thumb rule" in the context of smart governments refers to a general principle or heuristic that guides decision-making and the implementation of technology and innovation in governance. These rules are not rigid laws but serve as practical guidelines to ensure that the adoption and use of smart technologies align with the overarching goals of efficiency, transparency, accountability, and citizen-centric service delivery. Here are some key thumb rules for smart governments:

1. *Citizen-Centricity First*

- Prioritize User Experience: Always design and implement services with the citizen's needs and ease of use in mind. Services should be intuitive, accessible, and responsive to ensure widespread adoption and satisfaction.
- Feedback Mechanisms: Establish robust systems for collecting and responding to citizen feedback to continuously improve services.

2. *Data-Driven Decision Making*

- Evidence-Based Policies: Use data analytics to inform policy decisions and administrative actions. Ensure that decisions are based on accurate, timely, and comprehensive data.
- Open Data: Promote transparency by making non-sensitive government data publicly available, enabling citizens and third parties to use this data for innovation and accountability.

3. *Technology as an Enabler, Not a Solution*

- Purposeful Use of Technology: Adopt technology that directly addresses specific problems or improves existing processes. Avoid using technology for its own sake without clear benefits.
- Scalability and Flexibility: Choose technologies that can scale with increasing demand and adapt to changing circumstances and future innovations.

4. *Security and Privacy by Design*

- Robust Cybersecurity: Implement strong cybersecurity measures from the outset to protect against data breaches and cyber threats.
- Privacy Protection: Ensure that all technologies comply with privacy regulations and that personal data is handled responsibly and transparently.

5. *Interoperability and Integration*

- Seamless Systems: Ensure that different technologies and systems used across various government departments can work together seamlessly to provide a unified experience for users.
- Standardization: Adopt common standards and protocols to facilitate interoperability and data exchange between systems.

6. *Transparency and Accountability*

- Open Processes: Make government processes transparent to build trust and enable public scrutiny. Clearly communicate decisions, policies, and their rationales to the public.

- Performance Metrics: Regularly measure and publish performance metrics for government services to ensure accountability and continuous improvement.

7. *Inclusivity and Accessibility*

- Equitable Access: Ensure that digital services are accessible to all citizens, including those with disabilities and those in underserved areas. Address digital divide issues proactively.
- Diverse Representation: Involve a diverse range of stakeholders in the design and implementation of smart government initiatives to ensure that all voices are heard and considered.

8. *Sustainability*

- Environmental Responsibility: Integrate sustainable practices in the deployment of technology and the delivery of services. Aim for green technology solutions that minimize environmental impact.
- Long-Term Vision: Focus on long-term benefits and sustainability, ensuring that initiatives contribute to lasting improvements rather than short-term gains.

9. *Collaboration and Partnerships*

- Public-Private Collaboration: Foster partnerships with the private sector, non-profits, and academia to leverage expertise, resources, and innovative solutions.
- Citizen Engagement: Actively engage citizens in the governance process through participatory tools and platforms, encouraging their input and involvement.

These thumb rules serve as guiding principles to ensure that the implementation of smart government initiatives is effective, responsible, and aligned with the goal of enhancing public administration and service delivery. By adhering to these guidelines, governments can navigate the complexities of digital transformation and create a more efficient, transparent, and inclusive governance model.

UNIT SUMMARY

This unit initially emphasizes the need for Government Process Re-engineering (GPR) to enhance efficiency, transparency, and responsiveness in government operations. Then, it compares e-Governance with conventional approaches, detailing how GPR and Business Process Re-engineering (BPR) can improve service quality. The steps involved in GPR are outlined, illustrating a structured approach to re-engineering government processes. After that, the National e-Governance Plan (NeGP) for India is introduced, covering its vision, stakeholders, implementation strategy, mission mode projects (MMP), components, and required infrastructure. Finally, the unit explores the significance of SMART governments in the Indian bureaucracy, focusing on principles that ensure specific, measurable, achievable, relevant, and time-bound governance objectives, alongside best practices for effective decision-making and operational consistency.

EXERCISES

Q1 What is the primary goal of Government Process Re-engineering (GPR)?

A) Increase government revenue

B) Improve citizen services and reduce processing time

C) Promote foreign investment

D) Enhance government control

Q2 Which of the following best defines e-Governance?

A) Use of electronic devices for governance

B) Application of information technology to government processes

C) Internet voting system

D) Digital surveillance of citizens

Q3 What distinguishes conventional e-governance from modern e-governance?

A) Use of paper records

B) Focus on digital transactions

C) Lack of citizen interaction

D) Emphasis on transparency and efficiency

Q4 Which of the following is a key principle of Business Process Re-engineering (BPR)?

A) Incremental improvements

B) Radical redesign

C) Maintain existing processes

D) Focus on hierarchical control

Q5 What is the purpose of measuring Service Quality in e-governance?

A) To assess the number of transactions

B) To evaluate customer satisfaction and service efficiency

C) To increase government fees

D) To monitor employee performance

Q6 What is the vision of the National e-Governance Plan (NeGP) for India?

A) To digitalize all financial transactions

B) To make all government services accessible to the common man

C) To promote international trade

D) To centralize all government data

Q7 Who are the primary stakeholders in the National e-Governance Plan (NeGP)?

A) Citizens, Government, and Industry

B) Only the government

C) International agencies

D) Private corporations

Q8 What is the focus of Mission Mode Projects (MMP) in the context of NeGP?

A) To conduct government surveys

B) To implement specific e-governance initiatives

C) To create new government departments

D) To privatize government services

Q9 Which of the following is NOT a component of NeGP?

A) Common Service Centers (CSCs)

B) State Data Centers (SDCs)

C) National Highways

D) State Wide Area Networks (SWANs)

Q10 What is a key element of the NeGP Framework?

A) Focus on increasing taxes

B) Ensuring interoperability and integration of services

C) Reducing the number of government employees

D) Limiting citizen access to services

Q11 What kind of infrastructure support is required for effective e-governance?

A) Only physical office spaces

B) Robust IT infrastructure, connectivity, and data centers

C) Increased manual labor

D) Expansion of physical government offices

Q12 Which principle is NOT typically associated with SMART Governments?

A) Citizen-centric services

B) Transparency and accountability

C) Rigidity in processes

D) Responsiveness and efficiency

Q13 Which of the following is NOT a principle of SMART Government?

A) Specific

B) Measurable

C) Ambiguous

D) Time-bound

Answers

Q.N.	1	2	3	4	5	6	7	8	9	10	11	12	13
Option	B	B	D	B	B	B	A	B	C	B	B	C	C

Short Answer Type Questions

1. What is the main objective of Government Process Re-engineering (GPR)?
2. How does e-Governance differ from conventional governance approaches?
3. Define Business Process Re-engineering (BPR) and its relevance to GPR.
4. List the key steps involved in implementing GPR.
5. What are the benefits of re-engineering government processes?
6. What is the vision of the National e-Governance Plan (NeGP)?
7. Who are the primary stakeholders involved in NeGP?
8. Describe the e-Governance implementation strategy under NeGP.
9. What are Mission Mode Projects (MMP) in the context of NeGP?
10. Identify the main components of NeGP.
11. Explain the framework used for the implementation of NeGP.
12. What kind of infrastructure support is required for NeGP to be successful?
13. Why is the concept of SMART government significant in the context of Indian bureaucracy?
14. What do the principles of SMART governance stand for?
15. How do SMART principles contribute to effective decision-making in government?
16. Give an example of a thumb rule in the context of SMART governance.
17. What role do SMART principles play in creating a citizen-centric governance model?

Long Answer Type Questions

1. Compare and contrast e-Governance with conventional e-governance approaches. Discuss the advantages and disadvantages of each.
2. Explain the concept of Government Process Re-engineering (GPR). How does it aim to improve government operations and public service delivery?
3. Define Business Process Re-engineering (BPR). How does BPR differ from GPR, and how can BPR principles be applied to GPR initiatives?
4. Discuss the importance of understanding service quality in the context of GPR. How can improved service quality benefit both the government and citizens?

5. Explain the relationship between Business Process Re-engineering (BPR) and Government Process Re-engineering (GPR). Provide examples of how BPR principles can enhance GPR efforts.
6. Outline the key steps involved in implementing Government Process Re-engineering (GPR). Provide a detailed explanation of each step.
7. Evaluate the potential challenges and barriers to successful Government Process Re-engineering (GPR). How can these challenges be addressed?
8. Describe the vision of the National e-Governance Plan (NeGP). How does NeGP aim to transform public service delivery in India?
9. Identify and discuss the primary stakeholders involved in the National e-Governance Plan (NeGP). How do these stakeholders contribute to the success of NeGP?
10. Explain the e-Governance implementation strategy under the National e-Governance Plan (NeGP). What are the key components of this strategy?
11. Discuss the significance of Mission Mode Projects (MMP) within the framework of NeGP. Provide examples of successful MMPs and their impact on governance.
12. Analyze the main components of the National e-Governance Plan (NeGP). How do these components work together to achieve the goals of NeGP?
13. Describe the framework used for the implementation of NeGP. How does this framework ensure the effective delivery of e-Governance services?
14. Assess the infrastructure support required for the successful implementation of NeGP. What are the key challenges in building this infrastructure, and how can they be overcome?
15. Discuss the significance of SMART governments in the context of Indian bureaucracy. How can SMART principles enhance the efficiency and transparency of government operations?
16. Explain the principles of SMART governance. How do these principles ensure effective decision-making and operational consistency in government projects?

Dynamic QR code for further readings

REFERENCES AND SUGGESTED READINGS

1. E-Governance in India: Initiatives and Challenges" by R. P. Sinha, Concept Publishing Company, 2006.
2. Government Process Re-engineering: The Key to E-Governance Implementation" by Piyush Gupta and Sushil Kumar, The IUP Journal of Public Administration, 2008.
3. "E-Governance: Concepts and Case Studies" by C.S.R. Prabhu, Prentice-Hall of India Pvt. Ltd, 2004.
4. "The Implementation of E-Governance in India: An Analysis of the Mission Mode Projects (MMPs)" by Ashish Ghosh, India Infrastructure Report, 2012.
5. "SMART Governance: A New Paradigm for E-Governance in India" by R.K. Mittal and P. K. Bawa, Journal of Information Systems and Technology Management, 2012.
6. "Principles of SMART Government: A Framework for Implementing E-Governance in India" by S.K. Mishra and R.K. Jain, The IUP Journal of Systems Management, 2013.

3 Architecture and Models of e-Governance

UNIT SPECIFIES

Through this unit we discuss the following aspects:

- *Architecture and models of e-Governance including Public Private Partnership (PPP)*
- *Need for Innovation and Change Management in e-Governance*
- *Critical Success Factors; Major issue including corruption, resistance for change, e-Security*
- *Cyber laws*

RATIONALE

This unit include the architecture and models of e-Governance, containing Public Private Partnership (PPP), are crucial for designing efficient and scalable government services that leverage both public and private sector strengths. Innovation and change management in e-Governance are essential to adapt to technological advancements and evolving citizen needs, ensuring continuous improvement and relevance. Identifying critical success factors helps in focusing efforts on the most impactful areas. Addressing major issues such as corruption, resistance to change, e-Security, and compliance with cyber laws is vital for the integrity, acceptance, and security of e-Governance initiatives. These elements collectively foster a robust, secure, and citizen-centric governance framework.

PRE-REQUESITE

- *Contents of unit-1 and unit-2*

UNIT OUTCOMES

After completion of this unit the learner will be able to:

U3-O1: Understand the various layers used in e-governance architecture and models

U3-O2: Analyze the benefits and role of public private partnership (PPP)

U3-O3: Identify the need of change management in e-governance

U3-O4: Determine the various critical success factor for e-governance

Unit-3 Outcomes	Expected Mapping with Programme Outcomes (1- Weak Correlation; 2- Medium correlation; 3- Strong Correlation)					
	CO-1	CO-2	CO-3	CO-4	CO-5	CO-6
U3-O1	2	1	3	2	1	0

U3-O2	1	2	3	2	1	0
U3-O3	1	1	2	3	1	0
U3-O4	1	1	2	3	1	0

3.1 Architecture of e-Governance

e-Governance refers to the use of Information and Communication Technology (ICT) to deliver government services, enhance the efficiency of administrative processes, ensure transparency, and engage citizens in governance. The architecture of e-Governance encompasses a multi-layered structure involving hardware, software, networks, data, and various stakeholders to ensure smooth functioning and interaction between government agencies and the public. Below figure 3.1 shows the detailed look at the key components of e-Governance architecture.

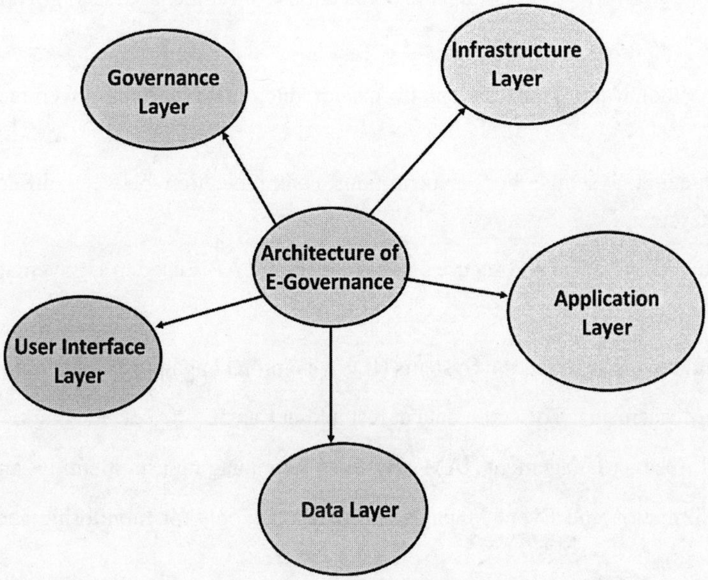

Figure 3.1 Key layers of e-Governance architecture.

3.1.1 Infrastructure layer

The infrastructure layer in e-governance architecture is a foundational component that supports the delivery of digital government services. This layer includes all the physical and virtual resources needed to ensure the efficient functioning, scalability, security, and reliability of e-governance systems. Here's a breakdown of the key components typically found in the infrastructure layer:

1. *Hardware*

- Servers: High-performance servers to host applications, databases, and websites.
- Storage Systems: Robust storage solutions to manage vast amounts of data securely and efficiently.

- Networking Equipment: Routers, switches, and other networking devices to ensure robust connectivity.
- End-user Devices: Computers, tablets, and other devices used by citizens and government employees.

2. *Data Centers*

- On-Premises Data Centers: Government-owned and operated data centers.
- Cloud Services: Use of public, private, or hybrid cloud services to enhance scalability and flexibility.
- Disaster Recovery Sites: Backup sites to ensure continuity in case of primary data center failure.

3. *Network Infrastructure*

- Internet Connectivity: High-speed internet connections to facilitate online services.
- Intranets: Secure internal networks for government communication and data exchange.
- Virtual Private Networks (VPNs): Secure connections for remote access to government systems.

4. *Middleware*

- Integration Middleware: Tools and platforms for integrating various government applications and services.
- Message Queuing Systems: For asynchronous communication between different parts of the e-governance system.
- API Gateways: To manage and secure access to different APIs used in e-governance applications.

5. *Security Infrastructure*

- Firewalls and Intrusion Detection Systems (IDS): To protect against external threats.
- Encryption Mechanisms: To secure data at rest and in transit.
- Identity and Access Management (IAM): Systems for managing user identities and access rights.
- Security Information and Event Management (SIEM): Tools for monitoring and managing security events.

6. *Software Platforms*

- Operating Systems: Stable and secure operating systems for servers and end-user devices.
- Database Management Systems (DBMS): Reliable and scalable databases to manage data.
- Application Servers: Platforms for deploying and managing e-governance applications.
- Content Management Systems (CMS): For managing digital content and websites.

7. *Service Management*

- Monitoring and Management Tools: To track the performance and health of infrastructure components.
- Service Desk Systems: For managing and resolving technical issues and requests.
- Configuration Management Databases (CMDB): To keep track of all infrastructure components and their relationships.

8. *Support Services*

- Technical Support: Teams and services to maintain and troubleshoot the infrastructure.
- Training and Documentation: Resources for training personnel and documenting procedures and systems.

3.1.2 Application Layer

The application layer in e-governance architecture is where the interaction between the government and its citizens, businesses, and other stakeholders takes place. This layer consists of various software applications and services that facilitate the delivery of digital government services, ensuring they are accessible, efficient, and user-friendly. Here's a detailed exploration of the components and functionalities of the application layer:

a) Citizen Services Applications

These are applications designed to provide services directly to citizens. They include:

- *Portals and Websites:* Centralized platforms where citizens can access information, submit forms, and interact with various government services. Examples include tax filing websites, healthcare portals, and educational platforms.
- *Mobile Applications:* Apps that provide on-the-go access to government services, ensuring that citizens can interact with government services via their smartphones and tablets.
- *Self-Service Kiosks:* Physical kiosks installed in public places to allow citizens to access e-governance services without needing personal devices or internet access.

b) Business Services Applications

- *These applications cater to the needs of businesses*, simplifying their interactions with government agencies. They include:
- *Business Registration and Licensing Systems:* Platforms that allow businesses to register, renew licenses, and comply with regulatory requirements online.
- *Taxation and Compliance Applications:* Tools for filing taxes, submitting compliance documents, and making payments.
- *Procurement and Tendering Systems:* Applications that facilitate government procurement processes, allowing businesses to participate in tenders and submit bids electronically.

c) Internal Government Applications

These are applications used by government employees and departments to streamline internal processes and improve efficiency. They include:

- *Enterprise Resource Planning (ERP) Systems:* Integrated software solutions that manage government resources, including finance, human resources, procurement, and inventory.
- *Document Management Systems (DMS):* Tools for storing, managing, and tracking electronic documents, ensuring efficient information retrieval and collaboration.
- *Workflow and Process Automation(WPA):* Applications that automate routine tasks and workflows, reducing manual intervention and improving process efficiency.

d) Communication and Collaboration Tools

These tools facilitate communication and collaboration within government departments and with external stakeholders. They include:

- *Email and Messaging Systems:* Secure platforms for internal and external communication.
- *Video Conferencing Tools:* Applications that enable virtual meetings, reducing the need for physical presence and travel.
- *Collaborative Platforms:* Tools like shared workspaces and project management applications that allow teams to work together more effectively.

e) Data Analytics and Decision Support Systems

These applications help in analyzing data and providing insights for informed decision-making. They include:

- *Business Intelligence (BI) Tools*: Platforms that aggregate and analyze data to generate reports, dashboards, and visualizations.
- *Geographic Information Systems (GIS):* Tools for spatial analysis and mapping, useful in urban planning, disaster management, and resource allocation.
- *Predictive Analytics:* Applications that use historical data to forecast future trends and outcomes, aiding in proactive governance.

f) Public Engagement and Feedback Systems

These systems facilitate interaction between the government and the public, allowing for feedback and engagement. They include:

- *Surveys and Polls:* Tools for collecting public opinions and feedback on various issues and policies.
- *Social Media Integration:* Applications that monitor and engage with citizens on social media platforms, ensuring real-time communication and responsiveness.
- *Feedback Portals:* Platforms where citizens can submit complaints, suggestions, and feedback regarding government services.

g) Interoperability and Integration Services

These services ensure that various applications within the e-governance ecosystem can communicate and work together seamlessly. They include:

- *Application Programming Interfaces (APIs):* Standardized interfaces that allow different software applications to exchange data and functionality.
- *Middleware Solutions:* Software that bridges the gap between different applications and systems, ensuring smooth data flow and integration.

3.1.3 Data Layer

The data layer in e-governance architecture is critical for the storage, management, and analysis of data. It serves as the foundation for making informed decisions, delivering personalized services, and ensuring transparency and accountability. This layer comprises various components that handle data collection, storage, processing, and retrieval. Here's a detailed breakdown of the data layer in e-governance architecture:

a) Data Sources

The data layer integrates multiple data sources, including:

- *Government Databases:* Centralized repositories that store data related to citizens, businesses, land records, taxes, health, education, etc.
- *External Data Sources:* Data from external entities like banks, telecom companies, healthcare providers, and other third-party organizations.
- *User-Generated Data:* Data collected from citizens through portals, surveys, feedback forms, and social media interactions.
- *IoT and Sensor Data:* Data from smart devices and sensors used in smart city projects, environmental monitoring, and infrastructure management.

b) Data Storage

Efficient and secure storage solutions are crucial for managing large volumes of data. This includes:

- *Relational Databases:* Structured storage systems like SQL databases for managing tabular data with predefined relationships.
- *NoSQL Databases:* Flexible storage systems like document, key-value, graph, and column-family databases for handling unstructured or semi-structured data.
- *Data Warehouses:* Central repositories that consolidate data from various sources, optimized for querying and analysis.
- *Data Lakes:* Scalable storage systems that store vast amounts of raw data in its native format, suitable for big data processing and advanced analytics.

c) Data Management

Data management ensures that data is accurate, consistent, and accessible. This includes:

- *Data Governance:* Policies and procedures to manage data integrity, quality, privacy, and security.
- *Master Data Management (MDM):* Processes to ensure a single, consistent view of key data entities like citizens, businesses, and assets across the organization.
- *Data Quality Management:* Tools and techniques for data cleansing, validation, and enrichment to maintain high-quality data.

d) Data Integration

Integrating data from various sources and systems is essential for a cohesive e-governance ecosystem. This includes:

- *ETL Processes:* Extract, Transform, Load (ETL) processes to consolidate data from different sources into a unified format for storage and analysis.

- *Data Integration Platforms:* Middleware and integration tools to facilitate seamless data exchange between disparate systems and applications.
- *APIs:* Application Programming Interfaces to enable data sharing and interoperability between different e-governance applications and services.

e) Data Processing and Analytics

Transforming raw data into actionable insights is a key function of the data layer. This includes:

- *Batch Processing:* Processing large volumes of data in batches at scheduled intervals for tasks like reporting and data migration.
- *Real-Time Processing:* Analyzing data in real-time for immediate insights and responses, crucial for applications like fraud detection and emergency response.
- *Data Analytics:* Techniques like descriptive, diagnostic, predictive, and prescriptive analytics to gain insights from data and support decision-making.
- *Big Data Technologies:* Tools like Hadoop, Spark, and Kafka to handle and process massive datasets efficiently.

f) Data Security and Privacy

Ensuring the security and privacy of data is paramount in e-governance. This includes:

- *Data Encryption:* Techniques to protect data at rest and in transit from unauthorized access.
- *Access Control:* Mechanisms to ensure that only authorized users can access and modify data, based on roles and permissions.
- *Auditing and Monitoring:* Tools to track and log data access and changes, ensuring compliance with legal and regulatory requirements.
- *Data Anonymization:* Techniques to protect sensitive information by anonymizing personal data when used for analysis and reporting.

g) Data Access and Retrieval

Efficient data access and retrieval mechanisms are necessary for timely and effective use of data. This includes:

- *Query Tools:* User-friendly tools and interfaces for querying databases and retrieving data as needed.
- *Reporting and Visualization*: Platforms that provide dashboards, reports, and visualizations to present data in an understandable and actionable format.
- *APIs and Data Services:* Services that allow applications and users to access data programmatically, enabling integration and interoperability.

3.1.4 User Interface Layer

The User Interface (UI) layer in e-governance architecture is crucial for ensuring that citizens, businesses, and government employees can effectively interact with digital government services. This layer encompasses all the elements that users interact with directly, including websites, mobile applications, portals, and other digital touchpoints. The primary goal of the UI layer is to provide a user-friendly, accessible, and engaging experience that facilitates seamless interaction with e-governance services. Here's a detailed exploration of the components and functionalities of the UI layer:

a) Web Portals

Web portals are centralized platforms where users can access various e-governance services and information. These portals are designed to be intuitive and user-friendly, offering easy navigation and search capabilities. Features include:

- *Homepages:* Clear and concise homepages that provide quick access to popular services, news, and updates.
- *Service Directories:* Organized listings of available services, categorized by type, user group, or department.
- *Interactive Forms:* Online forms for service applications, registrations, payments, and feedback submissions.

b) Mobile Applications

Mobile applications are essential for providing on-the-go access to e-governance services. They are designed to be responsive and user-friendly, ensuring a positive experience on various mobile devices. Features include:

- *Push Notifications:* Alerts and updates about service requests, deadlines, and important announcements.
- *Geolocation Services:* Location-based services such as finding the nearest government office or public facility.
- *Offline Access:* Limited functionality available without an internet connection, ensuring usability in areas with poor connectivity.

c) Self-Service Kiosks

Self-service kiosks are physical touchpoints installed in public places like government offices, community centers, and transportation hubs. They provide access to e-governance services for users who may not have personal devices or internet access. Features include:

- *Touchscreen Interfaces:* Intuitive and easy-to-use touchscreens for navigating services and information.
- *Multilingual Support:* Options to access services in multiple languages to cater to diverse populations.
- *Printing and Scanning:* Capabilities to print documents, receipts, and scan required documents for service applications.

d) Chatbots and Virtual Assistants

AI-powered chatbots and virtual assistants provide automated support and guidance to users, helping them navigate services and answer common queries. Features include:

- *Natural Language Processing (NLP):* Understanding and responding to user queries in natural language.
- *24/7 Availability:* Providing round-the-clock assistance without human intervention.
- *Seamless Integration:* Integrated within web portals, mobile apps, and social media platforms.

e) Accessibility Features

Ensuring that e-governance services are accessible to all users, including those with disabilities, is a key aspect of the UI layer. Features include:

- *Screen Readers:* Compatibility with screen reader software to assist visually impaired users.
- *Keyboard Navigation:* Ensuring all functions can be accessed using a keyboard.
- *High-Contrast Modes:* Options to enhance visibility for users with visual impairments.
- *Text-to-Speech:* Features that convert written text into spoken words for easier comprehension.

f) User Experience (UX) Design

A focus on UX design ensures that the UI layer is not only functional but also pleasant and engaging to use. This includes:

- *Consistent Design Language:* Using a consistent set of design elements, colors, and fonts to create a cohesive look and feel across all interfaces.
- *Responsive Design:* Ensuring that interfaces work well on a variety of devices and screen sizes.
- *Feedback Mechanisms:* Providing users with immediate feedback on their actions, such as form submissions or errors.
- *User Testing:* Conducting regular user testing and usability studies to identify and address pain points.

g) Security and Privacy

The UI layer must ensure that interactions are secure and that user privacy is protected. Features include:

- *Secure Login:* Using secure authentication methods such as two-factor authentication (2FA) to protect user accounts.
- *Data Encryption:* Ensuring that all data transmitted between the user and the system is encrypted.
- *Privacy Policies:* Clearly communicating how user data will be used and protected, and obtaining consent where necessary.

h) Multichannel Access

Providing consistent and unified access across multiple channels ensures that users can interact with e-governance services through their preferred medium. This includes:

- *Web Access:* Desktop and mobile web access through responsive websites.
- *Mobile Apps:* Dedicated applications for different platforms (iOS, Android).
- *Social Media Integration:* Offering services and updates through popular social media platforms.

- *Voice Assistants:* Integrating with voice-activated devices like Amazon Alexa or Google Assistant for hands-free interaction.

3.1.5 Governance Layer

The governance layer in e-governance architecture is critical for ensuring that digital government initiatives are managed effectively, ethically, and sustainably. This layer encompasses policies, frameworks, standards, and organizational structures that guide the planning, implementation, and management of e-governance projects. It ensures that e-governance systems are aligned with broader government goals, are transparent, accountable, and deliver value to citizens. Here's a detailed breakdown of the governance layer in e-governance architecture:

a) Policy and Regulatory Framework

The governance layer establishes the legal and regulatory foundations for e-governance initiatives. This includes:

- *Legislation:* Laws and regulations that provide a legal basis for e-governance activities, ensuring compliance with national and international standards.
- *Policies:* Government policies that define the strategic direction and priorities for e-governance, including data protection, privacy, cybersecurity, and digital inclusion.
- *Standards and Guidelines:* Technical and procedural standards that ensure interoperability, security, and quality across different e-governance systems and services.

b) Organizational Structures

Effective governance requires clear organizational structures and roles. This includes:

E-Governance Committees: High-level committees and task forces that oversee the strategic direction and coordination of e-governance initiatives.

- *Chief Information Officers (CIOs):* Senior officials responsible for the overall technology strategy and implementation within government departments.
- *Project Management Offices (PMOs):* Dedicated teams that manage e-governance projects, ensuring they are delivered on time, within budget, and to the required standards.

c) Strategic Planning

Strategic planning is essential for aligning e-governance initiatives with broader government objectives. This includes:

- *Vision and Mission Statements:* Clear articulation of the goals and aspirations for e-governance.
- *Roadmaps:* Detailed plans outlining the steps, milestones, and timelines for achieving e-governance objectives.
- *Resource Allocation:* Planning and allocation of financial, human, and technological resources to support e-governance projects.

d) Risk Management

Identifying and mitigating risks is a key aspect of governance. This includes:

- *Risk Assessment:* Regular assessments to identify potential risks to e-governance projects, including technological, operational, financial, and security risks.
- *Risk Mitigation Strategies:* Developing and implementing strategies to manage and mitigate identified risks, ensuring project resilience and continuity.

e) Performance Management

Monitoring and evaluating the performance of e-governance initiatives ensures they deliver expected benefits. This includes:

- *Key Performance Indicators (KPIs):* Metrics to measure the success and impact of e-governance projects, such as user satisfaction, service delivery times, and cost savings.
- *Continuous Improvement:* Processes for regularly reviewing and improving e-governance systems based on performance data and user feedback.
- *Audits and Reviews:* Independent assessments to ensure compliance with policies, standards, and best practices.

f) Stakeholder Engagement

Engaging with stakeholders is critical for the success of e-governance initiatives. This includes:

- *Citizen Participation:* Mechanisms to involve citizens in the design and evaluation of e-governance services, ensuring they meet user needs and expectations.
- *Public-Private Partnerships:* Partnerships with private sector organizations to leverage expertise, technology, and investment in e-governance projects.

g) Ethics and Accountability

Ensuring ethical conduct and accountability is vital for maintaining public trust in e-governance. This includes:

- *Transparency:* Providing clear and accessible information about e-governance initiatives, including objectives, progress, and outcomes.
- *Accountability Mechanisms:* Structures and processes to hold government officials and agencies accountable for the performance and impact of e-governance projects.
- *Ethical Standards:* Guidelines and codes of conduct to ensure ethical behavior in the design and implementation of e-governance systems, including the use of data and technology.

h) Capacity Building

Building the necessary skills and knowledge is essential for the sustainable success of e-governance. This includes:

- *Training and Development*: Programs to enhance the skills and knowledge of government employees and other stakeholders involved in e-governance.

- *Knowledge Sharing:* Platforms and networks for sharing best practices, lessons learned, and innovations in e-governance.
- *Change Management:* Strategies to manage the cultural and organizational changes required to adopt and sustain e-governance initiatives.

3.2 Models of e-Governance

Models of e-Governance refer to various approaches or frameworks adopted by governments to implement and manage digital services and interactions with citizens, businesses, and other stakeholders. These models evolve based on technological advancements, governance priorities, and the specific needs of different jurisdictions. Here are some common models of e-Governance given in figure 3.2.

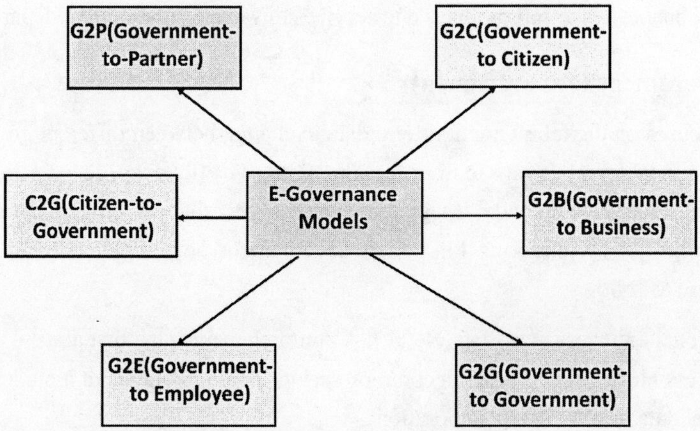

Figure 3.2 Various models of e-governance

3.2.1 G2C (Government-to-Citizen)

In the G2C model, the government delivers services and interacts directly with individual citizens through digital platforms. This includes online portals, mobile apps, and kiosks where citizens can access information, apply for permits/licenses, pay taxes, and avail of various public services. The focus is on enhancing convenience, transparency, and accessibility for citizens. Some of the common examples of G2C model are given below:

a) India's Digital India Initiative: Aims to transform India into a digitally empowered society and knowledge economy, providing various online services through platforms like the UMANG app.

b) Estonia's e-Residency Program: Offers a digital identity to global citizens, allowing them to access Estonian services such as company registration and banking.

c) USA's Healthcare.gov: Provides a platform for American citizens to compare and purchase health insurance plans under the Affordable Care Act.

3.2.2 G2B (Government-to-Business)

Under the G2B model, governments interact with businesses and enterprises electronically. This involves providing online portals and platforms for businesses to register, file taxes, obtain licenses, participate in government procurement processes, and comply with regulatory requirements. The aim is to streamline processes, reduce bureaucratic hurdles, and promote economic growth. Some examples of G2B model are as follows:

a) Singapore's BizFile+: An online business filing system that allows businesses to incorporate, file annual returns, and update information with the Accounting and Corporate Regulatory Authority (ACRA).

b) Australia's Business Registration Service (BRS): A one-stop-shop for business registration, offering services such as applying for an Australian Business Number (ABN) and registering for Goods and Services Tax (GST).

c) India's Government e-Marketplace (GeM): An e-procurement portal for government purchases, enabling businesses to sell products and services to various government departments and agencies.

3.2.3 G2G (Government-to-Government)

The G2G model focuses on digital interactions and data exchange between different government agencies at local, regional, or national levels. It aims to improve administrative efficiency, coordination, and collaboration across departments. Examples include integrated systems for sharing citizen data, inter-departmental workflows, and collaborative platforms for policy development and implementation. Some of common examples of G2G are as follows:

- India's National e-Governance Plan (NeGP): A comprehensive plan that aims to make all government services accessible to citizens through common service delivery outlets. It includes initiatives for inter-departmental data sharing and collaboration.
- USA's Integrated Justice Information Systems (IJIS): A program that facilitates information sharing and collaboration among various criminal justice agencies at federal, state, and local levels.
- European Union's eGovernment Action Plan: A strategy to improve the digital interaction between government entities within the European Union, promoting cross-border interoperability and data sharing.

3.2.4 G2E (Government-to-Employee)

In the G2E model, e-Governance initiatives target internal government operations and interactions with employees. This includes digital HR systems for managing payroll, leave, and benefits, as well as employee portals for accessing training resources, administrative tools, and communication platforms within the government workforce. Some G2E examples are as follows:

a) India's SPARROW System: An online system for the appraisal and review of performance reports of civil servants, promoting transparency and efficiency in performance management.

3.2.5 C2G (Citizen-to-Government)

The C2G model emphasizes citizen engagement and participation in governance processes through digital means. It includes platforms for citizen feedback, public consultations on policy decisions, online petitions, and social media channels where citizens can interact with government officials and provide input on public initiatives. This model promotes transparency, inclusivity, and responsiveness in governance. Some examples of C2G are as follows:

a) United Kingdom's GOV.UK: A single online platform that provides comprehensive government services and information for citizens, including tax filing, benefits claims, and public consultations.

b) Estonia's e-Residency Program: Allows non-Estonian citizens to access Estonian digital services and establish a business remotely, promoting global citizen engagement with the Estonian government.

c) Canada's Open Government Portal: Provides access to government data, information, and engagement opportunities, promoting transparency and collaboration with citizens.

3.2.6 G2P (Government-to-Partner)

In some contexts, there's a G2P model where governments collaborate with non-governmental organizations (NGOs), academia, research institutions, and other partners to deliver services and address societal challenges. This collaborative approach leverages digital platforms for sharing resources, conducting joint research, implementing projects, and achieving common goals. Some examples of G2P initiatives are as follows:

a) United Nations Development Programme (UNDP) Partnership for Sustainable Development Goals (SDGs): Collaborative initiatives with governments, NGOs, and private sector partners to achieve global SDGs through joint projects and advocacy.

b) Smart City Projects: Public-private partnerships in various cities worldwide to develop and implement smart technologies and solutions for urban development, such as transportation systems and energy efficiency.

c) Healthcare Initiatives: Collaborations between government health agencies, hospitals, pharmaceutical companies, and research institutions to improve public health services, develop vaccines, and address healthcare challenges.

3.3 Public Private Partnership (PPP)

Both at the global and local levels, e-Government has a significant impact on people's lives around the world. There is a lot of possibility for dramatic advancements in human growth from the flow of information about goods, people, capital, and ideas—especially when that movement is made possible by ICT. Consequently, e-Government has regularly shown its potential for Public-Private Partnerships.

Public Private Partnerships (PPPs) is now a potential business model to handle these factors irrespective of enhancing the financial visibility of e-Government initiatives. Public Private Partnerships are collaborative arrangements between government entities and private sector companies designed to fund, build, and operate projects that serve the public interest. These partnerships combine the strengths of both sectors to deliver public services or infrastructure more efficiently and effectively. In essence, PPPs leverage private sector investment and expertise while ensuring that public objectives are met. The private sector's role typically includes financing, designing, constructing, and operating the project, while the public sector focuses on regulatory oversight and ensuring that public needs are addressed.

A public and private partnership or PPP are related to the working of public and private sectors together to provide the services and infrastructure however that are originally provided by the government. The main goal is to improve public services through the building, management, and funding of important infrastructure by the private sector. PPP basically mean sharing a venture's gains and risks. The key features of PPPs are given as follows:

Public Private Partnerships (PPPs) have several distinct features that make them effective mechanisms for delivering public services and infrastructure. These features ensure that the strengths of both the public and private sectors are leveraged to achieve the best possible outcomes. Here are the key features of PPPs:

a) Shared Investment and Risk

- *Collaborative Financing*: Both the public and private sectors contribute financial resources to the project. This shared investment helps to spread financial risk and ensure mutual commitment.
- *Risk Allocation:* Risks are allocated to the party best able to manage them. For example, construction risks such as cost overruns might be borne by the private sector, while regulatory risks are usually managed by the public sector.

b) Long-Term Agreements

- *Sustained Collaboration:* PPPs typically involve long-term contracts, often spanning 20 to 30 years or more. This ensures a sustained collaboration between the parties and long-term commitment to the project's success.

c) Performance-Based Contracts

- *Incentive Structures*: Payments to the private sector are often linked to specific performance metrics. This ensures that the private sector has a strong incentive to deliver high-quality services and maintain operational efficiency throughout the project's lifecycle.

d) Focus on Outcomes

- *Result-Oriented:* PPPs emphasize achieving specific outcomes, such as improved public services, enhanced infrastructure, and economic development. This focus helps to align the goals of both the public and private sectors.

e) Diverse PPP Models

- *Variety of Structures:* There are several PPP models tailored to different types of projects and risk-sharing arrangements. Common models include:
- *Build-Operate-Transfer (BOT):* The private sector designs, builds, and operates a facility before transferring ownership to the public sector.
- *Design-Build-Finance-Operate (DBFO):* The private sector is responsible for the design, construction, financing, and operation of the project.
- *Concession:* The private sector operates and maintains a public service or infrastructure, collecting revenue from users or receiving payments from the government.

- *Lease-Develop-Operate (LDO):* The government leases an asset to a private entity, which then develops and operates it.
- *Joint Ventures:* Both public and private sectors co-invest and co-manage the project, sharing risks, costs, and benefits.

f) Efficiency and Innovation

- *Private Sector Expertise:* The involvement of the private sector can lead to increased efficiency and innovation in project delivery and service provision due to competitive pressures and profit incentives.

g) Access to Capital

- *Private Funding:* PPPs can mobilize private capital, reducing the need for public funding and borrowing. This can be particularly advantageous for cash-strapped governments looking to develop essential infrastructure.

h) Improved Service Delivery

- *Higher Standards:* The performance-based nature of PPP contracts often results in higher standards of service delivery and infrastructure maintenance, benefiting the public.

i) Economic Growth

- *Job Creation and Development:* PPP projects can stimulate economic development by creating jobs and improving infrastructure, which in turn can attract further investment.

j) Complex Negotiations and Management

- *Detailed Contracts:* Developing PPP agreements requires detailed and carefully negotiated contracts to clearly define the responsibilities, risks, and rewards for each party.
- *Effective Management:* Successful management of PPP projects necessitates robust oversight mechanisms to ensure that both parties adhere to their commitments and that the projects are delivered on time and within budget.

k) Accountability and Transparency

- *Public Scrutiny:* Ensuring transparency in PPP agreements and project implementation is crucial for maintaining public trust and preventing corruption. Clear reporting and accountability mechanisms are essential to monitor progress and performance.
- *Stakeholder Engagement:* Engaging with stakeholders, including the public, throughout the project lifecycle helps in addressing concerns and securing broader support for the project.

l) Flexibility and Adaptability

- *Contractual Flexibility:* PPP contracts often include provisions that allow for adjustments in response to changing circumstances. This flexibility helps in managing unforeseen challenges and ensuring project sustainability.

m) Legal and Regulatory Framework

- *Enabling Environment:* A robust legal and regulatory framework is essential for the successful implementation of PPPs. This includes clear guidelines on procurement processes, dispute resolution mechanisms, and regulatory oversight to ensure fair and transparent practices.

n) Sustainability Considerations

- *Environmental and Social Impact:* Modern PPP agreements increasingly incorporate sustainability criteria, ensuring that projects not only deliver economic benefits but also consider environmental and social impacts. This aligns with broader goals of sustainable development.

o) Innovation in Financing

- *Blended Finance:* PPPs often use innovative financing structures, including blended finance mechanisms that combine public, private, and philanthropic capital to enhance project viability and impact.

3.3.1 The Rationale for PPP

Governments make decisions on private sector involvement based on the following goals.

a) *Efficiency Gains:* Leverages private sector expertise for faster project completion and improved service delivery.

b) *Access to Capital:* Mobilizes private funds, reducing the need for public financing.

c) *Risk Sharing:* Allocates risks to the party best able to manage them.

d) *Innovation and Technology Transfer:* Encourages innovation and the adoption of advanced technologies.

e) *Improved Service Quality:* Incentivizes high standards through performance-based contracts.

f) *Economic Development:* Stimulates growth by creating jobs and improving infrastructure.

g) *Enhanced Public Sector Capacity:* Builds public sector capabilities through exposure to private sector practices.

h) *Long-Term Value for Money:* Promotes sustainable and cost-effective solutions.

i) *Flexibility and Scalability:* Adapts to various sectors and project scales.

j) *Public Benefit Focus:* Ensures projects deliver tangible public benefits.

k) *Fiscal Prudence:* Enables off-balance-sheet financing to manage public debt.

l) *Addressing Infrastructure Gaps:* Provides an alternative approach to meet infrastructure demands.

3.3.2 Benefits of PPPs

3.3.2.1 Benefits to Government

a) Access to private capital for large-scale projects without increasing public debt.

b) Transfer of significant project risks to the private sector, reducing financial exposure.

c) Efficient project delivery and improved service quality through private sector expertise.

d) Stimulates economic growth and job creation through infrastructure development.

e) Enhanced budget management with off-balance-sheet financing options.

f) Long-term maintenance and operation of infrastructure assets ensuring sustainability.

g) Alignment of projects with public priorities and efficient use of public resources.

h) Capacity building and technology transfer to enhance public sector capabilities.

3.3.2.2 Benefits to Citizens

a) Improved access to high-quality public services and infrastructure.

b) Enhanced efficiency and reliability of public services.

c) Creation of job opportunities through infrastructure development.

d) Stimulated local economies and improved living standards.

e) Long-term benefits from well-maintained infrastructure assets.

f) Innovation-driven improvements in service delivery and technology.

g) Greater accountability and transparency in project management.

h) Expanded access to diverse and upgraded public amenities

i) Contribution to local economic development and job creation.

3.3.2.3 Benefits to Private sector

a) Stable revenue streams and long-term income from government contracts.

b) Access to new markets and opportunities for business expansion.

c) Shared risks and responsibilities with the government, reducing overall project risk.

d) Incentives for innovation and adoption of advanced technologies.

e) Establishment of long-term partnerships with government entities.

f) Operational control and management of public infrastructure projects.

g) Enhancement of corporate reputation and credibility through successful PPP projects.

h) Contribution to local economic development and job creation.

3.3.3 Key design principles of PPP

The following fundamental Key design principles for Public Private Partnerships (PPPs) that establish a health relationship of government with private sector includes:

a) *Clear Objectives and Scope:* Define the project's goals, scope, and expected outcomes clearly to align with public needs and priorities.

b) *Risk Allocation:* Assign risks to the party best able to manage them, ensuring risks are appropriately balanced between the public and private sectors.

c) *Value for Money:* Ensure that the PPP provides cost-effective solutions over the project's lifecycle, considering both initial investment and long-term operational costs.

d) *Transparent Procurement and Contracting:* Implement transparent procurement processes and establish clear, enforceable contracts to mitigate risks and ensure accountability.

e) *Performance-Based Payment Mechanisms:* Link payments to performance metrics and outcomes to incentivize the private sector to meet specified standards and objectives.

f) *Legal and Regulatory Framework:* Establish a robust legal and regulatory framework that defines roles, responsibilities, and dispute resolution mechanisms for all stakeholders involved.

g) *Sustainable Development:* Integrate sustainability principles into project planning and execution, considering environmental, social, and economic impacts.

h) *Community Engagement and Stakeholder Management:* Engage stakeholders, including the public and affected communities, throughout the project lifecycle to ensure transparency, trust, and support.

i) *Flexibility and Adaptability:* Design PPP agreements to allow for adjustments in response to changing circumstances, ensuring resilience and adaptability over time.

j) *Long-Term Perspective:* Adopt a long-term perspective in project planning and financing to ensure the sustainability and continued benefit of the infrastructure or service provided.

These principles help guide the design and implementation of PPPs to maximize their effectiveness in delivering public infrastructure and services while managing risks and ensuring accountability.

3.3.4 Role of partners in PPP

In a Public Private Partnership (PPP), various partners play crucial roles, each contributing unique expertise, resources, and responsibilities to ensure the success of the project. Here's an overview of the roles typically fulfilled by different partners:

a) Government/Public Sector Parter

- *Policy Development and Regulation:* Sets policies, regulations, and frameworks governing PPPs.
- *Project Identification and Procurement:* Identifies projects suitable for PPPs and manages the procurement process.
- *Risk Management:* Assesses and manages political, regulatory, and public acceptance risks.
- *Oversight and Monitoring:* Monitors project implementation to ensure compliance with contractual terms and public interest.

b) Private Sector Partner(s)

- *Project Financing:* Provides funding for project development, construction, and operation.
- *Design and Construction:* Designs, builds, and implements the infrastructure or service according to agreed specifications.
- *Operation and Maintenance:* Manages ongoing operations, maintenance, and service delivery throughout the project lifecycle.
- *Innovation and Efficiency:* Introduces innovative technologies and management practices to optimize project performance.
- *Risk Management:* Assumes risks associated with construction, operational performance, and revenue generation.

3.4 Need for Innovation in e-governance

E-governance, or the use of digital technologies to improve the delivery of government services and democratic processes, has become increasingly vital in today's rapidly evolving digital landscape. The integration of innovative technologies in e-governance can enhance efficiency, transparency, and accessibility, making government services more responsive to the needs of citizens.

In an era where technology is advancing at an extraordinary pace, the traditional models of governance are often seen as slow, bureaucratic, and out of touch with the dynamic needs of society. Therefore, there is a pressing need for innovation in e-governance to ensure that public administration keeps pace with technological advancements and the expectations of digitally savvy citizens.

Innovations in e-governance are crucial for several reasons, as they can significantly enhance the efficiency, transparency, accessibility, and responsiveness of government services.

Here are some key reasons why innovations in e-governance are needed and benefited.

a) Improved Efficiency and Cost-Effectiveness: Innovations in e-governance streamline administrative processes, reducing the time and resources needed to deliver services. Automation of routine tasks, digital document management, and online service delivery minimize bureaucratic delays and operational costs.

b) Enhanced Transparency and Accountability: Digital platforms allow for real-time tracking and monitoring of government activities, making it easier to hold public officials accountable. Innovations such as blockchain for secure record-keeping and open data initiatives promote transparency, reducing opportunities for corruption.

c) Better Citizen Engagement and Participation: E-governance innovations provide citizens with easier access to information and government services. Interactive platforms, mobile applications, and social media integration enable more effective communication and engagement between citizens and the government, fostering a participatory governance culture.

d) Increased Accessibility to Services: Digital solutions make government services more accessible, particularly for individuals in remote or underserved areas. Mobile-friendly applications and multilingual support ensure that diverse population groups can access essential services without geographical or linguistic barriers.

e) Data-Driven Decision Making: Innovative e-governance solutions leverage big data analytics, artificial intelligence, and machine learning to gather insights and inform policy decisions. Data-driven approaches enable governments to better understand societal needs, forecast trends, and implement effective policies.

f) Enhanced Service Delivery: Innovations such as integrated service delivery platforms and personalized user interfaces improve the overall user experience. Citizens can access multiple services through single portals, reducing the need to navigate complex bureaucratic structures.

g) Resilience and Adaptability: The digital transformation of government services enhances resilience to crises, such as natural disasters or pandemics. For instance, during the COVID-19 pandemic, many governments quickly adapted to provide online services and information, highlighting the importance of robust e-governance infrastructure.

h) Support for Sustainable Development Goals (SDGs): E-governance innovations align with the United Nations' Sustainable Development Goals by promoting inclusive, transparent, and accountable institutions. Digital governance practices contribute to goals such as reducing inequality, ensuring quality education, and fostering innovation.

i) Security and Privacy: Innovations in cybersecurity and data protection are vital in e-governance to safeguard sensitive information and protect citizens' privacy. Advanced encryption, secure authentication methods, and robust data management practices ensure that digital interactions are safe and trustworthy.

j) Economic Development: Effective e-governance fosters a favorable business environment by simplifying regulatory procedures, enhancing ease of doing business, and attracting investment. This, in turn, stimulates economic growth and job creation.

In summary, innovations in e-governance are essential to modernize public administration, making it more efficient, transparent, and responsive to the needs of citizens and businesses. They enable governments to better serve their populations, promote inclusive development, and build trust in public institutions.

3.5 Need for Change Management in e-Governance

Change management in e-Governance is a critical aspect that involves the systematic approach to dealing with the transition or transformation of an organization's goals, processes, or technologies. The objective is to implement strategies for effecting change, controlling change, and helping people to adapt to change. It is particularly significant in e-Governance, where the shift from traditional governance methods to digital platforms requires careful planning, execution, and management to ensure success.

Change management in e-governance involves the structured approach to transitioning individuals, teams, and organizations from their current state to a desired future state to improve public services through digital means. It requires careful planning, communication, and execution to ensure the successful implementation of new technologies and processes.

The first step in effective change management for e-Governance is to establish a clear vision and objectives. This involves defining the goals of the e-Governance initiative, such as improving service delivery, increasing transparency, enhancing citizen engagement, or reducing costs. It is essential to communicate this vision effectively to all stakeholders, including government officials, employees, and citizens, to create a shared understanding and commitment. This communication helps to build trust and support for the initiative, which is crucial for overcoming resistance to change.

3.5.1 Definition of change management

Change management is a systematic approach to dealing with the transition or transformation of an organization's goals, processes, or technologies. The primary objective of change management is to implement strategies for effecting change, controlling change, and helping people adapt to change. It involves methods that redirect or redefine the use of resources, business processes, budget allocations, or other modes of operation that significantly reshape a company or organization.

Some of the key components of successful change management include.

a) Planning and Preparation: Identifying what needs to change and developing a structured plan to address these changes.

b) Communication: Clearly communicating the reasons for the change, the benefits, and the plan to all stakeholders.

c) Training and Support: Providing the necessary training and support to help employees adapt to the new systems, processes, or structures.

d) Implementation: Executing the change plan and managing the process to ensure it is carried out effectively.

e) Monitoring and Evaluation: Assessing the impact of the change and making necessary adjustments to ensure successful implementation.

Applying change management is often considered as having its most common beginning after the project has been conceived, created, and put into action. Change management is frequently incorporated after issues with the project start to arise. In actuality, we observe that change management procedures are started only after the implementation of the project has commenced in the majority of e-Government initiatives. Once more, this program is mostly implemented as a reactive rather than proactive approach and is not done so with a detailed knowledge of change management. The current CMF can be used to the project at any point in its lifecycle; however, it works best when the change management concerns are addressed at a high level in the project feasibility and conceptualization study. Second, the project plan needs to contain the actions related to the process of change management. Thirdly, it is advised that an outside competent consultant team assist in developing it if an internal team with the necessary level of skill develops it. Using both organizational and individual change management strategies is necessary to implement e-Government change management successfully. The people reaction to change management may be seen in following figure 3.3 which is given below.

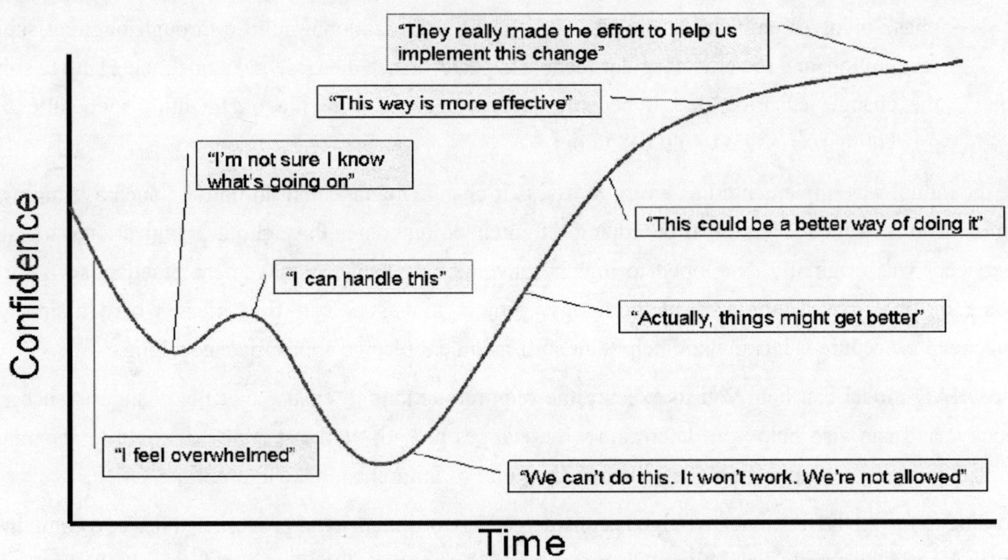

Figure 3.3 People reaction to change management

3.5.2 ADKAR – a model for change management

The ADKAR model is a well-regarded framework for managing organizational change, developed by Jeff Hiatt, founder of Prosci. The model is designed to guide individuals and organizations through the change process, ensuring successful transitions and sustainable outcomes. ADKAR is an acronym that stands for:

a) Awareness: Firstly, Awareness is about ensuring everyone involved understands the need for change. This phase focuses on communicating the reasons behind the change, the risks of not changing, and the benefits expected from the change. It is essential for stakeholders to grasp why the change is necessary to foster initial buy-in and reduce resistance.

b) Desire: Next, Desire is centered on motivating individuals to participate and support the change. This phase addresses the personal and emotional factors that influence people's willingness to engage with the change process. Strategies to build desire include aligning the change with individual and organizational goals, addressing fears and uncertainties, and involving people in the change process to create a sense of ownership.

c) Knowledge: pertains to equipping individuals with the information and training needed to implement the change. This stage involves educational initiatives, workshops, and training sessions that provide the skills and knowledge necessary to adapt to new systems, processes, or behaviors. Without adequate knowledge, even the most motivated individuals will struggle to make the change effectively.

d) Ability: The Ability phase ensures that individuals can implement the change on a day-to-day basis. This involves practical application, coaching, and support to help people develop the new skills required. Overcoming barriers to performance and providing the necessary resources are crucial at this stage to enable individuals to transition smoothly from old practices to new ones.

e) Reinforcement: Finally, Reinforcement is about sustaining the change over the long term. This phase involves embedding the change into the organizational culture through ongoing support, recognition, and rewards. Regular feedback, performance metrics, and adjustments help to solidify the change, ensuring that it becomes a permanent part of the organization's operations and preventing regression to old behaviors.

First, the model was implemented as a way to assess if change management initiatives, such as training and communications, were successful in producing the intended outcomes throughout organizational transition. The concept was originally developed to match conventional change management practices to a specific outcome or objective. Using this methodology, project managers can find areas where their change management procedure is lacking and help their staff members receive appropriate coaching.

The ADKAR model can help you to execute the required actions to ensure that the change is successful, productive and can also help you determine why changes are not working. You'll be able to separate the modification into its component pieces, identify the point of failure, and take appropriate action.

According to the ADKAR model, change is considered as two-dimensional process that has two components: the business and the people dimensions. Change is considered successful when it addresses both aspects at the same time. Figure 3.4 shows the phases of change project versus change of employees.

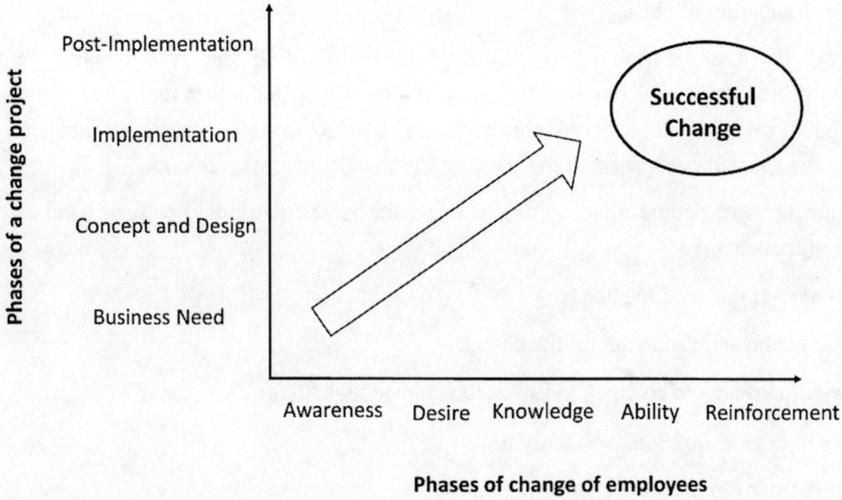

Figure 3.4 Phases of change project vs. phases of change of employee

3.5.3 Change Management design key principles

When creating a change management plan, the following factors need to be taken into consideration.

a) Clear Vision and Objectives: Define the vision and set measurable goals.

b) Leadership and Sponsorship: Ensure strong leadership and stakeholder engagement.

c) Communication: Maintain transparent and tailored communication.

d) Employee Involvement and Participation: Involve and empower employees early.

e) Training and Support: Provide necessary training and ongoing support.

f) Organizational Alignment: Align structures, systems, and policies with the change.

g) Change Readiness Assessment: Assess and enhance the organization's readiness.

h) Stakeholder Management: Identify and engage all stakeholders effectively.

i) Monitoring and Feedback: Continuously monitor progress and gather feedback.

j) Sustaining Change: Integrate changes into the culture and celebrate successes.

k) Adaptability and Flexibility: Be flexible and foster continuous improvement.

3.5.3.1 Organizational dimension of change

The business dimension of change normally includes the following project components.

- An opportunity or business necessity is determined.
- The project's goals and scope are established.
- New systems, procedures, and organizational structures are designed as part of the business solution.
- Systems and procedures are created from scratch.
- The organization adopts the solution.

3.5.3.2 People dimension of change

Research reveals that issues pertaining to the people dimension of change are frequently mentioned as the main causes of project failures. Effective employee change management was ranked as one of the top three project success factors overall in a research involving 248 companies. Assisting managers in becoming successful change sponsors was deemed the most important success factor overall.

Efficient management of people dimension of change, the ADKAR model needs to handle following five fundamental components.

- **Awareness** of the need to change
- **Desire** to contribute and support the change
- **Knowledge** of how to change (and what the change looks like)
- **Ability** to device the change on daily basis
- **Reinforcement** to keep the change in place

3.5.4 Communication in Change Management

Here are five key principles for effective communications.

Principle #1: Communication is essential for organizational change to take place.

Principle #2: Communication needs to happen concurrently and be completely integrated with the change process; it cannot happen as a stand-alone step or component.

Principle #3: Strategic planning for communication involves more than just following a recipe or cookbook when choosing approaches.

Principle #4: Communication with someone is not something you do for them. Good communication is a dialog-focused, two-way activity.

Principle #5: Professionals in communication implement the meticulous planning process, which includes determining the needs of stakeholders, crafting and guiding message delivery, and constructing feedback loops.

Following are some of the errors in communication in change management:

- No idea of stakeholders: Key audience or stakeholders
- Lack of Clarity: Providing vague or ambiguous information.
- Inconsistent Communication: Delivering mixed messages from different sources.
- Infrequent Updates: Failing to provide regular and timely updates.
- Ignoring Feedback: Not establishing channels for stakeholder feedback.
- Overloading with Information: Bombarding stakeholders with too much information at once.
- Over-dependence on traditional media
- Absence of strategic, high-level responsibility regarding communication
- Unpredictability in terms of communication channels
- Assume that private information will remain private

3.5.5 Key Reasons for failure of change initiatives

Key reasons for failures in change initiatives include:

a) Lack of Clear Vision: Absence of a well-defined and compelling vision for the change.

b) Inadequate Leadership: Insufficient support and commitment from top leadership.

c) Poor Communication: Ineffective communication leading to misunderstandings and resistance.

d) Employee Resistance: Strong opposition from employees due to fear, uncertainty, or lack of involvement.

e) Insufficient Training and Support: Failing to provide necessary training and resources for employees.

f) Inadequate Planning and Execution: Poorly planned and executed change strategies.

g) Ignoring Organizational Culture: Overlooking the importance of aligning the change with the existing organizational culture.

h) Lack of Monitoring and Feedback**:** Not monitoring progress and failing to gather and act on feedback.

i) Resource Constraints: Insufficient allocation of resources such as time, budget, and personnel.

j) Underestimating Complexity: Failing to recognize and address the complexity of the change process.

3.5.6 Approach for Change Management

Table 3.1 Essential elements of Change Management

S No.	Essential elements	Functions
1	Stakeholder Management	Ensure that all stakeholders are identified and their connections are effectively managed. Provide stakeholders with updates on progress, program needs, and benefits tracking. Collect and incorporate their feedback into the program.
2	Communication Management	Plan and execute communication throughout the organization using effective means and channels. Ensure that messages must reach the target audience promptly, providing just enough information to keep them informed and excited about the change, enabling them to implement it effectively.
3	Training	Assign training materials, trainers, and logistics. Ensure that the target audiences receive timely and sufficient training in the new ways of working, including data, processes, systems/tools, and governance.

The method to managing change in the execution of e-Government initiatives is summarized in this section. In order to accomplish the desired business or organizational objective and to successfully implement the business change within the social infrastructure of the workplace, change management refers to the process, tool, and techniques for managing the people-side of business change. Three main dimensions are the focus of change management in the implementation of e-Government programs.

The figure 3.5 offers an overview of the method for managing people change in the implementation of e-Government projects based on these essential components given in the table 3.1, and subsequent paragraphs provide a summary of the important activities carried out in each step of the approach.

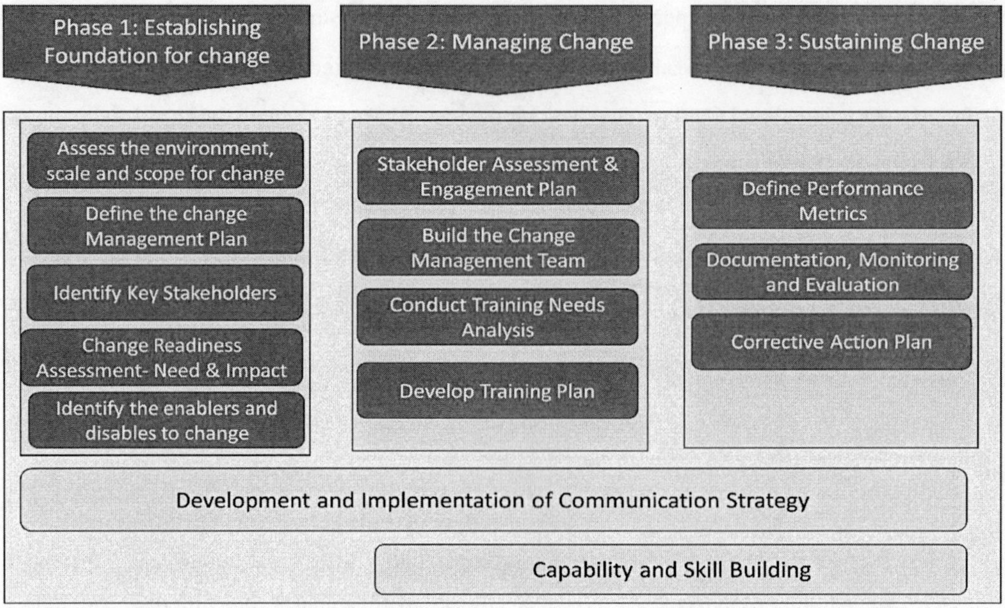

Figure 3.5 Overview of the method for managing people change in e-government

Stakeholder Management, Communication, and Capability Building (Training) span across the various phases of the Change Management Framework, highlighting their crucial role in the overall change management initiative. The following sections outline the key activities for each phase of the change management approach.

Phase I: Establishing foundation for change – key aspects

- Evaluating the scale of change, including the number of affected entities, users, and geographical distribution.
- Determining the scope of change concerning policy, processes, systems, and structure.
- Analyzing the current environment to assess 'Change Readiness' and conduct 'Culture' assessments.
- Developing a Change Management Plan.
- Identifying key stakeholders, both those impacted by and those who can influence the outcomes of the change initiatives.
- Recognizing the key enablers and barriers to change.

Phase II: Managing change – key aspects

- Evaluating stakeholders to understand their power, influence, impact, and support in the project.
- Planning of various stakeholders and stakeholder's groups.
- Forming the change management team to facilitate the change.
- Assigning the roles and responsibilities of the change team members.
- Providing training needs analysis to determine training objectives.
- Preparing a training plan to address identified training needs.

Phase III: Sustaining change – key aspects

- Determining the performance indicators that will be used to determine "Change's" effectiveness and sharing them with the relevant stakeholders.
- Measuring and assessing the metrics to determine the impact of the change and make the required adjustments.
- Creating a knowledge base or repository to house the documentation of the "Change".

3.5.7 Guiding principles for Change Planning

A Change Management Plan outlines the different phases, associated activities, tools, and mechanisms for assessing and monitoring changes, as well as the related deliverables involved in a change management initiative. The following principles serve as the guiding framework for effective change planning.

Table 3.2 Guiding principles of Change Planning in e-Governance

S No.	Guiding Principles	Detailed Descriptions
1	Guiding Principle 1: Formulate Change Vision	• A compelling vision for change is essential for the implementation of any change management initiative. • A vision serves as a connection between the current state and the desired future state. • It should be clearly defined and articulated at the beginning of the change management initiative.
2	Guiding Principle 2: Examine the Environment for Potential Changes	• Evaluate the environmental factors influencing the change process, such as legal, political, and social variables. Assess the government's or department's history, readiness, and capacity for change. • This assessment should be conducted in the early planning stages to identify risks and develop a mitigation plan.

3	Guiding Principle 3: Leadership Engagement	• The change agenda must be developed, advanced, and supported by the leadership. • Leaders need to use the ideas that make change effective and comprehend the dynamics of change management. Leadership engagement, including visibly leading the change, setting the tone, and reinforcing the government's commitment to the interventions, should be defined at the planning stage.
4	Guiding Principle 4: Stakeholder Engagement	• Decide who the stakeholders are and include them right away to reduce the resistance to the change and build support. • Collaborate and interact as much with the stakeholders impacted by the change.
5	Guiding Principle 5: Plan and Strategy for Communication	• Developing a targeted communication strategy is essential for e-Governance projects. • A communication strategy should be developed during the planning phase of change and needs to be revisited and refined throughout the change cycle. • Communication should be evaluated by considering the why, what, how, and when of the messaging. • The change program should aim to create awareness and gain support, involvement, and commitment.
6	Guiding Principle 6: Capacity Building	• Providing training to staff members at every level is essential for e-Government program to maintain change and develop capability. • Starting at the planning stage, the essential talents needed to lead and carry out the change project must be identified. • For the designated groups, a training schedule must be created, and specific instruction must be given. • It may not take much initial leadership training to give the leaders the tools they need to spearhead the transformation.
7	Guiding Principle 7: Monitoring and Evaluation	• Determine how far we have gone and how far we still need to go with the change endeavor by establishing metrics or a mechanism to track our progress. • The project team needs to create monitoring strategies and inform the stakeholders about them.

3.5.8 Tools for Change Planning

Change management involves various tools to facilitate the planning, execution, and monitoring of change initiatives. These tools help organizations navigate transitions smoothly and effectively.

a) Change Management Models : Change management models provide structured frameworks for managing change. The ADKAR Model focuses on Awareness, Desire, Knowledge, Ability, and Reinforcement, guiding individuals through the change process. Kotter's 8-Step Model includes steps such as creating urgency, forming a powerful coalition, and generating short-term wins to ensure comprehensive change implementation. Lewin's Change Management Model, with its stages of unfreeze, change, and refreeze, helps organizations understand and manage the dynamics of change.

b) Stakeholder Analysis Tools: Engaging stakeholders is crucial for successful change management. Stakeholder Mapping helps identify stakeholders and assess their influence and interest, ensuring that key players are involved and informed. The RACI Matrix clarifies roles and responsibilities, designating who is Responsible, Accountable, Consulted, and Informed for each task, which enhances accountability and coordination.

c) Communication Tools: Effective communication is vital during change initiatives. A Communication Plan outlines what will be communicated, to whom, when, and how, ensuring consistency and clarity. Message Mapping ensures that all communications are aligned and clear, helping to manage expectations and reduce resistance.

d) Training and Development Tools: Training and development are essential for equipping employees with the necessary skills and knowledge. Training Needs Analysis (TNA) identifies gaps that training can address, while Learning Management Systems (LMS) deliver and track training programs, ensuring that employees are prepared for the changes ahead.

e) Project Management Tools: Project management tools help in planning and tracking the progress of change initiatives. Gantt Charts provide a visual representation of project timelines and milestones, making it easier to manage tasks and deadlines. PERT Charts analyze and represent the tasks involved, helping to identify dependencies and potential bottlenecks.

f) Monitoring and Evaluation Tools: Monitoring and evaluation tools are used to track the effectiveness of change initiatives. The Balanced Scorecard measures organizational performance against strategic goals, providing a comprehensive view of progress. KPI Dashboards offer real-time tracking of key performance indicators, enabling timely adjustments.

g) Risk Management Tools: Identifying and mitigating risks is critical in change management. A Risk Assessment Matrix evaluates potential risks and their impact, helping to develop strategies to address them. SWOT analysis assesses strengths, weaknesses, opportunities, and threats, providing a comprehensive view of the internal and external factors affecting the change.

h) Feedback and Assessment Tools: Gathering feedback is essential for understanding the impact of change. Surveys and Questionnaires collect input from employees and stakeholders, while focus groups facilitate in-depth discussions, providing valuable insights into the change process.

i) Change Readiness Assessment Tools: Assessing readiness for change helps in planning and executing change initiatives. Readiness surveys evaluate the organization's preparedness, and Force Field Analysis identifies driving and restraining forces, providing a clear picture of the factors influencing change.

j) Collaboration and Engagement Tools: Collaboration and engagement tools foster teamwork and participation. Workshops and Brainstorming Sessions facilitate collaborative planning and problem-solving, while Collaboration Platforms, such as Microsoft Teams and Slack, enhance communication and coordination.

k) Documentation and Tracking Tools: Standardized documentation and tracking tools ensure consistency and accountability. Change request forms standardize the process of requesting changes, while issue tracking systems monitor and manage issues that arise, ensuring they are addressed promptly.

l) Incentive and Reward Programs: Incentive and reward programs motivate employees and reinforce positive behavior. Recognition Programs acknowledge contributions, boosting morale, while incentive plans provide tangible rewards for achieving change-related goals, encouraging active participation and commitment.

These tools collectively support a structured, systematic approach to change management, enhancing the likelihood of successful outcomes and sustainable improvements

3.6 Critical Success Factor

The successful implementation of e-governance initiatives depends on several critical success factors (CSFs). These factors encompass strategic, operational, and technological aspects, ensuring that e-governance projects achieve their objectives and deliver value to citizens and other stakeholders. Here are some key CSFs for implementing e-governance:

3.6.1 Political Will and Leadership

Political will and leadership are fundamental to the success of e-governance initiatives. Strong political will signifies a commitment from the highest levels of government to pursue digital transformation and implement necessary reforms, even in the face of potential resistance or challenges. Leadership in e-governance involves setting clear priorities, supporting the vision, and mobilizing resources and stakeholders to achieve the desired outcomes.

3.6.2 Clear Vision and Strategy

Clear vision and strategy are critical success factors for e-governance as they provide essential guidance and direction for the implementation of digital government initiatives. A clear vision articulates a long-term goal that aligns the efforts of various government departments and stakeholders, ensuring that all actions contribute towards a common objective. This vision inspires and motivates, setting a benchmark for what the government aims to achieve through its digital transformation.

Meanwhile, a well-defined strategy outlines the specific steps and actions needed to realize this vision, serving as a roadmap for efficient resource allocation, prioritization of projects, and performance measurement. It ensures that financial, human, and technological resources are used effectively and that progress can be monitored and adjusted as necessary.

3.6.3 Adequate Funding and Resources

Adequate funding and resources are vital for the successful implementation and sustainability of e-governance initiatives. Sufficient financial investment is needed to develop, deploy, and maintain the necessary digital infrastructure, including hardware, software, and cybersecurity measures. Resources also encompass skilled personnel who can manage and operate e-governance systems, provide training, and offer technical support to ensure smooth functioning. Adequate funding enables the government to adopt innovative technologies, conduct pilot projects, and scale successful solutions across various departments and regions.

Moreover, consistent financial backing is crucial for continuous improvements and upgrades, keeping the e-governance systems up-to-date with evolving technological advancements and user needs. Without adequate funding and resources, e-governance projects risk being incomplete, underperforming, or becoming obsolete. Therefore, securing sufficient and sustained funding, along with strategically allocating resources, is essential to achieving the objectives of e-governance, improving service delivery, and enhancing citizen engagement and satisfaction.

3.6.4 ICT Infrastructure

ICT infrastructure is the backbone of e-governance, providing the technological foundation necessary for digital transformation in government services. Robust ICT infrastructure includes reliable internet connectivity, data centers, cloud services, and secure networks, which are essential for supporting the vast array of digital services offered to citizens. High-quality infrastructure ensures that government platforms are accessible, efficient, and resilient, capable of handling large volumes of data and user interactions seamlessly. It also facilitates interoperability between different government departments, enabling the seamless exchange of information and coordination of services.

Additionally, strong ICT infrastructure supports the integration of advanced technologies like artificial intelligence, big data analytics, and the Internet of Things (IoT), which can enhance the effectiveness and efficiency of e-governance initiatives. Without a solid ICT foundation, e-governance efforts can be hindered by technical issues, security vulnerabilities, and limited reach, ultimately impacting the quality and reliability of public services. Therefore, investing and continuously upgrading ICT infrastructure is crucial for the success and sustainability of e-governance, driving innovation, improving service delivery, and ensuring that citizens can fully benefited from digital government services.

3.6.5 Awareness

Awareness plays a pivotal role in the successful adoption and utilization of e-governance initiatives. In the context of e-governance, awareness refers to informing and educating citizens about the availability, benefits, and usage of digital government services. Effective awareness campaigns aim to increase public knowledge and understanding of how to access and interact with government services online, thereby promoting greater participation and engagement. When citizens are informed about the e-governance services available to them, they are more likely to utilize these services. This heightened engagement ensures that the benefits of e-governance—such as increased efficiency, transparency, and accessibility—are fully realized. Without adequate awareness, even the most well-designed e-governance systems can go underutilized, failing to achieve their intended impact.

Furthermore, awareness initiatives often include elements of digital literacy, which are essential in regions where a significant portion of the population may not be familiar with digital platforms. By educating citizens on how to navigate and use e-governance services, these initiatives bridge the gap between technology and the user, ensuring that more people can benefit from digital government services. This education fosters trust and confidence in e-governance systems, as informed citizens are more likely to trust the services they understand and see the value in.

In addition to increasing user participation and digital literacy, awareness also facilitates a feedback loop between the government and its citizens. When people are aware of and actively using e-governance services, they can provide valuable feedback that can be used to improve these services. This feedback is crucial for the continuous improvement and adaptation of e-governance systems to better meet the needs of the public. Thus, awareness not only drives the initial adoption of e-governance services but also their ongoing enhancement.

Inclusivity is another vital aspect supported by awareness in e-governance. Awareness campaigns can reach out to marginalized and underserved communities, ensuring that everyone has equal access to e-governance services. This inclusivity is essential for the overall success of e-governance initiatives, as it ensures that the benefits of digital government are distributed equitably across all segments of society. By promoting awareness, governments can work towards closing the digital divide and creating a more inclusive society.

Finally, awareness leads to more efficient utilization of resources. When citizens are well-informed and actively using e-governance services, it reduces the burden on traditional government offices and processes, often resulting in cost savings and faster service delivery. This efficient use of resources allows governments to allocate their efforts and funds more effectively, further enhancing the overall governance process. In summary, awareness is foundational to the success of e-governance, driving engagement, inclusivity, and continuous improvement while ensuring efficient resource utilization.

3.6.6 E-Skills

E-skills, or digital skills, are a critical success factor in e-governance because they enable citizens to effectively access and utilize digital government services. In an era where governance increasingly relies on digital platforms for service delivery, the ability of citizens to navigate these platforms is paramount. E-skills encompass a range of competencies, from basic digital literacy to advanced technical expertise, and are essential for ensuring that all segments of the population can engage with e-governance systems. Without these skills, even the most sophisticated e-governance initiatives may fail to reach their full potential, as a significant portion of the population could be excluded from digital services.

Moreover, e-skills empower citizens to participate more actively in the democratic process. By being proficient in digital tools, individuals can access information more readily, communicate with government officials, and contribute to public discourse through online platforms. This increased engagement fosters a more informed and involved citizenry, which is crucial for the success of democratic governance. E-skills also enable citizens to benefit from the transparency and accountability that e-governance promises, as they can independently verify and scrutinize government actions and data available online.

In addition to enhancing citizen engagement, e-skills are vital for the efficiency and effectiveness of e-governance. Public servants and government employees must possess strong digital competencies to manage and deliver digital services effectively. Training government personnel in e-skills ensures that they can operate and maintain e-governance systems, troubleshoot issues, and innovate processes. This capability is essential for the seamless delivery of services and the continuous improvement of digital governance platforms.

E-skills also play a significant role in economic development. As governments transition to digital service delivery, there is an increasing demand for a workforce skilled in Information and Communication Technology (ICT). By investing in e-skills, governments can stimulate job creation and economic growth, as individuals with these competencies are better positioned to take advantage of new opportunities in the digital economy. Furthermore, a digitally skilled population can drive innovation, leading to the development of new technologies and services that can further enhance e-governance.

3.6.7 Transparency and accountability

Transparency and accountability are critical success factors in e-governance because they build trust between the government and its citizens, ensuring that digital governance initiatives are credible and effective. By providing open access to information, e-governance platforms enable citizens to monitor government activities, decisions, and expenditures, thereby reducing the potential for corruption and misuse of power. This openness fosters a culture of accountability, where government officials are held responsible for their actions, leading to more ethical and efficient public service delivery. Furthermore, transparency in e-governance promotes informed citizen participation, as individuals are better equipped with the knowledge needed to engage in democratic processes and advocate for their rights. Ultimately, transparency and accountability enhance the legitimacy of e-governance systems, driving greater public trust, compliance, and active participation in digital governance initiatives.

3.6.8 Adequate Legal Regulatory Framework

An adequate legal regulatory framework is a critical success factor in e-governance as it provides the necessary legal foundation to support and sustain digital government initiatives. Such a framework ensures that there are clear guidelines and regulations governing the use of digital technologies, data protection, privacy, cybersecurity, and the ethical use of information. By establishing these legal parameters, governments can protect citizens' rights, maintain public trust, and ensure that e-governance services are secure and reliable. Additionally, a robust legal framework facilitates the smooth implementation and operation of e-governance by defining the roles and responsibilities of various stakeholders, setting standards for interoperability, and ensuring compliance with national and international laws. This legal clarity not only promotes consistency and fairness in the delivery of digital services but also encourages innovation and investment in e-governance initiatives, ultimately leading to more efficient, transparent, and accountable governance.

3.6.9 Top Management and Government Support

Top management and government support are critical success factors in e-governance because they provide the strategic direction, resources, and leadership necessary for the successful implementation of digital governance initiatives. When top leaders and government officials are committed to e-governance, they can drive the necessary policy changes, allocate sufficient funding, and foster a culture of innovation and accountability within public institutions. Their support is essential for overcoming resistance to change, coordinating efforts across various government departments, and ensuring that e-governance projects align with broader national development goals. Furthermore, strong leadership from the top helps to communicate the importance and benefits of e-governance to the public and other stakeholders, building widespread support and engagement. This high-level backing not only accelerates the adoption and integration of digital technologies in governance but also ensures the sustainability and scalability of e-governance initiatives over time.

3.6.10 Capacity Building and Training

Capacity building and training are critical success factors in e-governance because they ensure that both government employees and citizens possess the necessary skills and knowledge to effectively use and manage digital government services. For government employees, targeted training programs enhance their technical competencies, enabling them to develop, maintain, and innovate e-governance systems. This proficiency is crucial for delivering efficient and high-quality services to the public. For citizens, capacity building initiatives, such as digital literacy programs, empower them to access and benefit from e-governance services, fostering greater engagement and inclusion. By investing in ongoing capacity building and training, governments can create a skilled workforce and an informed citizenry, both of which are essential for the sustainable success and evolution of e-governance initiatives. This continuous development ensures that all stakeholders can effectively adapt to new technologies and processes, thereby maximizing the overall impact and efficiency of e-governance.

3.6.11 User-Centric Approach

A user-centric approach is a critical success factor in e-governance because it ensures that digital government services are designed with the needs, preferences, and experiences of the users at the forefront. By focusing on the user, e-governance initiatives can create more intuitive, accessible, and responsive services that are easy to navigate and understand. This approach involves engaging citizens throughout the design and implementation process, gathering feedback, and continuously improving services based on user input. By prioritizing the user experience, government can enhance satisfaction, increase adoption rates, and foster trust in digital services. Additionally, a user-centric approach helps to address the diverse needs of different segments of the population, including those with limited digital skills or access, thereby promoting inclusivity and equity. Ultimately, a focus on the user ensures that e-governance initiatives are more effective, relevant, and sustainable, delivering greater value to all stakeholders.

3.6.12 Citizen Empowerment

Citizen empowerment is a critical success factor in e-governance because it enables individuals to actively participate in and influence governmental processes and decisions. Empowered citizens, equipped with access to information and digital tools, can hold governments accountable, advocate for their rights, and contribute to public policy debates. E-governance initiatives that focus on citizen empowerment provide platforms for direct communication and feedback, fostering a more transparent and responsive government. By facilitating greater citizen engagement, these initiatives help build trust and legitimacy in government actions. Empowerment also ensures that diverse voices and perspectives are included in governance, leading to more inclusive and equitable policy outcomes. Ultimately, citizen empowerment in e-governance not only enhances democratic participation but also drives the continuous improvement of public services, aligning them more closely with the needs and aspirations of the population.

3.6.13 Change Management

Change management is a critical success factor in e-governance because it addresses the complexities of implementing digital transformation within government institutions. E-governance initiatives often involve significant shifts in processes, technologies, and organizational culture, which can encounter resistance and challenges. Effective change management strategies help navigate these transitions by systematically planning, communicating, and guiding stakeholders through the change process.

Key aspects of change management in e-governance include stakeholder engagement, where leaders and managers communicate the benefits of digital transformation and actively involve employees and citizens in decision-making. Training and capacity building are also crucial, ensuring that staff have the skills and knowledge to adopt new technologies and procedures seamlessly. Additionally, change management involves managing risks, addressing concerns, and providing support to mitigate disruptions during the transition period.

By prioritizing change management, governments can minimize resistance to change, enhance organizational readiness, and increase the likelihood of successful e-governance implementation. It enables government agencies to adapt to new technologies and operational models more effectively, improving service delivery, efficiency, and responsiveness to citizen needs. Ultimately, robust change management practices in e-governance facilitate a smoother transition towards digital governance, fostering innovation and continuous improvement in public administration.

3.6.14 Public Awareness and Outreach

Public awareness and outreach are critical success factors in e-governance initiatives. Effective e-governance hinges not only on the deployment of technology but also on ensuring that citizens are informed and engaged. By raising public awareness, governments can educate citizens about available digital services, their rights, and how to participate in governance processes online. Outreach efforts can include campaigns, workshops, and community engagement activities designed to bridge the digital divide and ensure equitable access to information and services. This proactive approach not only enhances transparency and accountability but also fosters trust between citizens and government institutions, thereby strengthening the overall effectiveness of e-governance initiatives.

3.6.15 Effective Project Management

Effective project management is a cornerstone of successful e-governance initiatives. In the context of digital transformation in government, meticulous project management ensures that complex technological deployments and policy changes are implemented smoothly and efficiently. Key aspects include clear goal setting, stakeholder engagement, rigorous planning, and robust risk management strategies.

Project managers in e-governance must navigate various challenges, such as balancing technical requirements with user needs, adhering to timelines and budgets, and maintaining high standards of data security and privacy. Effective communication channels and regular progress monitoring are essential to keep all stakeholders informed and aligned throughout the project lifecycle.

Moreover, agile methodologies often play a crucial role in e-governance projects, allowing for iterative development, rapid adaptation to changing requirements, and continuous improvement based on user feedback. By prioritizing effective project management practices, governments can maximize the impact of their e-governance initiatives, ensuring they deliver tangible benefits to citizens while fostering innovation and efficiency in public service delivery.

3.6.16 Monitoring and Evaluation

Monitoring and evaluation (M&E) are indispensable factors for the success of e-governance initiatives. These processes provide governments with the tools to assess the effectiveness, efficiency, and impact of their digital transformation efforts. Through systematic monitoring, governments can track key performance indicators (KPIs), such as user adoption rates, service delivery times, and cost savings, to gauge whether objectives are being met.

Evaluation goes beyond mere data collection, focusing on analyzing outcomes and assessing the overall success of e-governance projects against predefined goals. This involves gathering feedback from stakeholders, including citizens, to understand their experiences and satisfaction levels with digital services.

By incorporating M&E into e-governance strategies, governments can identify strengths, weaknesses, and areas for improvement, enabling informed decision-making and course corrections as needed. Additionally, transparent reporting of M&E findings fosters accountability and enhances public trust in government initiatives. Ultimately, effective monitoring and evaluation not only optimize resource allocation but also drive continuous improvement and innovation in e-governance, ensuring that digital solutions meet the evolving needs of citizens and deliver tangible benefits to society as a whole.

3.6.17 Adaptability and Innovation

Adaptability and innovation are pivotal success factors in the realm of e-governance, where rapid technological advancements and evolving citizen expectations necessitate flexible approaches. Governments must continuously adapt their strategies and systems to harness emerging technologies effectively and address new challenges.

Innovation in e-governance involves not only the introduction of cutting-edge technologies but also the creative reimagining of processes and services to enhance efficiency, accessibility, and user experience. This could mean leveraging artificial intelligence (AI) for personalized citizen services, adopting blockchain for secure and transparent transactions, or implementing data analytics to derive actionable insights for policymaking.

Moreover, adaptability encompasses the agility to respond swiftly to changing circumstances, such as shifts in user demographics or unexpected technological disruptions. Flexible governance frameworks and agile project management methodologies enable governments to iterate and refine solutions based on real-time feedback and evolving needs.

By prioritizing adaptability and fostering a culture of innovation, governments can stay ahead of the curve in e-governance, delivering responsive and citizen-centric services that improve overall governance effectiveness and public trust. This proactive approach not only future-proofs digital initiatives but also positions governments to lead in leveraging technology for inclusive and sustainable development.

3.6.18 Stakeholder Engagement and Collaboration

Stakeholder engagement and collaboration represent critical success factors in e-governance, emphasizing the importance of involving diverse stakeholders in decision-making processes and implementation efforts. Effective e-governance initiatives require the active participation of various groups, including government agencies, private sector partners, civil society organizations, and, most importantly, citizens themselves.

Engagement begins with understanding stakeholders' needs, concerns, and expectations regarding digital services and governance reforms. By involving stakeholders from the outset, governments can co-create solutions that are responsive to real-world challenges and reflect the diverse interests of the community. This collaborative approach not only enhances the relevance and acceptance of e-governance initiatives but also builds trust and legitimacy among stakeholders.

Furthermore, sustained collaboration throughout the project lifecycle ensures that resources are leveraged efficiently, risks are managed collectively, and expertise is shared to overcome complex challenges. Platforms for dialogue, feedback mechanisms, and transparent communication channels play a crucial role in fostering continuous engagement and alignment of goals across stakeholders.

Ultimately, robust stakeholder engagement and collaboration in e-governance foster a supportive ecosystem where innovations thrive, policies are informed by diverse perspectives, and the benefits of digital transformation are equitably distributed. By nurturing these relationships, governments can strengthen governance outcomes, promote inclusivity, and drive sustainable development in the digital age.

3.7 Major issue including corruption and resistance for change

Implementing e-governance initiatives can face several challenges and issues, which can vary depending on the context and the specific project. Some major issues include.

3.7.1 Citizen Engagement and Trust

Citizen engagement and trust are pivotal in the successful implementation of e-governance initiatives. One of the primary challenges lies in ensuring that citizens are not only aware of these digital services but also trust them enough to actively participate. This requires transparent communication about the benefits and functionalities of e-governance platforms, as well as efforts to make them accessible and user-friendly for diverse demographics. Building trust also depends on robust data privacy measures and cybersecurity protocols to protect citizen information. Governments must establish effective feedback mechanisms and demonstrate responsiveness to citizen input, fostering a sense of inclusivity and accountability. Additionally, addressing the digital divide and ensuring equitable access to technology and digital literacy are crucial steps toward enhancing citizen engagement. Ultimately, nurturing a culture of openness, consultation, and continuous improvement in e-governance practices is essential for cultivating enduring trust and participation among citizens.

3.7.2 Digital Divide

The digital divide poses a significant challenge in the implementation of e-governance initiatives, creating disparities in access to and utilization of digital services among different socioeconomic groups and geographic regions. In urban areas, access to high-speed internet and digital devices may be relatively widespread, enabling easier adoption of e-governance platforms. However, rural and remote areas often face infrastructural limitations, such as inadequate internet connectivity and limited availability of digital devices, which hinder access to online government services. Moreover, disparities in digital literacy levels further increase the divide. Citizens with lower levels of digital literacy may struggle to navigate complex e-governance interfaces or understand the procedures required to access services online. Bridging the digital divide requires comprehensive strategies, including infrastructure development to improve internet connectivity in underserved areas, provision of affordable digital devices, and targeted digital literacy programs to empower citizens with the skills needed to effectively engage with e-governance platforms. Addressing these challenges is crucial for ensuring equitable access to government services and promoting inclusive participation in the digital economy.

3.7.3 Financial Constraints

Financial constraints pose a significant challenge in the implementation of e-governance initiatives, impacting the ability of governments to develop, deploy, and sustain digital platforms and services effectively. E-governance projects require substantial investments in various areas, including infrastructure development, software procurement, cybersecurity measures, capacity building, and ongoing maintenance. Limited financial resources can restrict the scope and quality of these initiatives, delaying project timelines or compromising the functionality of digital systems. Moreover, the costs associated with upgrading existing IT infrastructure to support e-governance functionalities can be prohibitive, especially for governments facing budgetary pressures or competing priorities.

In addition to initial investment costs, the sustainability of e-governance initiatives over the long term is contingent upon securing adequate funding for operational expenses and continuous improvements. Governments must allocate resources strategically to prioritize key areas such as cybersecurity, data protection, and digital skills training, while also ensuring affordability and accessibility of digital services for all citizens. Innovative financing mechanisms, partnerships with private sector entities, and leveraging international assistance can provide avenues to mitigate financial constraints and enhance the resilience of e-governance projects. Overcoming these financial challenges requires careful planning, efficient resource management, and a commitment to prioritizing investments in digital infrastructure as a cornerstone of modern governance.

3.7.4 Privacy and Security

Privacy and security are paramount concerns in the implementation of e-governance initiatives, influencing citizen trust and the overall success of digital government services. The collection, storage, and use of personal data in e-governance systems necessitate stringent measures to safeguard against unauthorized access, data breaches, and misuse. Governments must adhere to robust data protection laws and regulations to ensure that citizens' sensitive information, such as personal identifiers and transaction details, remains secure.

One of the primary challenges is maintaining the confidentiality and integrity of data across various stages of its lifecycle, from collection through to storage and eventual disposal. Weaknesses in cybersecurity infrastructure, including inadequate encryption protocols or vulnerabilities in software applications, can expose e-governance systems to cyber threats and malicious attacks. Such incidents not only compromise individual privacy but also erode public confidence in digital government services.

Moreover, ensuring transparency and accountability in how government agencies handle citizen data is crucial for building and maintaining trust. Citizens need assurance that their information is being used responsibly and only for authorized purposes. Implementing effective data governance frameworks, conducting regular audits of security protocols, and providing clear information about data handling practices are essential steps in mitigating privacy and security risks in e-governance.

3.7.5 Infrastructure

Implementing e-governance often faces significant infrastructure challenges that can prevent its effectiveness and reach. One critical issue is the lack of robust digital infrastructure in many regions. This includes inadequate internet connectivity, especially in rural and remote areas, which limits access to online services. Without reliable connectivity, citizens cannot fully benefit from e-governance platforms, impacting inclusivity and equity in service delivery.

Moreover, outdated or incompatible IT systems within government departments pose another hurdle. These systems may not integrate well with new e-governance initiatives, leading to inefficiencies, data silos, and compromised service delivery. Upgrading these systems requires substantial investment in both technology and human resources, which can strain budgets and delay implementation.

Security concerns also appear large. E-governance platforms handle sensitive citizen data, making them prime targets for cyber threats. Ensuring robust cybersecurity measures is essential but challenging, especially for governments with limited expertise and resources in this area.

3.7.6 Interoperability and Standards

Implementing e-governance faces significant challenges related to interoperability and standards, which are crucial for seamless operation and integration of various government systems and services. One of the primary issues is the lack of standardized protocols and formats for data exchange among different government agencies and departments. Without uniform standards, data sharing becomes cumbersome, leading to inefficiencies, duplication of efforts, and delays in service delivery.

Moreover, disparate IT systems used by different government entities making it difficult to integrate data and processes across departments. This fragmentation hampers the ability to provide coherent and holistic services to citizens, as information may not be readily available or accessible when needed.

Interoperability challenges also arise from legacy IT systems that are outdated and incompatible with modern e-governance platforms. Integrating these systems with new technologies and standards requires significant effort and resources, potentially delaying the rollout of e-governance initiatives.

Additionally, varying levels of digital maturity among government agencies further complicate interoperability efforts. Some departments may be more advanced in their digital transformation journey, while others lag behind, creating disparities in service delivery and citizen experience.

To address these challenges, governments need to establish robust interoperability frameworks and enforce standards for data exchange and system integration. This includes adopting open standards and APIs (Application Programming Interfaces) that facilitate seamless communication between different systems. Collaborative efforts among government agencies, along with partnerships with the private sector and international organizations, can help establish common interoperability guidelines and best practices.

3.7.7 Lack of Awareness

The lack of awareness poses a significant challenge in the effective implementation of e-governance initiatives. Despite technological advancements and the potential benefits of digital platforms in enhancing government services, many citizens remain uninformed about these initiatives. This lack of awareness can be from various factors, including limited access to information channels, inadequate digital literacy among the population, and insufficient efforts by government agencies to promote and educate the public about available e-governance services.

Without proper awareness, citizens may not fully utilize digital platforms for accessing government services, resulting in underutilization of resources and missed opportunities for efficiency gains. Moreover, the success of e-governance depends heavily on active citizen participation and feedback, which are delayed when people are unaware of the tools and resources available to them.

3.7.8 Low computer literacy

The issue of low computer literacy poses a significant challenge in the implementation of e-governance initiatives. E-governance aims to leverage digital technologies to improve the efficiency, transparency, and accessibility of government services. However, in many regions, particularly in rural and less developed areas, a large portion of the population lacks the necessary skills to effectively use computers and navigate online platforms.

This lack of computer literacy creates barriers to access e-governance services, as citizens struggle to understand and interact with digital interfaces for tasks such as applying for permits, paying taxes, or accessing vital information. Moreover, addressing low computer literacy requires comprehensive strategies, including targeted digital literacy programs, user-friendly interfaces, and support systems to assist citizens in using e-governance platforms effectively. Without these interventions, the potential of e-governance to democratize access to government services and foster inclusive development may remain unrealized in many communities.

3.7.9 Technical issue

One of the critical technical issues delaying the implementation of e-governance initiatives is the compatibility and interoperability of systems. E-governance relies heavily on various digital platforms, databases, and communication technologies to deliver services efficiently and transparently. However, governmental agencies often operate with disparate systems that may not communicate seamlessly with each other.

This lack of interoperability can lead to inefficiencies and delays in service delivery. For instance, a citizen might need to interact with multiple government departments for different services, each with its own separate system and interface. This fragmentation not only complicates the user experience but also hampers the ability of agencies to share data securely and in real-time.

Moreover, technical issues such as outdated infrastructure, inadequate cybersecurity measures, and insufficient bandwidth in rural areas further enhance the challenges. These issues not only affect the reliability of e-governance services but also pose risks to the privacy and security of citizen data.

Addressing these technical challenges requires significant investment in upgrading digital infrastructure, establishing common standards for data exchange, and implementing robust cybersecurity protocols. Additionally, fostering a culture of innovation and continuous improvement within governmental agencies is crucial to adapt to evolving technologies and maintain the effectiveness of e-governance initiatives over time. By overcoming these technical barriers, governments can enhance the accessibility, efficiency, and responsiveness of digital services for all citizens.

3.7.10 Economic and social issues

The implementation of e-governance initiatives often encounters economic challenges that can hinder their effectiveness and widespread adoption. One of the primary economic issues is the initial cost of infrastructure development and technology deployment. Building robust digital platforms, upgrading existing systems, and ensuring sufficient internet connectivity require substantial financial investments, especially for governments operating with limited budgets.

Another economic challenge is the digital divide, where disparities in access to technology and internet connectivity exist among different socioeconomic groups. Marginalized communities, rural areas, and low-income households may lack the necessary infrastructure or financial means to access and benefit from e-governance services. This inequality increases social exclusion and limits the potential of e-governance to enhance citizen engagement and improve service delivery equitably across all demographics.

Moreover, the return on investment (ROI) from e-governance initiatives may not always be immediately apparent or easily quantifiable. While digital transformation promises long-term benefits such as increased efficiency, reduced administrative costs, and enhanced transparency, measuring and realizing these benefits requires careful planning, monitoring, and evaluation over extended periods.

To address these economic challenges, governments need to adopt a strategic approach that balances short-term costs with long-term benefits. This includes prioritizing investments in digital infrastructure, promoting public-private partnerships to share costs and expertise, and implementing policies that promote equitable access to technology. By leveraging e-governance to streamline operations, improve service delivery, and foster economic growth, governments can maximize the impact of their investments and ensure sustainable development for all citizens.

3.7.11 Resistance for Change

Resistance for change is a common hurdle in the implementation of e-governance initiatives. Despite the potential benefits such as increased efficiency, transparency, and accessibility, many stakeholders within government bodies and the public sector often exhibit reluctance towards adopting new technologies and processes. This resistance can be from various factors, including fear of job loss due to automation, concerns about data security and privacy, lack of familiarity with technology, and a preference for traditional methods. Overcoming these challenges requires not only robust technical solutions and infrastructure but also comprehensive change management strategies.

In summary, overcoming resistance for change in e-governance implementations demands a holistic approach that tackles both technical and human factors. By addressing concerns, providing adequate support, and fostering a culture of openness to innovation, governments can successfully navigate the challenges and realize the full potential of digital transformation in public service delivery.

3.8 e-security and Cyber Laws

E-security, or electronic security, refers to the protection of information systems, digital data, and electronic infrastructure from unauthorized access, disruption, or damage. It encompasses a broad range of practices, technologies, and policies designed to safeguard information assets in the digital domain. With the increasing dependance on digital systems for communication, commerce, governance, and personal activities, e-security has become a critical aspect of modern life.

The foundation of e-security lies in ensuring the confidentiality, integrity, and availability of information. Confidentiality involves protecting sensitive data from unauthorized access and disclosure. This is often achieved through encryption, access controls, and strict authentication protocols. Integrity ensures that data remains accurate and unaltered during storage or transmission. Techniques like cryptographic hashing and digital signatures are used to verify data integrity and detect any unauthorized modifications. Availability ensures that information and systems are accessible to authorized users when needed, which involves implementing redundancy, regular backups, and robust disaster recovery plans.

Authentication and authorization are key components of e-security. Authentication verifies the identity of users and devices, typically through methods such as passwords, biometrics, or multi-factor authentication (MFA). Authorization, on the other hand, determines what an authenticated user is allowed to do, ensuring that they have the necessary permissions to access specific resources. These measures are vital in preventing unauthorized access and ensuring that users only have access to the information and systems necessary for their roles.

Technological measures play a crucial role in e-security. Firewalls monitor and control the incoming and outgoing network traffic based on predetermined security rules, acting as a barrier against unauthorized access. Intrusion detection and prevention systems (IDPS) continuously monitor networks and systems for malicious activities or policy violations, providing alerts and taking actions to mitigate potential threats. Anti-malware and anti-virus software detect, prevent, and remove malicious software, protecting systems from infections that could lead to data breaches or system damage.

In conclusion, e-security is an essential aspect of protecting digital information and systems in an increasingly interconnected world. By implementing a combination of technological measures, strict authentication and authorization protocols, and continuous education and assessment, organizations can effectively safeguard their information assets against a wide range of threats.

3.8.1 Role of e-security

E-security plays a pivotal role in e-governance, ensuring the secure, reliable, and efficient delivery of government services to citizens. As government increasingly adopt digital platforms to enhance transparency, accessibility, and convenience, the importance of robust e-security measures cannot be overstated. Here are several key roles of e-security in e-governance:

a) Protecting sensitive data: E-governance systems handle vast amounts of sensitive data, including personal information, financial records, and confidential government documents. E-security measures, such as encryption and access controls, protect this data from unauthorized access, ensuring that citizens' privacy is maintained and sensitive information is not compromised.

b) Ensuring service availability: Government services must be consistently available to the public. E-security helps prevent disruptions caused by cyberattacks, such as Distributed Denial of Service (DDoS) attacks, which can disable government websites and online services. By implementing robust security protocols, governments can ensure the continuous availability of their services.

c) Maintaining data integrity: Accurate and unaltered data is crucial for effective governance. E-security measures, including cryptographic hashes and digital signatures, help maintain data integrity by preventing unauthorized modifications. This ensures that the information provided to and from citizens is reliable and trustworthy.

d) Building citizen trust: Trust is fundamental for the success of e-governance initiatives. Citizens need to trust that their interactions with government digital services are secure. Effective e-security practices foster this trust by protecting against data breaches and cyber threats, thereby encouraging greater use of e-governance platforms.

e) Facilitating secure communication: Secure communication channels are essential for interactions between government entities and citizens. E-security ensures that communications, such as emails, online forms, and transactions, are encrypted and protected from interception by malicious actors.

f) Compliance with legal and regulatory requirements: Governments must comply with various legal and regulatory frameworks related to data protection and privacy. E-security measures help ensure that e-governance systems adhere to these requirements, avoiding legal effects and maintaining public trust.

g) Preventing fraud and corruption: E-governance aims to increase transparency and reduce opportunities for fraud and corruption. E-security plays a critical role in this by implementing measures like audit trails, which track all actions and changes within the system, making it easier to detect and investigate fraudulent activities.

h) Enabling efficient incident response: In the event of a security breach, having robust e-security measures in place allows for efficient incident response. This includes identifying the breach, mitigating its impact, and restoring affected services quickly, minimizing disruption and maintaining public confidence.

i) Supporting digital transformation: As governments undergo digital transformation, e-security ensures that new digital services are launched securely. This involves securing new platforms and applications from the ground up, integrating security into the development lifecycle, and continuously monitoring for vulnerabilities.

E-security is fundamental to the successful implementation and operation of e-governance. By protecting sensitive data, ensuring service availability, maintaining data integrity, and fostering trust, e-security enables governments to provide secure, reliable, and efficient digital services to their citizens. As digital transformation continues to evolve, the role of e-security in e-governance will only become more critical, requiring continuous advancements and vigilance to address emerging threats.

3.8.2 Importance of e-security

E-security is crucial in e-governance for several reasons, ensuring that digital government services are secure, reliable, and trustworthy. First, it protects sensitive personal and governmental data from unauthorized access and cyber threats, thereby safeguarding citizens' privacy and maintaining the confidentiality of government operations. Second, e-security ensures the integrity of data, making sure that information remains accurate and unaltered, which is vital for informed decision-making and public trust. Third, it guarantees the availability of essential services by preventing disruptions caused by cyberattacks, ensuring that citizens can consistently access digital government services without interruption. Additionally, e-security supports compliance with legal and regulatory requirements, reducing the risk of legal issues and penalties. It also helps in detecting and preventing fraud and corruption by implementing robust monitoring and audit mechanisms.

Overall, e-security is fundamental to building and maintaining trust in e-governance, enabling secure communication, protecting data, and ensuring the smooth, efficient, and reliable delivery of digital government services.

3.8.3 classification of e-security system

E-security in e-governance can be classified into several key categories, each addressing different aspects of protecting digital government services and data. These classifications ensure a comprehensive security strategy that covers all potential vulnerabilities and threats. Here are the main classifications:

a) Network Security

- *Firewalls:* Devices or software that filter incoming and outgoing network traffic based on security rules.
- *Intrusion Detection and Prevention Systems (IDPS):* Tools that monitor network traffic for suspicious activities and take action to prevent breaches.
- *Virtual Private Networks (VPNs):* Secure communication channels that encrypt data transmitted over public networks.

b) Application Security

- *Secure Coding Practices:* Techniques used during software development to prevent security vulnerabilities.

- *Web Application Firewalls (WAF)*: Filters that protect web applications by monitoring and filtering HTTP traffic.
- *Regular Patch Management:* Timely updates and patches to fix security vulnerabilities in software applications.

c) Endpoint Security

- *Anti-Malware Software:* Programs that detect and remove malicious code from computers and other devices.
- *Endpoint Detection and Response (EDR):* Solutions that continuously monitor and respond to threats on endpoints such as computers and mobile devices.
- *Device Encryption:* Encrypting data stored on devices to prevent unauthorized access if the device is lost or stolen.

d) Data Security

- *Data Encryption:* Protecting data at rest and in transit using encryption algorithms.
- *Data Masking:* Techniques to hide sensitive data, showing only non-sensitive information to users.
- *Access Controls:* Implementing role-based access controls (RBAC) to restrict data access to authorized users.

e) Identity and Access Management (IAM)

- *Authentication Methods:* Techniques such as passwords, biometrics, and multi-factor authentication (MFA) to verify user identities.
- *Authorization Protocols:* Ensuring users have the appropriate permissions for their roles.
- *Single Sign-On (SSO):* Systems that allow users to log in once and gain access to multiple applications without re-authenticating.

f) Operational Security

- *Security Policies and Procedures:* Documented guidelines for managing and protecting information systems.
- *Incident Response Plans:* Prepared strategies for detecting, responding to, and recovering from security incidents.
- *Regular Security Audits:* Assessments to evaluate the effectiveness of security measures and identify vulnerabilities.

g) Physical Security

- *Controlled Access to Facilities:* Restricting physical access to data centers and other sensitive locations.

- *Surveillance Systems:* Cameras and monitoring systems to detect and prevent unauthorized physical access.
- *Environmental Controls:* Measures to protect hardware from environmental hazards such as fire, flood, and extreme temperatures.

h) User Education and Awareness

- *Security Training Programs:* Educating employees and users on security best practices and threat recognition.
- *Phishing Simulations:* Testing users' ability to recognize and respond to phishing attacks.
- *Regular Updates and Reminders:* Keeping users informed about new security threats and preventive measures.

i) Compliance and Regulatory Security

- *Adherence to Legal Standards:* Ensuring compliance with laws and regulations such as GDPR, HIPAA, and others.
- *Industry Standards:* Implementing best practices from standards such as ISO/IEC 27001, NIST, and COBIT.
- *Regular Compliance Audits:* Conducting audits to verify adherence to regulatory requirements.

j) Disaster Recovery and Business Continuity

- *Backup Solutions:* Regularly backing up data to secure locations.
- *Disaster Recovery Plans:* Strategies to restore systems and data after a security breach or disaster.
- *Business Continuity Planning:* Ensuring that critical government functions can continue during and after a security incident.
- By addressing e-security through these classifications, e-governance can achieve a holistic security posture that protects against a wide range of threats and ensures the continuous, secure delivery of government services.

3.8.4 Applications of e-security

e-security in e-governance finds numerous applications across various aspects of digital government operations, aiming to ensure the confidentiality, integrity, and availability of data and services. Here are some key applications of e-security in e-governance.

a) Protecting Sensitive Data: Encryption and access controls safeguard personal and government information from unauthorized access.

b) Securing Digital Transactions: Secure authentication and encryption ensure safe online transactions for services like tax payments and licenses.

c) Managing Citizen Identities: Biometric authentication and identity verification systems validate citizens' identities securely online.

d) Ensuring Secure Communication: Encrypted emails, VPNs, and secure messaging platforms protect sensitive government communications.

e) Defending Against Cyber Threats: Firewalls, IDS, and antivirus software safeguard government networks and systems from cyber-attacks.

3.8.5 Examples of e-security systems

Below are some examples of e-security in e-governance include:

a) Estonia's e-Residency Program: Uses blockchain technology to secure digital identities and authenticate users accessing government services online.

b) Singapore's SingPass: Provides a single sign-on (SSO) system with two-factor authentication (2FA) for secure access to various government e-services.

c) India's Aadhaar System: Uses biometric authentication (fingerprint and iris scans) to verify identities securely for accessing government services and benefits.

d) Norway's Altinn Platform: Ensures secure online filing of taxes and submission of business-related documents through encrypted connections and authentication measures.

e) Australia's myGov Platform: Provides secure access to multiple government services with strong authentication and encryption to protect personal information and transactions.

These examples highlight how governments worldwide implement e-security measures to protect data, authenticate users securely, and ensure the integrity of digital interactions in e-governance.

3.9 Cyber Laws

Cyber laws, also known as cybersecurity laws or information technology laws, encompass legal measures and regulations that govern the use of computers, networks, and the internet. These laws are designed to protect individuals, organizations, and governments from cybercrimes, ensure data privacy, regulate electronic commerce, and establish guidelines for the secure use of digital technologies. Key components of cyber laws include.

a) Data Protection and Privacy: Laws that regulate the collection, storage, and use of personal and sensitive information to prevent unauthorized access and ensure individuals' privacy rights are protected (e.g., GDPR in Europe, CCPA in California).

b) Cybercrime Prevention: Legislation that criminalizes various forms of cybercrimes such as hacking, identity theft, phishing, malware distribution, and denial-of-service attacks, with penalties and enforcement mechanisms in place to prevent offenders.

c) Electronic Transactions and Commerce: Regulations that govern electronic contracts, digital signatures, online payments, and other aspects of electronic commerce to ensure legality, security, and consumer protection in digital transactions.

d) Intellectual Property Rights: Laws that protect intellectual property in the digital realm, including copyrights, trademarks, and patents, and address issues such as online privacy and digital rights management (DRM).

e) Cybersecurity Standards and Practices: Legal frameworks that mandate cybersecurity measures for organizations and businesses to protect their networks, systems, and data from cyber threats, often aligning with industry standards and best practices.

f) Government Surveillance and National Security: Laws that govern the collection, monitoring, and interception of electronic communications by government agencies for national security purposes, balancing security needs with civil liberties and privacy rights.

g) Cross-Border Data Transfers: Regulations that address the transfer of personal data across international borders, ensuring compliance with data protection laws and safeguarding data privacy rights across jurisdictions.

h) Incident Reporting and Response: Legal requirements for organizations to report data breaches and cyber incidents promptly, along with guidelines for incident response, remediation, and notification to affected parties.

Cyber laws vary significantly from country to country based on legal traditions, cultural norms, technological advancements, and geopolitical considerations. As digital technologies continue to evolve, cyber laws are continually updated to address emerging cyber threats and protect individuals and organizations in the digital age.

UNIT SUMMARY

The unit starts with discussing the architecture of e-Governance encompasses several layers: Infrastructure, Application, Data, User Interface, and Governance. Then, various models like G2C, G2B, G2G, G2E, C2G, and G2P facilitate interactions between government, citizens, businesses, employees, and partners were discussed. After that the Public-Private Partnerships (PPPs) which are integral, offering benefits through collaboration and adhering to key design principles were deliberated. The unit also contains innovation and change management which are crucial for evolving e-governance, with models like ADKAR guiding the process. Critical success factors include political will, ICT infrastructure, clear vision, transparency, legal frameworks, and capacity building. Challenges like corruption, resistance for change, digital divide, financial constraints, and privacy concerns are addressed. Finally, e-security and cyber laws play a pivotal role in safeguarding digital interactions, emphasizing the need for robust security systems and legal frameworks are deliberated.

EXERCISES

Q1 Which layer in the e-Governance architecture is primarily responsible for the storage and management of data?

a) Infrastructure Layer

b) Application Layer

c) Data Layer

d) User Interface Layer

Q2 The Governance Layer in the e-Governance architecture is responsible for:

a) Managing the infrastructure and network

b) Implementing policies and regulations

c) Providing applications for users

d) Handling user interfaces

Q3 Which model in e-Governance focuses on the interaction between government and citizens?

a) G2C b) G2B c) B2G d) G2E

Q4 The G2B model in e-Governance refers to

a) Government-to-Banking

b) Government-to-Business

c) Government-to-Beneficiaries

d) Government-to-Bureaucrats

Q5 What does the PPP in e-Governance stand for?

a) Public Private Partnership

b) Public Policy Program

c) Private Public Policy

d) Partnership for Public Programs

Q6 One of the key benefits of PPP in e-Governance is:

a) Reduced transparency

b) Increased operational risk

c) Enhanced resource efficiency

d) Diminished accountability

Q7 The ADKAR model in Change Management stands for:

a) Awareness, Desire, Knowledge, Ability, Reinforcement

b) Analysis, Design, Knowledge, Action, Review

c) Accountability, Development, Knowledge, Application, Response

d) Assessment, Development, Knowledge, Action, Reinforcement

Q8 Which of the following is NOT a critical success factor for e-Governance?

a) Clear Vision and Strategy

b) E-Skills

c) Lack of Infrastructure

d) Transparency and Accountability

Q9 In the context of e-Governance, 'Citizen Empowerment' refers to:

a) Providing government employees with better tools
b) Enabling citizens to access and participate in government processes
c) Reducing citizen participation in decision-making
d) Centralizing power within government institutions

Q10 Which of the following is a major issue in implementing e-Governance?

a) Increased digital literacy
b) High financial investments
c) Strong political will
d) Universal access to the internet

Q11 What is the role of e-security in e-Governance?

a) To increase the complexity of systems
b) To protect data and ensure secure communication
c) To reduce the need for data protection
d) To simplify governance processes

Q12 Which of the following is an example of a G2E (Government-to-Employee) interaction in e-Governance?

a) Tax filing by citizens
b) Pension management systems for government employees
c) Business registration processes
d) Online public grievance systems

Q13 The Digital Divide in the context of e-Governance refers to:

a) The gap between government services and business processes
b) The disparity in access to digital technologies among different population groups
c) The difference in software used by various government departments
d) The division between urban and rural internet services

Q14 Which of the following is a key reason for the failure of change initiatives in e-Governance?

a) Lack of top management support
b) Adequate training and capacity building
c) Clear communication strategies
d) Strong legal regulatory framework

Q15 What is the primary importance of Cyber Laws in e-Governance?

a) To regulate online shopping

b) To establish legal frameworks for online interactions and protect data privacy

c) To provide discounts for online services

d) To restrict internet access for citizens

Answers

Q.N.	1	2	3	4	5	6	7	8	9	10	11	12	13	14	15
Option	D	B	A	B	A	C	A	C	B	B	B	B	B	A	B

Short Answer Type Questions

1. What are the main components of the infrastructure layer in e-Governance architecture?
2. Explain the role of the application layer in e-Governance.
3. What is the significance of the data layer in an e-Governance system?
4. Describe the user interface layer in e-Governance architecture.
5. What is the governance layer, and how does it contribute to e-Governance?
6. Differentiate between G2C and G2B models in e-Governance.
7. What is the purpose of the G2G model in e-Governance?
8. How does the G2E model facilitate interaction between the government and employees?
9. Explain the rationale behind Public-Private Partnerships (PPP) in e-Governance.
10. List three key benefits of implementing PPPs in e-Governance projects.
11. What are the key design principles of PPP in the context of e-Governance?
12. Why is innovation important in the field of e-Governance?
13. Define change management in the context of e-Governance.
14. What is the ADKAR model, and how does it apply to change management in e-Governance?
15. What are the critical success factors for the effective implementation of e-Governance?

Long Answer Type Questions

1. Discuss the key components of the e-Governance architecture. How do these components interact to deliver effective governance?
2. Explain the infrastructure layer in e-Governance. What are its critical elements, and how do they support the overall system?

3. Analyze the role of the application layer in e-Governance. Provide examples of applications that operate within this layer.
4. What is the significance of the data layer in e-Governance? How does data management impact the efficiency of e-Governance services?
5. Describe the user interface layer in e-Governance. How does user-centric design enhance the effectiveness of e-Governance platforms?
6. Examine the governance layer in the context of e-Governance architecture. How does it ensure compliance and regulatory oversight?
7. Compare and contrast the G2C, G2B, and G2G models in e-Governance. What are the unique challenges and benefits associated with each model?
8. How does the G2E model facilitate effective communication and services between the government and its employees? Provide examples of G2E applications.
9. Evaluate the role of Public-Private Partnerships (PPP) in e-Governance. What are the main drivers for implementing PPPs in this domain?
10. Discuss the benefits of Public-Private Partnerships (PPP) in e-Governance projects. How do these partnerships contribute to the success of e-Governance initiatives?
11. What are the key design principles of PPP in e-Governance? How can these principles be applied to ensure sustainable and effective partnerships?
12. Analyze the need for innovation in e-Governance. What are the potential areas where innovation can significantly impact governance?
13. Explain the concept of change management in e-Governance. How does the ADKAR model facilitate effective change management in e-Governance projects?
14. Identify and discuss the critical success factors for implementing e-Governance initiatives. How do these factors influence the outcomes of e-Governance projects?
15. Examine the major challenges faced in e-Governance, including corruption and resistance to change. What strategies can be employed to overcome these challenges?

Dynamic QR code for further readings

REFERENCES AND SUGGESTED READINGS

1. "E-Governance: Concepts and Case Studies" by C.S.R. Prabhu - This book provides a detailed examination of the architecture of e-Governance systems, covering infrastructure, application, data, and governance layers. (Prentice Hall India Learning, 2013)

2. "E-Government: From Vision to Implementation" by Subhash Bhatnagar - This book explores various e-Governance models, including G2C, G2B, G2G, and G2E, with Indian case studies. (SAGE Publications, 2004)

3. "Public-Private Partnership in Infrastructure: Managing the Challenges" by P.K. Agarwal and Sunil Sharma - Explores the nuances of PPP in various sectors, including e-Governance. (SAGE Publications, 2018)

4. "Innovation and Best Practices in Public Sector Reforms: Ideas, Challenges, and Perspectives" edited by P.K. Mohanty - Discusses various innovative practices in public administration, including e-Governance. (SAGE Publications, 2018)

5. "Change Management in the Public Sector: Indian Perspectives" by Rajesh Kumar Shukla - Focuses on the application of change management theories and practices in the Indian public sector, with a chapter on e-Governance. (Oxford University Press, 2020)

6. "Digital Transformation and Public Service Delivery: A Study of Critical Success Factors in India" by Piyush Gupta - Examines key success factors such as political will, leadership, and ICT infrastructure in the success of e-Governance projects. (Routledge India, 2021)

7. "Corruption and Governance in India: Challenges and Prospects" by N. Vittal - Provides an in-depth analysis of corruption in India and its impact on e-Governance. (Oxford University Press, 2012)

8. "Cyber Laws and IT Protection" by Harish Chander - This book covers the cyber laws relevant to e-Governance in India and the importance of e-security. (PHI Learning, 2012)

4 Focus on Indian Initiatives

UNIT SPECIFIES

Through this unit we discuss the following aspects:

- *Focusing on Indian initiatives and their impact on citizens*
- *Sharing of case studies to highlight best practices in managing e-Governance projects in Indian context*
- *Visits to local e-governance sites (CSC, eSeva, Post Office, Passport Seva Kendra, etc) as part of Tutorials.*

RATIONALE

This unit include the architecture and models of e-Governance, containing Public Private Partnership (PPP), are crucial for designing efficient and scalable government services that leverage both public and private sector strengths. Innovation and change management in e-Governance are essential to adapt to technological advancements and evolving citizen needs, ensuring continuous improvement and relevance. Identifying critical success factors helps in focusing efforts on the most impactful areas. Addressing major issues such as corruption, resistance to change, e-Security, and compliance with cyber laws is vital for the integrity, acceptance, and security of e-Governance initiatives. These elements collectively foster a robust, secure, and citizen-centric governance framework.

PRE-REQUESITE

- *Contents of unit-1, 2 and unit-3*

UNIT OUTCOMES

After completion of this unit the learner will be able to:

U4-O1: Understand the various Indian initiatives and their impact on Indian citizen

U4-O2: Understand the application of best practices in e-governance project management

U4-O3: Use hands-on experience with e-governance platforms

U4-O4: Analyze the services provided by various Indian Initiatives

Unit-4 Outcomes	Expected Mapping with Programme Outcomes (1- Weak Correlation; 2- Medium correlation; 3- Strong Correlation)					
	CO-1	CO-2	CO-3	CO-4	CO-5	CO-6
U4-O1	1	0	1	1	3	0
U4-O2	1	1	1	1	1	1
U4-O3	1	0	1	1	1	1
U4-O4	1	0	1	2	2	1

4.1 Focusing on Indian initiatives and their impact on citizens

India has undertaken several initiatives in recent years to foster development and improve the quality of life for its citizens. These initiatives span across various sectors including health, education, infrastructure, technology, and social welfare. The impact of these efforts is substantial, affecting millions of lives and contributing to the country's progress on multiple fronts. Over the years, strategic programs have been launched to tackle these issues, resulting in significant positive outcomes for citizens across the country.

One of the earliest and most transformative initiatives in independent India was the Green Revolution, launched in the 1960s. Faced with severe food shortages and an agrarian crisis, the government introduced high-yielding varieties of seeds, improved irrigation techniques, and modern agricultural practices. This revolution not only made India self-sufficient in food production but also turned it into a significant agricultural exporter. Millions of farmers benefited from increased crop yields and incomes, which in turn, contributed to rural development and poverty reduction.

Fast forward to recent decades, the focus has shifted towards inclusive growth and digital empowerment. The computerization of government services, such as land records, income certificates, building licenses, pensions, road transport, property registration, railway services, and income tax payments, has also improved the efficiency with which the government operates and made life easier, more efficient, and transparent for the people.

The establishment of the National Informatics Centre (NIC) in 1977 marked a significant milestone towards the development of e-Government in India and marked the beginning of the e-governance boom. Numerous efforts were then introduced to assist in the expansion of e-governance in India. The introduction of NICNET in 1987 served as one of the motivations behind e-Government. Figure 4.1 shows some Indian initiatives that are taken by Indian government.

The Indian initiative as shown in figure 4.1 are broadly classified in nine categories which are given below and discussed one-by-one subsequently.

1. Nation e-governance Plan
2. Government to Citizen (G2C) Initiatives
3. Government to Business (G2B) Initiatives

4. Government to Government (G2G) Initiatives
5. Central government initiatives as mission mode projects (MMP)
6. State Mission Mode projects
7. Integrated Mission Mode Projects
8. Recent Initiatives
9. Government initiatives for m-governance

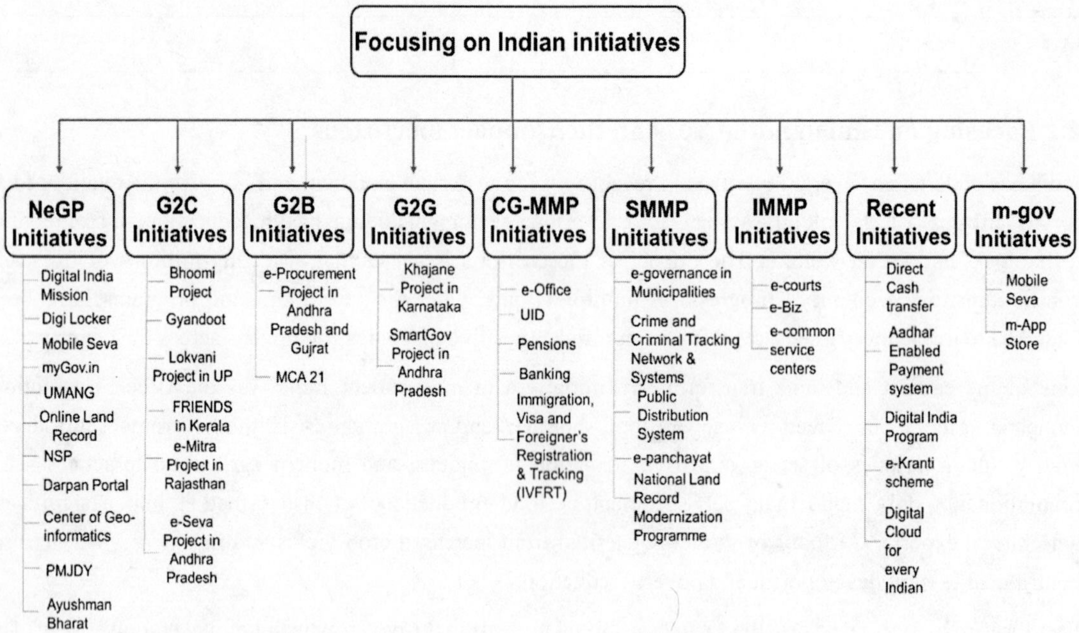

Figure 4.1 Some of Indian initiatives in diverse domain

4.1.1 National e-governance Plan (NeGP)

The National e-Governance Plan (NeGP) is an initiative by the Government of India aimed at making all government services accessible to the common man in his locality, ensuring efficiency, transparency, and reliability at affordable costs to realize the basic needs of the common man. Launched in 2006, the NeGP encompasses a number of Mission Mode Projects (MMPs) and core infrastructure components aimed at transforming the delivery of government services using Information and Communication Technology (ICT). Below are few objectives of NeGP:

a) Simplify Service Delivery: To make government services accessible and efficient by leveraging technology.

b) Enhance Transparency: To ensure transparency in government functions and services.

c) Improve Accountability: To improve accountability in the delivery of government services.

d) Increase Reach and Coverage: To make services available to all citizens, especially in rural and remote areas.

e) Reduce Costs: To lower the costs of delivering government services.

Below are some NeGP initiatives as follows.

a) Digital India Mission:

The Digital India Mission, launched by the Government of India on July 1, 2015, aims to transform India into a digitally empowered society and knowledge economy. It focuses on providing high-speed internet access, ensuring electronic delivery of government services, and enhancing digital literacy. The mission encompasses various pillars such as broadband highways, universal mobile connectivity, public internet access, e-governance, electronic delivery of services (e-Kranti), information for all, electronics manufacturing, IT for jobs, and early harvest programmes.

Key initiatives include Aadhaar for unique identification, BharatNet for rural internet connectivity, DigiLocker for secure document storage, UMANG for unified mobile governance, and BHIM for digital payments. The mission has significantly increased internet penetration, promoted digital transactions, and improved access to government services, while also creating jobs in the IT and electronics sectors. Despite its achievements, challenges such as bridging the digital divide, enhancing cybersecurity, and improving digital infrastructure remain critical for the mission's future success.

b) DigiLocker:

Digi Locker, an initiative under the Digital India Mission, was launched by the Government of India to provide a secure, cloud-based platform for storing, sharing, and verifying documents and certificates. The platform allows citizens to access their important documents such as driving licenses, vehicle registration certificates, academic records, and other government-issued documents online. By linking DigiLocker accounts to Aadhaar, users can authenticate and share their documents with various agencies electronically, eliminating the need for physical copies and reducing administrative overhead. This initiative enhances convenience, reduces the risk of document loss, and promotes paperless governance, making services more efficient and accessible. DigiLocker also ensures data security and privacy, contributing to a more transparent and digitally empowered society.

c) Mobile Seva

The Mobile Seva initiative, launched by the Government of India, aims to provide government services to citizens through mobile devices, enhancing accessibility and convenience. This initiative leverages the widespread use of mobile phones to deliver various services, information, and applications directly to users' devices. Mobile Seva includes services such as SMS notifications, mobile applications, and a unified platform for m-Governance (m-Governance Service Delivery Gateway). It facilitates real-time access to essential services like healthcare, education, agriculture, and public grievance redressal, making government interactions more efficient and user-friendly. By utilizing mobile technology, Mobile Seva bridges the digital divide, particularly benefiting citizens in rural and remote areas, and promotes a more inclusive approach to governance.

d) myGov.in

MyGov.in, launched by the Government of India, is a citizen engagement platform designed to foster participatory governance by involving citizens in decision-making processes. This digital initiative encourages individuals to contribute ideas, suggestions, and feedback on various government policies and programs. Through discussions, polls, and tasks, MyGov.in enables direct interaction between the government and the public, promoting transparency and accountability. The platform covers diverse areas such as healthcare, education, environment, and infrastructure, allowing citizens to share their insights and collaborate on solutions. MyGov.in empowers citizens to play an active role in shaping policies and initiatives, thereby enhancing the democratic process and fostering a sense of ownership and responsibility towards national development.

e) UMANG

The UMANG (Unified Mobile Application for New-age Governance) initiative, launched by the Government of India, is a comprehensive mobile app designed to provide citizens with access to a wide range of government services and information from a single platform. Integrating over 1,200 services from various central, state, and local government departments and agencies, UMANG offers services across sectors such as healthcare, education, agriculture, transport, and utilities. The app aims to simplify the process of accessing government services, making it more user-friendly and efficient. By bringing multiple services under one umbrella, UMANG enhances convenience, promotes digital governance, and bridges the gap between citizens and the government, particularly benefiting those in rural and remote areas with easy access to essential services.

f) Computerization of Land Records

The Computerization of Land Records initiative by the Government of India aims to digitize and modernize the management of land records, ensuring greater transparency, efficiency, and accessibility. This initiative involves the creation of a comprehensive database of land records, including ownership details, plot boundaries, and transaction history, which can be accessed online by citizens and government officials. By eliminating manual record-keeping, it reduces the scope for errors, fraud, and disputes, while also expediting the process of land registration and transfer. This digital transformation supports the goals of e-governance, providing citizens with secure, reliable, and easily accessible land information, thereby promoting better land management and planning.

g) National Scholarships Portal (NSP).

The National Scholarships Portal (NSP) is an initiative by the Government of India designed to streamline the scholarship application process for students across the country. It serves as a single, unified platform for various scholarships offered by central and state governments, as well as other government agencies. NSP aims to simplify the application process, ensuring transparency and efficiency in the disbursement of scholarship funds. Students can register, apply, and track their applications online, reducing paperwork and administrative delays. By consolidating multiple scholarships under one portal, NSP helps in ensuring that financial assistance reaches deserving students, promoting higher education and reducing dropout rates. This initiative significantly contributes to making education more accessible and equitable for students from diverse socio-economic backgrounds.

h) Darpan Portal

The Darpan Portal, an initiative by the Government of India, is designed to enhance the transparency and accountability of Non-Governmental Organizations (NGOs) and Voluntary Organizations (VOs) operating in the country. This digital platform allows NGOs and VOs to register and update their information, providing a comprehensive database accessible to government departments, donors, and the general public. Through the Darpan Portal, stakeholders can easily verify the credentials, track the performance, and assess the impact of various NGOs and VOs, ensuring that resources and support are directed towards credible and effective organizations. By facilitating better monitoring and collaboration, the Darpan Portal promotes a more transparent and efficient ecosystem for the voluntary sector in India, thereby enhancing its contribution to social development and community welfare.

i) National Center of Geo-informatics (NCoG)

The National Center of Geo-informatics (NCoG) is an initiative by the Government of India aimed at harnessing the potential of geospatial technology for national development and governance. Established under the Ministry of Electronics and Information Technology (MeitY), NCoG serves as a centralized platform for integrating and analyzing geospatial data from various government departments and agencies. The center facilitates the creation of spatial databases, maps, and applications that enable informed decision-making across sectors such as agriculture, urban planning, disaster management, infrastructure development, and environmental conservation.

NCoG plays a crucial role in coordinating and standardizing geospatial data across the country, ensuring interoperability and accessibility to stakeholders at different levels of governance. By leveraging advanced technologies like Geographic Information System (GIS) and Remote Sensing, NCoG supports evidence-based policy formulation, resource management, and monitoring of developmental projects. The initiative aims to enhance efficiency, transparency, and sustainability in governance by harnessing the power of geoinformatics to address complex socio-economic challenges and promote inclusive growth.

j) Pradhan Mantri Jan Dhan Yojana (PMJDY)

Pradhan Mantri Jan Dhan Yojana (PMJDY) is a national financial inclusion initiative launched by the Government of India in August 2014. The scheme aims to provide universal access to banking facilities for all households in the country, particularly focusing on the unbanked and underbanked populations. Under PMJDY, individuals can open a bank account with minimal documentation and no minimum balance requirement. The accounts come with a RuPay debit card, providing access to banking services such as deposits, withdrawals, remittances, and access to credit and insurance facilities.

PMJDY also promotes financial literacy and awareness among beneficiaries through various programs and initiatives. The scheme encourages direct benefit transfers (DBT) for subsidies and welfare payments, reducing leakages and ensuring that benefits reach the intended beneficiaries efficiently. It aims to bring marginalized sections of society into the formal banking system, thereby promoting financial empowerment, reducing poverty, and fostering economic growth. As of now, PMJDY has made significant strides in expanding financial access across the country, with millions of accounts opened and transactions facilitated through its robust banking infrastructure.

k) Ayushman Bharat Initiative

Ayushman Bharat, launched by the Government of India in September 2018, is one of the largest health insurance schemes globally aimed at providing affordable healthcare to millions of vulnerable and economically disadvantaged individuals in India. It comprises two main components:

i. *Pradhan Mantri Jan Arogya Yojana (PM-JAY):* Also known as Ayushman Bharat-PMJAY, this component provides health insurance coverage of up to ₹5 lakh per family per year for secondary and tertiary care hospitalization. It covers over 10 crore poor and vulnerable families (approximately 50 crore beneficiaries) based on the Socio-Economic Caste Census (SECC) data.

ii. *Health and Wellness Centres (HWCs):* Under this component, the government aims to transform and strengthen the primary healthcare infrastructure by converting existing sub-health centres and primary health centres into Health and Wellness Centres. These centres provide comprehensive primary healthcare services, including preventive, promotive, and curative care.

Ayushman Bharat seeks to address the healthcare needs of the population by focusing on preventive healthcare, providing financial protection against catastrophic health expenditures, and improving access to quality healthcare services. It aims to reduce out-of-pocket health expenditures, which often push families into poverty, and promote universal health coverage across the country.

Since its launch, Ayushman Bharat has significantly expanded access to healthcare services, particularly in underserved and rural areas. It has facilitated millions of hospital admissions and surgeries, providing critical financial protection to vulnerable families. The initiative continues to evolve, with ongoing efforts to enhance the quality and reach of healthcare services and improve health outcomes for all citizens of India.

4.1.2 Government to Citizen (G2C) Initiatives

Government to Citizen (G2C) initiatives are efforts made by government agencies to provide public services directly to citizens through digital means. These initiatives aim to enhance the efficiency, accessibility, and transparency of government services, thereby improving the overall experience for citizens. Examples of G2C initiatives include Gyandoot, Lokvani Project in Uttar Pradesh, Project FRIENDS in Kerala, e-Mitra Project in Rajasthan, e-Seva (Andhra Pradesh) schemes which have been discussed in subsequent sections. By leveraging technology, G2C initiatives help reduce bureaucratic hurdles, minimize the need for physical visits to government offices, and ensure timely delivery of services. These initiatives are particularly beneficial in bridging the digital divide, ensuring that all segments of society, including those in remote and underserved areas, have access to essential government services. The Government to Citizen (G2C) initiatives are discussed below one by one.

a) Bhoomi Project

The Bhoomi Project is a revolutionary initiative by the Government of India aimed at digitizing land records to enhance transparency, efficiency, and accessibility in land management. Launched in Karnataka, this project involves the computerized management of land records, providing a transparent, efficient, and accessible system for landowners and stakeholders. The Bhoomi Project allows citizens to easily access their land records online, reducing the need for middlemen and minimizing corruption. It provides services such as mutation requests, issuance of Record of Rights, Tenancy and Crops (RTC), and enables quick and accurate updating of land records. By streamlining the process and ensuring that land records are updated in real-time, the Bhoomi Project significantly reduces disputes related to land ownership and provides a reliable database for planning and development activities. This initiative serves as a model for other states in India, showcasing the potential of technology in transforming public service delivery.

b) Gyandoot

The Gyandoot initiative, launched by the Government of India, is an innovative project aimed at providing rural citizens with access to government services and information through Information and Communication Technology (ICT). Initiated in the Dhar district of Madhya Pradesh, Gyandoot established a network of internet kiosks in rural areas, operated by local entrepreneurs, to deliver a wide range of services. These kiosks offer access to vital information such as market prices for agricultural products, healthcare advice, educational resources, and government schemes. Additionally, citizens can file grievances, access land records, and apply for various certificates through the kiosks. The Gyandoot initiative not only bridges the digital divide by bringing technology to remote areas but also empowers rural communities by enhancing their access to crucial information and services, thereby promoting transparency, efficiency, and local development.

c) Lokvani Project in Uttar Pradesh

The Lokvani Project is an exemplary e-governance initiative by the Government of Uttar Pradesh, aimed at providing transparent, efficient, and accessible government services to rural citizens. Launched in the Sitapur district, Lokvani centers are established as internet kiosks that serve as one-stop shops for a wide range of public services. These centers enable citizens to access information related to government schemes, lodge complaints, track the status of their applications, and obtain essential certificates such as birth and death certificates. Additionally, Lokvani centers provide services like land record management and public grievance redressal. By leveraging technology, the Lokvani Project significantly reduces the need for physical visits to government offices, controls corruption, and enhances service delivery. This initiative empowers rural communities by ensuring that they have easy and timely access to vital government services, thereby promoting transparency and accountability in governance.

d) Project FRIENDS in Kerala

The FRIENDS (Fast, Reliable, Instant, Efficient Network for Disbursement of Services) Project is an innovative e-governance initiative by the Government of Kerala, designed to provide citizens with a hassle-free and efficient way to access government services. Launched across various districts in Kerala, the FRIENDS centers act as single-window service counters where citizens can pay utility bills, property taxes, and license fees, as well as access various government-related services. These centers are equipped with modern technology to ensure quick and accurate processing of transactions, significantly reducing wait times and the need for multiple visits to different government offices. The FRIENDS Project aims to enhance the overall experience of public service delivery by making it more user-friendly, transparent, and efficient. By consolidating various services under one roof, this initiative not only saves time and effort for citizens but also promotes accountability and reduces the scope for corruption, thereby setting a benchmark for other states to follow.

e) e-Mitra Project in Rajasthan

The e-Mitra Project is a flagship e-governance initiative by the Government of Rajasthan, aimed at providing seamless access to a wide array of government services for citizens through digital means. Established with the vision of enhancing the convenience and efficiency of public service delivery, e-Mitra centers are set up across urban and rural areas of Rajasthan. These centers serve as single-window platforms where citizens can avail themselves of various services such as utility bill payments, issuance of certificates, application submissions for government schemes, and access to land records. The e-Mitra Project leverages technology to minimize bureaucratic red tape, reduce the need for physical visits to government offices, and promote transparency and accountability in governance. By bringing essential services closer to the citizens, especially those in remote and underserved areas, the e-Mitra Project significantly improves the reach and quality of public service delivery, fostering inclusive development and digital empowerment across the state.

f) e-Seva (Andhra Pradesh)

The e-Seva initiative is a pioneering e-governance project launched by the Government of Andhra Pradesh to provide citizens with easy and efficient access to a wide range of public services. e-Seva centers are established across the state, offering a single-window platform where citizens can conduct transactions such as paying utility bills, property taxes, and obtaining various documents including birth, death, and income certificates. Additionally, these centers facilitate the submission of applications for government schemes, issuance of licenses, and access to land records. The e-Seva initiative leverages advanced technology to ensure quick and accurate service delivery, significantly reducing the need for physical visits to multiple government offices and minimizing bureaucratic delays. By promoting transparency, reducing corruption, and enhancing the convenience of accessing government services, e-Seva has become a model for effective public service delivery, contributing to the overall digital empowerment and development of Andhra Pradesh.

4.1.3 Government to Business (G2B) Initiatives

Government to Business (G2B) initiatives are designed to facilitate and streamline interactions between government agencies and businesses through the use of digital technologies. These initiatives aim to create a more efficient, transparent, and supportive environment for businesses to operate in. Examples of G2B initiatives include online business registration and licensing portals, e-procurement systems, electronic tax filing, and compliance reporting platforms. By digitizing these processes, governments can reduce administrative burdens, minimize delays, and lower the costs associated with compliance and regulatory requirements for businesses. Additionally, G2B initiatives often provide businesses with access to valuable data and resources, such as market research, investment opportunities, and government tenders. This fosters a more helpful business environment, encourages entrepreneurship, and stimulates economic growth. Ultimately, G2B initiatives play a crucial role in enhancing the ease of doing business, fostering innovation, and improving the overall competitiveness of the economy. The main G2B initiatives are e-Procurement Project in Andhra Pradesh and Gujarat and MCA21 which are discussed below.

a) e-Procurement Project in Andhra Pradesh and Gujarat

The e-Procurement Project in Andhra Pradesh and Gujarat represents a transformative e-governance initiative aimed at modernizing and enhancing the efficiency of public procurement processes through digital platforms. In Andhra Pradesh, the e-Procurement platform was launched to digitize the entire procurement lifecycle, from tender creation to contract management and payment processing. This initiative aims to streamline processes, increase transparency, and ensure accountability in government procurement.

Similarly, Gujarat's e-Procurement initiative focuses on creating a transparent and competitive bidding environment for government contracts. It enables vendors to register online, submit bids electronically, and track the status of their bids in real-time. By automating procurement processes, Gujarat aims to reduce administrative costs, minimize delays, and improve the overall quality of goods and services procured by government agencies.

Both states have implemented robust e-Procurement systems that not only enhance efficiency but also foster fair competition among vendors, leading to better value for public money. These initiatives demonstrate the commitment of Andhra Pradesh and Gujarat to leveraging technology for good governance, promoting economic growth, and ensuring effective utilization of public funds.

b) MCA21

MCA21 is a significant initiative undertaken by the Ministry of Corporate Affairs (MCA) in India. It stands for "Mission Mode Project on Corporate Governance, Transparency and Investor Services," and it represents a comprehensive e-governance initiative aimed at modernizing the processes related to company incorporation, compliance, and regulation in India.

Launched in 2006, MCA21 has transformed the way corporate affairs are managed in India by introducing online services for company registration, filing of annual returns, financial statements, and other statutory documents. The project aims to enhance transparency, improve regulatory compliance, and provide efficient services to businesses and stakeholders. It also includes initiatives like the e-governance portal for corporate governance and the Ministry's efforts to implement electronic filing, payment of stamp duty, and other legal formalities.

MCA21 has significantly reduced the time taken for various company-related processes, minimized paperwork, and improved ease of doing business in India. By leveraging technology and digital platforms, MCA21 has played a crucial role in promoting corporate governance, transparency, and investor confidence in the Indian market.

4.1.4 Government to Government (G2G) Initiatives

Government to Government (G2G) initiatives are collaborative efforts between different government agencies, Government to Government (G2G) initiatives refer to collective endeavor between different government entities aimed at improving efficiency, effectiveness, and service delivery within the public sector. These initiatives typically involve the integration of digital technologies to streamline inter-agency communication, data sharing, and operational coordination. By facilitating seamless information exchange and decision-making processes, G2G initiatives help reduce redundancy, minimize bureaucratic hurdles, and enhance overall governance.

One prominent example of a G2G initiative is the establishment of integrated e-governance platforms that enable various government departments and agencies to interact and share data in real-time. Such platforms not only improve administrative efficiency but also enhance the transparency and accountability of government operations. For instance, initiatives like India's National e-Governance Plan (NeGP) have promoted the adoption of standardized ICT infrastructure across different government levels, facilitating smoother inter-departmental collaboration and service delivery.

Moreover, G2G initiatives often include joint projects and partnerships between federal, state, and local governments to address common challenges and deliver public services more effectively. These collaborations can range from shared infrastructure projects to collaborative policy development efforts, aiming to optimize resource allocation and enhance public service outcomes. Internationally, G2G initiatives also foster cooperation between governments on global issues such as climate change, trade facilitation, and security, promoting mutual understanding and shared solutions. The two major G2G initiative Khajane Project in Karnataka and SmartGov in Andhra Pradesh are discussed below.

a) Khajane Project in Karnataka

The Khajane Project, implemented by the Government of Karnataka, is a transformative e-governance initiative aimed at modernizing and centralizing the state's treasury operations. Launched to streamline financial transactions and enhance transparency in public finance management, the project consolidates all treasury-related activities onto a unified digital platform. This platform enables real-time monitoring and management of government funds, facilitating efficient disbursement and reconciliation processes across various departments and agencies.

One of the key objectives of the Khajane Project is to eliminate manual processes and reduce paperwork associated with financial transactions. By digitizing treasury operations, the project minimizes the risk of errors, delays, and financial discrepancies, thereby improving the overall fiscal discipline of the state government. It also enhances accountability by providing stakeholders with instant access to financial data and transaction details, ensuring greater transparency in the utilization of public funds.

Furthermore, the Khajane Project supports the government's efforts towards digital transformation and good governance practices. It enables seamless integration with other e-governance initiatives in Karnataka, such as online service delivery portals and electronic payment systems, thereby enhancing the efficiency and effectiveness of public service delivery. Overall, the Khajane Project stands as a testament to Karnataka's commitment to leveraging technology for financial management reforms, ensuring better fiscal control, and promoting transparency in government operations.

b) SmartGov (Andhra Pradesh)

The launch of SmartGov, the online secretariat project by the Andhra Pradesh government, scheduled for November 1, the state formation day, indicates a significant step towards digital transformation and efficiency in governance. This initiative aims to streamline administrative processes, enhance transparency, and improve service delivery within the state government.

SmartGov is expected to centralize and digitize various administrative functions of the secretariat, facilitating smoother workflows and faster decision-making processes. By leveraging technology, the project aims to reduce bureaucratic hurdles, enhance accountability, and optimize resource utilization across departments.

The launch of SmartGov underscores the Andhra Pradesh government's commitment to leveraging digital solutions to modernize governance and improve citizen services. It aligns with broader national initiatives such as Digital India, emphasizing the role of technology in promoting inclusive growth and efficient public administration.

In essence, G2G initiatives play a pivotal role in modernizing governance structures, promoting innovation, and improving the overall responsiveness of governments to citizen needs. By leveraging digital advancements and fostering collaborative relationships, these initiatives contribute to building more efficient, transparent, and resilient public sector frameworks that benefit societies at large.

4.1.5 Central government initiatives as mission mode projects (MMP)

The Indian central government has launched several Mission Mode Projects (MMPs) under the National e-Governance Plan (NeGP) to enhance service delivery through technology. Key initiatives include e-office, Immigration, Visa and Foreigner's Registration & Tracking (IVFRT), UID and Pensions. These projects collectively aim to make government operations more efficient, transparent, and responsive to citizen needs through technology adoption. These MMPs initiatives are discussed in details in below section.

a) e-office

The Government of India has implemented the e-Office initiative to modernize the functioning of government offices and improve efficiency, transparency, and accountability. The e-Office initiative is a part of the broader Digital India program and aims to transform traditional paper-based office procedures into a more efficient, digital workflow. Key components of e-Office include e-File, which enables electronic movement and tracking of files, e-Leave for online leave management, e-Tour for managing official tours and travels, and Knowledge Management System (KMS) for sharing and managing knowledge resources. The initiative also includes the implementation of e-Sign for secure digital signatures and the use of a Centralized Personnel Information System (CPIS) for managing employee records. By digitizing these processes, the e-Office initiative reduces the reliance on physical files, speeds up decision-making, and enhances the overall productivity of government offices, making them more citizen-centric and service-oriented.

b) Immigration, Visa and Foreigner's Registration & Tracking (IVFRT)

The Immigration, Visa and Foreigner's Registration & Tracking (IVFRT) initiative by the Government of India aims to enhance the security and efficiency of immigration and visa services. Implemented under the Ministry of Home Affairs, IVFRT integrates multiple functions such as visa issuance, immigration control, and foreigner registration into a unified system. This initiative leverages advanced technology to streamline and automate processes, ensuring faster and more accurate processing of visa applications and registration. It includes features like online visa applications, electronic travel authorization, real-time tracking of visa status, and automated alerts for visa expiry. Additionally, IVFRT facilitates seamless data sharing between immigration authorities and other stakeholders, enhancing national security and improving the overall experience for foreign visitors. This initiative not only strengthens the management of foreign nationals entering and staying in India but also contributes to the government's broader goals of fostering global connectivity and tourism.

c) UID

The Aadhaar Unique Identification (UID) initiative by the Government of India aims to provide a unique identification number to every resident of the country. Managed by the Unique Identification Authority of India (UIDAI), Aadhaar assigns a 12-digit unique number based on biometric (fingerprints and iris scan) and demographic data. This initiative streamlines the delivery of various government services and subsidies, ensuring accurate identification and eliminating duplicate and fake identities. Aadhaar serves as a proof of identity and address, simplifying access to government schemes, opening bank accounts, and verifying identity for mobile connections and other services. As a cornerstone of India's Digital India program, the Aadhaar UID initiative drives digital inclusion and promotes transparency, efficiency, and accountability in public service delivery, significantly impacting citizens' lives by making processes more straightforward and accessible.

d) Pensions

Government of India has implemented several pension initiatives to ensure financial security for various segments of society, particularly the elderly, disabled, and economically disadvantaged. One prominent initiative is the National Pension System (NPS), a voluntary, defined contribution retirement savings scheme that allows individuals to save systematically during their working years, providing them with a steady income post-retirement. The Atal Pension Yojana (APY) is another significant scheme targeting the unorganized sector, offering guaranteed minimum monthly pensions to subscribers upon reaching 60 years of age. Additionally, the Pradhan Mantri Vaya Vandana Yojana (PMVVY) is a pension scheme specifically designed for senior citizens, providing a guaranteed return on investments for a fixed term. Furthermore, the Indira Gandhi National Old Age Pension Scheme (IGNOAPS) provides monthly pensions to elderly individuals living below the poverty line. These initiatives collectively aim to promote a culture of savings and financial planning, ensuring a stable and dignified post-retirement life for all citizens while reducing dependency on traditional social security measures. Through these programs, the government seeks to enhance the social safety net and promote inclusive economic growth.

e) Banking

The Government of India has undertaken several banking initiatives aimed at promoting financial inclusion, enhancing digital transactions, and improving access to banking services across the country. One of the notable initiatives is the *Pradhan Mantri Jan Dhan Yojana (PMJDY)*, launched to ensure access to financial services such as savings accounts, remittances, credit, insurance, and pension in an affordable manner. PMJDY aims to provide banking facilities to the unbanked population, particularly in rural and remote areas.

Additionally, the Digital India program has been pivotal in transforming the banking sector by promoting digital payments, mobile banking, and electronic fund transfers. It includes initiatives like the Unified Payments Interface (UPI), which facilitates instant and seamless transfer of funds between bank accounts using mobile phones.

Moreover, initiatives such as the *Direct Benefit Transfer (DBT)* scheme enable the direct transfer of subsidies and welfare benefits into beneficiaries' bank accounts, reducing leakages and ensuring efficient delivery of government benefits.

Furthermore, the *Financial Inclusion Fund (FIF)* and the *Financial Literacy and Credit Counseling Centers (FLCCs)* have been established to promote financial literacy and awareness among marginalized and underbanked communities, empowering them to make informed financial decisions.

These initiatives collectively aim to strengthen the banking infrastructure, expand access to financial services, and promote inclusive economic growth across India.

4.1.6 State Mission Mode Projects

State Mission Mode Projects (MMPs) are initiatives by the Government of India aimed at transforming governance and service delivery at the state level through the use of information technology. These projects are tailored to address specific regional challenges and improve the efficiency, transparency, and accessibility of public services. Each state may prioritize different sectors based on local needs, but common areas include e-governance, education, healthcare, agriculture, and infrastructure development.

For instance, states may implement e-governance projects similar to the national e-District initiative, which digitizes services like certificates, licenses, and utility payments to streamline citizen interactions with government offices. In education, MMPs could focus on enhancing digital literacy, improving school management systems, and providing e-learning resources. Healthcare MMPs aim to modernize hospitals, implement electronic health records, and enhance patient care through technology integration.

Agricultural MMPs may include initiatives to provide farmers with real-time market information, weather forecasts, and digital platforms for accessing agricultural subsidies and loans. Infrastructure MMPs focus on digitizing land records, improving transportation networks, and promoting smart city development. A few of MMP initiative by state government such as e-Governance in Municipalities, Crime and Criminal Tracking Network & Systems, Public Distribution System, e-panchayat, e-District and National Land Records Modernization Programme (NLRMP) have been discussed in below section.

a) e-Governance in Municipalities

The Government of India has initiated several e-Governance projects aimed at modernizing municipal administration and enhancing service delivery in urban areas. These initiatives focus on leveraging information technology to improve transparency, efficiency, and citizen engagement within municipalities. Key projects include the *Smart Cities Mission*, which aims to develop 100 cities across the country into smart cities by integrating technology for sustainable urban development. These cities implement various e-Governance solutions such as smart metering, intelligent traffic management, and digital governance platforms to improve urban infrastructure and quality of life.

Additionally, the *AMRUT (Atal Mission for Rejuvenation and Urban Transformation)* initiative focuses on providing basic urban services like water supply, sewerage, and urban transport in cities and towns. AMRUT emphasizes the adoption of e-Governance for better project management, monitoring, and citizen feedback mechanisms.

Furthermore, the *Swachh Bharat Mission (Urban)* incorporates e-Governance tools for monitoring and ensuring cleanliness in urban areas, including the use of mobile apps for citizen reporting and monitoring of sanitation services.

These initiatives are supported by digital platforms that enable online payment of taxes, issuance of birth and death certificates, property registration, and grievance redressal systems. By promoting e-Governance in municipalities, the government aims to improve administrative efficiency, accountability, and citizen satisfaction while fostering sustainable urban development across India.

b) Crime and Criminal Tracking Network & Systems

The Crime and Criminal Tracking Network & Systems (CCTNS) initiative by the Government of India is a comprehensive e-Governance project aimed at modernizing and integrating the country's law enforcement system. Launched to enhance the efficiency and effectiveness of policing, CCTNS facilitates real-time sharing of crime and criminal information among all police stations and higher law enforcement agencies across the nation. This integration helps in improving crime investigation, crime prevention, and law enforcement response times.

Under CCTNS, police stations are equipped with computerized systems to register FIRs (first information reports), maintain records of criminals and suspects, and manage investigations digitally. The system also enables seamless exchange of information between states and central agencies, enhancing coordination in tackling crime and ensuring swift action against criminals.

Moreover, CCTNS includes components for citizen-centric services such as online reporting of crimes, status tracking of complaints, and access to police services through digital platforms. This initiative plays a crucial role in enhancing transparency, accountability, and public trust in law enforcement agencies by providing citizens with easier access to police services and improving the overall effectiveness of crime management in India.

c) Public Distribution System

The Public Distribution System (PDS) initiatives by the Government of India aim to ensure food security for the nation's economically vulnerable populations. PDS is a foundation of India's social welfare programs, providing subsidized food grains, primarily rice, wheat, and coarse grains, to eligible beneficiaries through a network of fair price shops (FPS) across the country. The government undertakes several initiatives to streamline and improve the efficiency of PDS, including the adoption of technology-driven solutions.

One such initiative is the *End-to-End Computerization* of PDS Operations, which involves digitizing the supply chain from procurement to distribution. This includes online allocation of food grains to states, computerized tracking of transportation, and electronic weighing at FPS to prevent leakages and ensure transparency in grain distribution. The Integrated Management of PDS (IMPDS) enables portability of ration cards across states, allowing beneficiaries to access their entitled food grains from any FPS nationwide.

Furthermore, the *Direct Benefit Transfer (DBT)* in PDS initiative aims to transfer food subsidies directly into the bank accounts of beneficiaries, reducing leakages and ensuring that subsidies reach the intended recipients. This system also helps in eliminating duplicate and ghost beneficiaries from the PDS list through Aadhaar authentication.

Additionally, the *National Food Security Act (NFSA)* provides a legal framework for the PDS, ensuring that subsidized food grains are made available to eligible households at affordable prices. Under NFSA, priority households are entitled to receive food grains at highly subsidized rates, thereby enhancing food security and reducing hunger among vulnerable populations.

These initiatives collectively aim to improve the accessibility, efficiency, and transparency of the Public Distribution System, ensuring that food grains reach the intended beneficiaries effectively and contribute to alleviating poverty and malnutrition across India.

d) e-panchayat

The e-Panchayat initiative by the Government of India aims to strengthen rural governance through the application of Information and Communication Technology (ICT). Launched under the National e-

Governance Plan (NeGP), this initiative focuses on digitizing and automating the functioning of Panchayati Raj Institutions (PRIs) at the grassroots level.

Key objectives of the e-Panchayat initiative include improving transparency, efficiency, and accountability in the delivery of public services to rural citizens. It involves the development and deployment of various e-Governance applications such as PRIASoft (Panchayat Raj Institutions Accounting Software) for financial management, PlanPlus for decentralized planning, and National Panchayat Portal for information dissemination.

Through these digital platforms, elected representatives and officials at the Panchayat level can manage administrative functions more effectively, including financial planning, budgeting, and monitoring of developmental projects. Citizens benefit from improved access to services such as birth and death certificates, property tax payments, and grievance redressal mechanisms through online portals and mobile applications.

The e-Panchayat initiative aims to empower PRIs with the tools and capabilities needed to enhance rural development outcomes, promote local self-governance, and foster inclusive growth in rural India. By leveraging ICT, the government seeks to bridge the digital divide and ensure that rural communities have equitable access to governance and public services, thereby contributing to socio-economic development at the grassroots level.

e) e-District

The e-District initiative by the Government of India aims to bring essential government services closer to citizens through digital platforms, particularly at the district level. Launched under the National e-Governance Plan (NeGP), this initiative focuses on transforming service delivery mechanisms by leveraging Information and Communication Technology (ICT).

The primary objective of e-District is to simplify and streamline the process of accessing various government services such as issuance of certificates, licenses, permits, and other essential documents. It involves the digitization of service delivery mechanisms, enabling citizens to apply for and receive these services online, thereby reducing bureaucratic delays and improving efficiency.

Key components of the e-District initiative include the development of online portals and mobile applications where citizens can submit applications, track their status in real-time, and receive notifications electronically. This not only enhances transparency and accountability in service delivery but also empowers citizens by providing them with easy access to government services from anywhere and at any time.

Furthermore, e-District integrates with other national initiatives like Digital India to ensure interoperability and seamless service delivery across different levels of government. By promoting digital governance at the district level, the e-District initiative contributes to the overall goal of enhancing citizen-centric service delivery, fostering transparency, and improving administrative efficiency in India's governance framework.

f) National Land Records Modernization Programme (NLRMP)

The National Land Records Modernization Programme (NLRMP) initiated by the Government of India aims to modernize land administration systems across the country. Launched under the Digital India and National e-Governance Plan (NeGP), NLRMP seeks to streamline land record management, minimize disputes over land & property, and enhance transparency in land transactions.

Key objectives of NLRMP include computerization of land records, digitization of cadastral maps, and integration of these records with Registration and Revenue departments. By digitizing land records, the program facilitates easier access to property information for citizens, reduces administrative inefficiencies, and ensures quicker resolution of disputes.

Moreover, NLRMP promotes the use of Geographic Information System (GIS) technology for accurate mapping of land parcels and enables online access to land records through dedicated portals and mobile applications. This initiative also includes capacity building programs for officials involved in land administration to enhance their skills in managing digital records and utilizing modern technologies effectively.

Overall, NLRMP plays a crucial role in modernizing India's land management infrastructure, promoting land reforms, and supporting socio-economic development by providing a reliable and transparent land administration system that benefits both citizens and government agencies alike.

4.1.7 Integrated Mission Mode Projects

The National Land Records Modernization Programme (NLRMP), initiated by the Government of India, aims to upgrade the country's land administration systems. As part of the Digital India initiative and the National e-Governance Plan (NeGP), NLRMP focuses on modernizing land record management, reducing disputes related to land and property, and promoting transparency in land transactions.

The main goals of the NLRMP include the computerization of land records, the digitization of cadastral maps, and the integration of these records with the Registration and Revenue departments. Through digitizing land records, the program enables citizens to access property information more easily, reduces administrative inefficiencies, and ensures faster resolution of disputes.

Moreover, NLRMP promotes the use of Geographic Information System (GIS) technology for accurate mapping of land parcels and enables online access to land records through dedicated portals and mobile applications. This initiative also includes capacity building programs for officials involved in land administration to enhance their skills in managing digital records and utilizing modern technologies effectively.

Overall, NLRMP plays a crucial role in modernizing India's land management infrastructure, promoting land reforms, and supporting socio-economic development by providing a reliable and transparent land administration system that benefits both citizens and government agencies alike. Some common initiatives such as e-Courts, e-Biz and Common Service Centres are discussed below

a) e-courts

The e-Courts initiative by the Government of India is a transformative effort aimed at modernizing the judicial system through the use of information technology. Launched under the National e-Governance Plan (NeGP), e-Courts seeks to enhance the efficiency, transparency, and accessibility of the judiciary while reducing procedural delays and improving judicial services delivery.

Key objectives of the e-Courts initiative include digitizing court proceedings, case management, and records management across all levels of the judiciary. It involves the development and implementation of a unified National Judicial Data Grid (NJDG), which serves as a comprehensive database of case information from district courts to the supreme court. This allows for real-time monitoring of case status, tracking of court proceedings, and efficient management of judicial processes.

Moreover, e-Courts facilitate electronic filing (e-filing) of cases, online payment of court fees, scheduling of hearings, and electronic issuance of summons and notices. These digital interventions not only streamline administrative processes but also improve access to justice for litigants and stakeholders by reducing the need for physical presence in courts and enabling remote participation in legal proceedings.

Furthermore, the initiative includes capacity building programs for judicial officers and court staff to enhance their skills in using digital tools effectively. By promoting transparency, accountability, and efficiency in the judiciary, e-Courts contribute to strengthening the rule of law and ensuring timely dispensation of justice, thereby advancing the overall judicial reforms agenda in India.

b) e-Biz

The e-Biz initiative by the Government of India is a comprehensive online platform aimed at simplifying the process of starting and operating businesses in the country. Launched under the National e-Governance Plan (NeGP), e-Biz seeks to facilitate a business-friendly environment by integrating and streamlining regulatory services across various ministries and departments.

Key objectives of the e-Biz platform include providing a single-window clearance mechanism for business-related approvals, licenses, permits, and registrations. It enables entrepreneurs and businesses to apply for and obtain necessary clearances electronically, reducing bureaucratic hurdles and transaction costs. This initiative significantly improves the ease of doing business in India by enhancing transparency, efficiency, and speed in obtaining regulatory approvals.

The e-Biz platform offers a wide range of services such as company incorporation, tax registrations, industrial licenses, environmental clearances, and intellectual property rights registrations. It integrates multiple government services into a unified digital interface, allowing stakeholders to track the status of their applications in real-time and receive electronic notifications.

Moreover, e-Biz promotes digital governance by supporting online payments, electronic document submission, and digital signatures, thereby eliminating the need for physical visits to government offices and paperwork. This initiative plays a crucial role in attracting investments, promoting entrepreneurship, and fostering economic growth by creating a conducive environment for business development and expansion in India.

c) Common Services Centres

The Common Services Centres (CSC) initiative by the Government of India, launched under the Digital India Programme, aims to provide essential government and public services to citizens in rural and remote areas through digital means. These centres, operated by local entrepreneurs known as Village Level Entrepreneurs (VLEs), serve as access points for a wide range of services including public utility services, social welfare schemes, healthcare, financial services, education, and agricultural services. By leveraging technology, CSCs play a pivotal role in bridging the digital divide, enabling rural communities to access and benefit from various digital services that improve their quality of life and promote inclusive development across India.

4.1.8 Recent Initiatives

In addition to the wide range of government projects that were previously covered, this section also covers several initiatives including Direct Cash Transfer, the Aadhar Enabled Payment System (AEPS), the Digital India program, the E-Kranti plan, and Digital Cloud for every Indian have been discussed here. These initiatives collectively aim to leverage technology for inclusive growth, enhance efficiency in governance, and promote digital empowerment across India.

Here are brief explanations of some recent initiatives taken by the Government of India are as follows:

a) Direct Cash Transfer

The Government of India has implemented several Direct Cash Transfer (DCT) initiatives to enhance the efficiency and transparency of welfare programs. One prominent example is the Pradhan Mantri Jan Dhan Yojana (PMJDY), which facilitates the opening of bank accounts for unbanked households, ensuring that subsidies and benefits can be directly transferred to beneficiaries. The Direct Benefit Transfer (DBT) scheme extends this further by transferring subsidies for food, fertilizers, and other essentials directly to the bank accounts of beneficiaries, thereby reducing leakages and ensuring that aid reaches the intended recipients. The Mahatma Gandhi National Rural Employment Guarantee Act (MGNREGA) also uses DCT to directly deposit wages into workers' bank accounts. Additionally, the PM-KISAN scheme provides income support to farmers by depositing ₹6,000 annually in three installments directly into their bank accounts. These initiatives, facilitated by the widespread adoption of Aadhaar, the world's largest biometric identification system, and the proliferation of banking infrastructure, have significantly improved the delivery of welfare benefits, reducing corruption and ensuring that funds are efficiently utilized.

b) Aadhaar Enabled Payment System (AEPS)

The Aadhaar Enabled Payment System (AEPS) initiative by the Government of India is a groundbreaking effort to facilitate financial inclusion and empower citizens through seamless, secure, and convenient financial transactions. AEPS leverages the Aadhaar biometric authentication system, allowing individuals to perform banking transactions using their Aadhaar number and fingerprint or iris scan, without the need for a physical bank card. This system enables a range of banking services, including cash withdrawals, balance inquiries, and fund transfers, at micro-ATMs and banking correspondents. By simplifying access to financial services, AEPS aims to bring banking to the doorstep of every Indian, particularly in rural and underserved areas, thus promoting a more inclusive and digitally connected economy.

c) Digital India Program

The Digital India Program, an ambitious initiative by the Government of India, aims to transform the country into a digitally empowered society and knowledge economy. Launched in 2015, this program seeks to provide universal digital infrastructure, enhance digital literacy, and deliver government services electronically to citizens. Key components include the expansion of broadband connectivity to rural areas, promoting digital literacy through training programs, and ensuring digital access to essential services such as healthcare, education, and banking. By fostering innovation and technology, the Digital India Program strives to create an inclusive digital landscape that bridges the digital divide and drives economic growth and development across the nation.

d) E-Kranti plan

The E-Kranti plan, an integral part of the Digital India initiative, aims to transform the delivery of government services across India through the use of technology. It focuses on electronic delivery of services to ensure efficiency, transparency, and accountability. Key initiatives under E-Kranti include the establishment of a unified mobile app called UMANG (Unified Mobile Application for New-age Governance), which provides access to over 1,200 government services across multiple sectors like healthcare, agriculture, education, and financial services. The plan also promotes the use of electronic health records (EHR) to enhance the quality and accessibility of healthcare. Additionally, the e-Hospital project enables online registration, appointment scheduling, and availability of diagnostic reports for patients in various government hospitals. The e-Sign framework allows citizens to digitally sign documents online using Aadhaar authentication. E-Kranti also focuses on digital literacy through the National Digital Literacy Mission (NDLM) to ensure that at least one person in every household is digitally literate. By leveraging these digital solutions, the E-Kranti plan aims to bridge the digital divide and provide seamless, efficient, and inclusive governance to all citizens.

e) Digital Cloud for every Indian

The Government of India's "Digital Cloud for every Indian" initiative aims to revolutionize the way citizens store and access their personal documents. Under this initiative, each citizen will have access to a secure digital storage space where they can store important documents such as educational certificates, medical records, and other personal documents. This digital repository will be accessible online, ensuring that citizens can easily retrieve their documents anytime and anywhere, reducing the reliance on physical copies. The initiative is part of a broader push towards a digitally empowered society, promoting efficiency, transparency, and convenience in document management for all Indians.

4.1.9 Government of India for m-governance

The Government of India has undertaken several initiatives to promote mobile governance (m-governance), enhancing the accessibility, efficiency, and user-friendliness of public services through mobile devices. Key initiatives include the mobile seva and mobile application store (m-App Store), which integrates over 1,200 services from various government bodies into a single platform, and mKisan, which provides farmers with agricultural information via SMS and mobile apps. The mPassport Seva app streamlines passport services, while Aarogya Setu, developed during the COVID-19 pandemic, aids in contact tracing and health information dissemination are some examples under mobile seva and mobile application store(m-App Store) initiatives, which are described in below section.

a) Mobile seva

The Government of India's Mobile Seva initiative is a pioneering effort aimed at integrating mobile technology into the delivery of public services, thereby enhancing accessibility and efficiency. Launched by the Department of Electronics and Information Technology (DeitY), Mobile Seva provides a centralized platform for government departments and agencies to offer their services through mobile devices. This initiative includes features such as SMS-based services, mobile applications, and interactive voice response systems, enabling citizens to access a wide range of services, including healthcare, education, and utility bill payments, directly from their mobile phones. By simplifying access to government services and ensuring that essential services are available to citizens anytime and anywhere, Mobile Seva plays a crucial role in promoting digital inclusion and making governance more citizen-centric.

b) Mobile Applications Store (m-App Store)

The Government of India's Mobile Applications Store (m-App Store) initiative is a strategic effort to centralize and streamline the delivery of mobile-based public services. Managed by the Department of Electronics and Information Technology (DeitY), the m-App Store serves as a unified platform where citizens can easily download and access a wide array of government mobile applications. These apps cover various domains such as healthcare, education, agriculture, and public utilities, ensuring that essential services are accessible to everyone, especially those in remote and underserved areas. By providing a single, secure, and user-friendly repository for government mobile applications, the m-App Store enhances the reach and effectiveness of m-governance, promoting greater digital inclusion and making it easier for citizens to interact with government services on-the-go.

4.2 Sharing of case studies to highlight best practices in managing e-Governance projects in Indian context

Case studies illustrate the practical implementation of e-Governance, highlighting both successes and challenges, as well as innovation, design, and lessons learned. They demonstrate the capacity of Governments to develop and execute e-Governance programs. Various theoretical frameworks are applied to assess these new initiatives and their distinctions from existing ones. Our evaluation of the case studies will consider not only whether these projects empower underserved populations and provide substantial value but also their sustainability, scalability, and potential for replication within the state. The following eight case studies have been discussed to highlight best practices in managing projects in Indian context.

1. Akshaya –An IT dissemination Project – An Initiative of the Kerala Government
2. KAVERI An Initiative of the Karnataka Government
3. Implementation of e-Procurement Exchange for Government of Andhra Pradesh
4. Nagarpalika - An initiative of the Gujarat Government
5. E-Agricultural Marketing ("EKVI") An Initiative of the Madhya Pradesh Government
6. Lokvani-An effort to empower citizens An Initiative of the UP Government
7. Tamilnilam - The Land Records Computerization Project of Tamil Nadu
8. e-Kosh- computerization of the Treasury Department–An Initiative of the Chattisgarh Government

Let's look each case study one by one highlighting the best practices in managing the project in Indian context.

4.2.1 Akshaya – An IT dissemination Project an Initiative of the Kerala Government

a) Background

The Akshaya project was launched by the Kerala government with the primary objective to make 6.5 million people. The initiative was driven by Kerala's unique position, characterized by its high literacy rate and relatively advanced telecom infrastructure. These conditions provided a fertile ground for a project aimed at bridging the digital divide and promoting socio-economic development through information and communication technology (ICT).

The conceptualization of Akshaya began at the grassroots level in Malappuram district in April 2002. It was initiated in response to the local community's demand for affordable computer education, as existing computer training centers were charging prohibitively high fees. The proposal was to establish a network of tele-centres that would provide a variety of ICT services, thereby democratizing access to technology and information.

The project was designed as a Public-Private Partnership (PPP), with significant involvement from local village councils, known as panchayats. This partnership model was crucial in ensuring the project's financial viability while simultaneously achieving its social development goals. The initiative aimed to create a sustainable business model by encouraging local entrepreneurship and community ownership.

The initial phase of the project involved extensive engagement with local communities to assess their needs and tailor the services accordingly. This grassroots approach ensured that the project was relevant and responsive to the specific requirements of the population it aimed to serve. The pilot implementation in Malappuram served as a test bed for the project, providing valuable insights and lessons that informed its subsequent expansion across other districts in Kerala.

b) Key Objectives

The primary objectives of the Akshaya project were to:

- Facilitate universal access to technology.
- Develop IT competence and skill set among all societal segments.
- Provide locally relevant content in Malayalam.
- Empower citizens by enhancing their digital literacy and access to e-governance services.
- Project Formulation/Conceptualization at the grassroot level
- The project began at the grassroots level in Malappuram district in April 2002, initiated by local village councils. It was driven by the community's demand for affordable computer education, as existing options were too expensive. The proposal included establishing a network of tele-centres to offer various ICT services, with Malappuram serving as the pilot area.

c) Business Model

The Akshaya project was conceived as a Public-Private Partnership (PPP) involving significant participation from local panchayats. The model emphasized financial viability through market-driven entrepreneurship, balancing social development goals with the need for sustainability.

d) Selection of Location

Malappuram district was chosen as the pilot location due to its proactive village councils and the community's expressed need for accessible computer education. The success of the pilot would later allow for replication in other districts of Kerala.

e) Selection of Entrepreneurs

Local entrepreneurs were selected and trained to manage the tele-centres. This approach ensured that the project was locally owned and operated, fostering community involvement and creating job opportunities for local residents.

f) Role of State Government and Entrepreneurs

The State Government played a crucial role in providing the necessary infrastructure, policy support, and initial funding for the project. Entrepreneurs were responsible for the day-to-day operations of the tele-centres, including delivering training programs and maintaining the facilities. This partnership ensured both governance oversight and local entrepreneurship.

g) Implementation Details

In the initial phase, the project involved extensive local engagement to assess and address community needs. Local entrepreneurs were trained to run the tele-centres, ensuring that the project was locally owned and managed. Community outreach programs promoted the use of ICT and the services provided by the tele-centres. Services offered included e-literacy programs, internet access, e-governance services, information dissemination, and online applications for government services. Educational content was developed in Malayalam to ensure accessibility, focusing on topics of local relevance such as agriculture, health, and education.

h) Sustainability Issues

Sustainability was a critical challenge for the Akshaya project. Balancing social objectives with financial viability required continuous effort. Ensuring ongoing funding, maintaining infrastructure, and keeping community interest high were essential for the long-term success of the project. The PPP model aimed to address these issues by leveraging both public support and private entrepreneurship.

i) Benefits

The Akshaya project achieved significant success in increasing e-literacy rates and empowering individuals with digital skills. It improves access to information and government services, thereby enhancing the quality of life for many rural residents. The project's community-driven approach and focus on local relevance contributed to its positive impact.

Conclusion: The Akshaya project stands as a landmark initiative in e-Governance, demonstrating the potential of ICT in transforming rural communities and bridging the digital divide. Its success in Malappuram led to replication across other districts in Kerala, serving as a benchmark for similar initiatives in other states. Despite challenges in sustainability, the project showcased the effectiveness of a community-centric, PPP model in achieving large-scale digital empowerment.

4.2.2 KAVERI An Initiative of the Karnataka Government

a) Background

The Karnataka Valuation and e-Registration (KAVERI) project was initiated to address significant challenges in the Department of Registration and Stamps, Karnataka. Prior attempts at computerizing the department's processes had only partial success due to a variety of issues. These challenges included a cumbersome registration process, lengthy delays in delivering registered documents, and the inability to develop and implement integrated software effectively. The manual processes were time-consuming, and delivering documents on the same day of registration was not feasible, often taking up to 45 days instead.

Another major obstacle was the substantial investment required to fully computerize all 201 sub-registries in the state. The government estimated that completing this task would take 10 to 15 years, contingent on the availability of funds. The existing infrastructure and processes were inadequate to handle the growing demand for efficient and transparent registration services.

Recognizing these challenges, the Karnataka government sought to reengineer the entire business process of the Department of Registration and Stamps. The aim was to create a more efficient, transparent, and user-friendly system. This led to the development of the KAVERI project, which was conceived as a comprehensive solution to streamline the registration process, reduce delays, and improve service delivery. The project marked a significant shift towards full automation and represented the first public-private partnership initiative in Karnataka aimed at overhauling the registration workflow.

b) KAVERI- A Business Process Reengineering Model

KAVERI (Karnataka Valuation and e-Registration) is an example of a Business Process Reengineering (BPR) model aimed at reorienting the Department of Registration and Stamps towards full automation of the registration process. The initiative seeks to ensure that registered documents are delivered to applicants within 30 minutes of submission, in stark contrast to the previous 45-day period.

c) Key Objectives

KAVERI represents the first public-private partnership project in Karnataka since 2003, designed to streamline and automate the registration workflow. The system's key objectives include providing conclusive proof of document authenticity, publicizing transactions, preventing fraud, enabling the verification of property transactions, and securing deeds and titles. The project aims to enhance transparency, facilitate effective monitoring, improve revenue collection, and create a user-friendly administration.

d) Business Model / Revenue Model

The KAVERI project follows a Build-Operate-Transfer (BOT) strategy, involving a private partner who installs, operates, and maintains hardware across all offices, recovering investments through service fees charged to clients. The contract period for this arrangement is five years. The government invested approximately Rs 1.10 crore in software development, while service providers invested around Rs 40 crore in hardware, data entry, and furniture. The service providers are responsible for project execution, administration, and maintenance, charging Rs 30 per page as a scanning fee, of which Rs 5 is remitted to the government.

e) New Model

The KAVERI application suite manages the entire registration process, including report generation and property valuation. The project retained the existing five-step registration procedure to benefit users familiar with it. Sub-Registrars' offices were equipped with Citizen Care Centres (CCCs) providing kiosks with touchscreen interfaces to inform the public about document requirements and property costs according to government rules. The electronic token system improved workflow by assigning specific times for document presentation, reducing wait times and crowding.

f) Benefits

Kiosks (CCCs) reduced the burden on department employees by ensuring applicants presented complete documents, thus decreasing pending paperwork. The electronic token system streamlined document registration, and private sector involvement increased departmental productivity. The project also facilitated data transmission to District Registrars' offices and reduced storage demands on application software.

Conclusion: Initially designed for property registration, KAVERI has expanded to include the registration of firms, societies, and marriages. Efforts are underway to link it with the Bhoomi Project for land record access. The KAVERI project received the "Best e-Governance Project" award for 2004 at the 40th annual conference of the Computer Society of India .

4.2.3 Implementation of e-Procurement Exchange for Government of Andhra Pradesh

a) Background

The e-Procurement initiative for the Government of Andhra Pradesh was launched to address inefficiencies in the traditional procurement processes. These inefficiencies included delays, lack of transparency, and corruption. The government aimed to streamline procurement activities, improve transparency, reduce the cycle time, and enhance overall efficiency through the implementation of an electronic procurement system.

b) New Initiative

The e-Procurement system was a groundbreaking initiative aimed at transforming the way government procurement was conducted. It involved developing an electronic marketplace that enabled suppliers and government departments to conduct procurement transactions online. This new approach sought to replace the traditional, paper-based methods with a more efficient and transparent electronic system.

c) Key Objectives of e-Procurement

The primary objectives of the e-Procurement system were:

- To enhance transparency and accountability in the procurement process.
- To reduce the procurement cycle time and associated costs.
- To eliminate corruption by ensuring all transactions are traceable and auditable.
- To provide equal opportunities for all suppliers, fostering a competitive environment.
- To improve overall efficiency and effectiveness of government procurement.
- Core Functionality of the e-Procurement Marketplace

d) The core functionalities of the e-Procurement marketplace included:

- Electronic tendering: allowing the entire tender process to be conducted online.
- Bid submission and evaluation: enabling suppliers to submit bids electronically and facilitating online evaluation by government officials.
- Contract management: supporting the creation, execution, and management of procurement contracts.

- Supplier registration and management: providing a platform for suppliers to register and manage their profiles.
- Audit trails and reporting: ensuring all transactions are recorded and can be audited, with comprehensive reporting capabilities.

e) Business Model

The business model of the e-Procurement system was based on a Public-Private Partnership (PPP). This model involved collaboration between the government and a private sector partner responsible for developing, operating, and maintaining the e-Procurement platform. The government provided regulatory oversight and policy direction, while the private partner handled the technical and operational aspects.

f) Revenue Model

The revenue model for the e-Procurement system included fees charged to suppliers for participating in the procurement process. These fees covered services such as registration, bid submission, and transaction processing. The revenue generated from these fees was used to maintain and enhance the e-Procurement platform, ensuring its sustainability and continuous improvement.

g) Implementation Details

The implementation of the e-Procurement system involved several key steps:

- Development of the e-Procurement platform in collaboration with the private sector partner.
- Training and capacity building for government officials and suppliers to ensure effective use of the system.
- Pilot testing in select departments to identify and address any issues before full-scale deployment.
- Gradual rollout across all government departments to ensure a smooth transition to the new system.

h) Steps to Facilitate Speedy Adoption

To facilitate the speedy adoption of the e-Procurement system, the government undertook several initiatives:

- Comprehensive training programs for all stakeholders, including government officials and suppliers.
- Awareness campaigns to inform suppliers about the benefits of the new system.
- Providing technical support and assistance to users during the transition phase.
- Implementing user-friendly interfaces and features to encourage participation and ease of use.

i) Business Process Reengineering

The implementation of the e-Procurement system involved significant business process reengineering. This included:

- Redesigning procurement workflows to align with the capabilities of the electronic system.
- Streamlining approval processes to reduce delays and improve efficiency.
- Standardizing procurement documentation and procedures to ensure consistency.

- Integrating the e-Procurement system with existing financial and administrative systems for seamless operation.

j) Outcome of the Initiative

The e-Procurement initiative resulted in several positive outcomes:

- Increased transparency and accountability in the procurement process.
- Reduced cycle times and lower costs associated with procurement activities.
- Enhanced competitiveness among suppliers, leading to better value for money for the government.
- Improved efficiency and effectiveness of government procurement operations.
- Greater trust and confidence in the procurement process among stakeholders.

k) Benefits of the e-Procurement System

The e-Procurement system delivered numerous benefits, including:

- Elimination of corruption and malpractices in the procurement process.
- Significant time and cost savings for both the government and suppliers.
- Improved access to procurement opportunities for small and medium enterprises (SMEs).
- Enhanced data security and integrity through electronic record-keeping.
- Better decision-making capabilities through comprehensive reporting and analytics.

l) Recognition of the Project

The e-Procurement initiative received widespread recognition for its innovative approach and positive impact. It was awarded the "Golden Icon" for exemplary implementation of e-Governance initiatives by the Government of India. The project was also highlighted as a best practice model in various national and international forums.

Conclusion: The implementation of the e-Procurement system for the Government of Andhra Pradesh represents a significant advancement in public procurement. It has transformed the traditional procurement processes, delivering increased transparency, efficiency, and effectiveness. The success of the initiative serves as a benchmark for other states and countries looking to modernize their procurement practices through the use of technology.

4.2.4 Nagarpalika - an initiative of the Gujarat Government

a) Background

The e-Nagarpalika initiative, launched by the Gujarat Government, is a pioneering project aimed at revolutionizing urban governance through digital transformation. The initiative was conceptualized against the environment of a rapidly urbanizing Gujarat, where increasing population density in cities necessitated more efficient and transparent municipal services. Traditional methods of municipal administration were often plagued by bureaucratic inefficiencies, delays, and lack of accessibility for the common citizen. Recognizing these challenges, the Gujarat Government embarked on the e-Nagarpalika initiative to leverage the power of information technology to address these issues.

The primary motivation behind this initiative was to enhance the delivery of municipal services by making them more accessible, efficient, and transparent. By digitizing various municipal functions, the government aimed to reduce the dependency on physical visits to municipal offices, thereby saving time and resources for both citizens and municipal authorities. The initiative sought to create a more citizen-centric approach to urban governance, ensuring that residents could access essential services from the comfort of their homes.

The e-Nagarpalika initiative also aligns with broader national goals of promoting Digital India and Smart Cities, where the integration of technology in governance is seen as a critical factor in achieving sustainable urban development. By implementing this project, Gujarat aimed to set a benchmark in digital governance, providing a model that other states in India could emulate.

b) e-Nagarpalika Initiative

The e-Nagarpalika initiative by the Gujarat Government is designed to modernize and streamline urban governance through the use of digital technology. This initiative aims to transform the delivery of municipal services, making them more accessible, efficient, and transparent for the citizens of Gujarat.

c) Key objectives

The key objective of the e-Nagarpalika initiative is to digitize municipal services to provide citizens with easier, faster, and more transparent access to these services. By leveraging information technology, the project aims to streamline various municipal processes, reducing the time and effort required to obtain services and minimizing the need for physical visits to municipal offices. This initiative not only seeks to enhance the efficiency of service delivery but also aims to increase transparency and accountability in municipal operations, thereby reducing opportunities for corruption and ensuring that citizens are well-informed and empowered in their interactions with municipal authorities.

d) Services offered

The e-Nagarpalika initiative offers a wide range of digital municipal services designed to meet the needs of urban residents. These services include online payment systems for property taxes, water bills, and other municipal fees, which eliminate the need for in-person transactions and save valuable time for citizens. Additionally, the initiative provides for the online issuance of birth and death certificates, streamlining these essential processes. Building plan approvals can also be submitted and processed online, significantly reducing wait times and simplifying the approval process. The initiative features a digital platform for grievance redressal, allowing citizens to lodge complaints and track their status, ensuring timely resolution of issues.

Furthermore, citizens can access information and apply for various civic amenities, such as parks and community halls, through the online platform. Licensing and permit applications, such as trade licenses and health permits, can also be handled digitally, further enhancing convenience. By offering these services online, the e-Nagarpalika initiative aims to create a seamless, efficient, and responsive interaction between municipal authorities and citizens, fostering a more effective and accountable urban governance system.

e) Revenue and Business models

Both revenue & business models ensure both operational efficiency and financial sustainability. At its core, the initiative employs a public-private partnership (PPP) model, where the government collaborates with private IT firms to develop, implement, and maintain the digital infrastructure necessary for the project. This partnership leverages the expertise and technological capabilities of the private sector while the government provides regulatory oversight and ensures that the services align with public needs. This synergy not only accelerates the implementation process but also enhances the quality and reliability of the services offered.

The revenue model for the e-Nagarpalika initiative is multifaceted, designed to cover operational costs and ensure long-term sustainability. Primarily, the initiative generates revenue through nominal service charges for various online transactions, such as the payment of property taxes, water bills, and other municipal fees. These charges are kept minimal to encourage widespread adoption among citizens while ensuring that the system remains financially viable. Additionally, the initiative offers premium services for faster processing and additional conveniences, which come with higher fees. Government funding also plays a critical role, particularly in the initial setup and ongoing maintenance of the digital infrastructure. Grants and subsidies from both state and central governments help in offsetting costs and expanding the reach of the initiative. By diversifying its revenue streams, the e-Nagarpalika initiative aims to create a robust financial foundation that supports continuous improvements and scalability.

f) Viability and Sustainability

The viability of the e-Nagarpalika initiative by the Gujarat Government is ensured through the use of scalable technology. By adopting modern and flexible IT solutions, the initiative can expand its services and handle increasing user demand efficiently. Regular updates and maintenance of the digital platform keep the system secure and capable of meeting evolving requirements, thus maintaining high service quality.

Financial sustainability is achieved through a multi-dimensional revenue model, including nominal service charges, fees for premium services, and government funding. This balanced approach ensures the initiative can cover operational costs while keeping services affordable for citizens. Initial government grants and subsidies help offset the substantial initial investment in digital infrastructure, and as more citizens adopt the services, the revenue generated increases, further supporting financial stability.

Stakeholder engagement and capacity building are also crucial for sustainability. Continuous training programs for municipal staff ensure proficiency with the new digital tools, enhancing service delivery efficiency. The initiative actively seeks citizen feedback to refine and improve services, creating a dynamic interaction that supports long-term sustainability. This robust ecosystem involving the government, municipal employees, and citizens ensures the initiative's ongoing success.

g) Implementation details

The implementation of the e-Nagarpalika initiative by the Gujarat Government involves a comprehensive strategy to digitize municipal services. This includes the development of a user-friendly online portal and a mobile application, both designed to provide easy access to various services such as payment of taxes, issuance of certificates, and grievance redressal. The digital infrastructure is carefully integrated with existing municipal systems to ensure seamless service delivery.

To facilitate smooth adoption, the initiative has established help desks and support centers across cities to assist citizens in navigating these new digital platforms. Furthermore, extensive capacity-building programs are conducted to train municipal employees, ensuring they are proficient in using the new technology and can effectively assist citizens.

h) Current Status

As of the current status, the e-Nagarpalika initiative has been successfully deployed in numerous cities across Gujarat, with a significant number of citizens actively using the digital services. The initiative has received positive feedback for its efficiency and ease of use, indicating successful adoption by the public. Continuous monitoring and evaluation processes are in place to assess the performance of the initiative, identify areas for improvement, and implement necessary adjustments. This ongoing evaluation helps in maintaining high service standards and addressing any challenges that may arise. The success of the initiative is reflected in the increasing number of online transactions and the growing satisfaction among citizens.

Conclusion:

The e-Nagarpalika initiative is a landmark project in the modernization of urban governance in Gujarat. By leveraging digital technology, the initiative has significantly enhanced the efficiency, transparency, and accessibility of municipal services. The strategic implementation, supported by robust infrastructure and continuous improvements, ensures the long-term success and sustainability of the project. The initiative not only addresses the immediate needs of urban residents but also sets a precedent for other regions to follow. It exemplifies how digital transformation can effectively tackle the challenges of urban governance, fostering a more responsive and accountable municipal administration.

4.2.5 E-Agricultural Marketing ("EKVI") An Initiative of the Madhya Pradesh Government

a) Background

The E-Agricultural Marketing ("EKVI") initiative by the Madhya Pradesh Government is a forward-thinking project aimed at revolutionizing the agricultural sector through digital transformation. Recognizing the challenges faced by farmers in accessing fair and transparent markets, the initiative was launched to streamline agricultural marketing processes and enhance the efficiency of the supply chain. EKVI seeks to eliminate the traditional barriers and inefficiencies associated with agricultural marketing by leveraging digital platforms to connect farmers directly with buyers, thus ensuring better price realization for their products. This initiative is part of the broader efforts by the Madhya Pradesh Government to modernize agriculture, boost farmer incomes, and create a more resilient and transparent agricultural economy. By providing a digital marketplace, EKVI aims to empower farmers with real-time information, reduce dependency on intermediaries, and promote a more competitive and equitable agricultural market landscape.

b) Computerization of Mandis

The computerization of mandis under the E-Agricultural Marketing ("EKVI") initiative by the Madhya Pradesh Government aims to modernize agricultural trading practices. By digitizing traditional mandis through online platforms and mobile apps, the initiative enhances market transparency, efficiency, and accessibility for farmers. It provides real-time market information, facilitates direct farmer-buyer interactions, and reduces bureaucratic delays and intermediary costs. This digital transformation seeks to empower farmers with fairer prices and better market access, thereby fostering a more competitive and sustainable agricultural economy in Madhya Pradesh.

c) EKVI project

The EKVI project, an initiative of the Madhya Pradesh Government, represents a pivotal effort in modernizing agricultural marketing within the state. Aimed at transforming traditional agricultural practices through digital innovation, EKVI focuses on creating a streamlined and transparent marketplace for farmers. The project leverages digital platforms to connect farmers directly with buyers, reducing the role of intermediaries and ensuring fairer pricing for agricultural produce. By computerizing mandis and integrating them into an online ecosystem, EKVI provides farmers with real-time market information and facilitates efficient trading processes. This initiative not only aims to enhance market accessibility and efficiency but also aims to empower farmers by enabling them to make informed decisions and improve their income opportunities. Through EKVI, the Madhya Pradesh Government aims to boost agricultural productivity, increase farmer incomes, and create a sustainable and resilient agricultural sector in the state.

d) Business and Revenue Model

The business model of the E-Agricultural Marketing ("EKVI") initiative by the Madhya Pradesh Government revolves around creating a digital marketplace that connects farmers directly with buyers. It involves developing and maintaining online platforms and mobile applications to facilitate transparent and efficient agricultural trading. The revenue model primarily includes nominal fees for transactions conducted through the digital platform, ensuring affordability for farmers while generating revenue to sustain the initiative. Additionally, government funding supports initial setup and operational costs, emphasizing financial sustainability and scalability of the project. This model aims to empower farmers with better market access and fairer prices, contributing to the overall modernization and growth of the agricultural sector in Madhya Pradesh.

e) Implementation details

The implementation of the E-Agricultural Marketing ("EKVI") initiative by the Madhya Pradesh Government involves the deployment of digital platforms to streamline agricultural marketing processes. This includes the development of user-friendly online portals and mobile applications that connect farmers directly with buyers. The initiative focuses on computerizing traditional mandis (agricultural markets) to provide real-time market information, facilitate transparent transactions, and reduce dependency on intermediaries. Extensive training programs are conducted to educate farmers and stakeholders on using the digital tools effectively. The implementation also includes setting up support centers to assist farmers in navigating the new technology and resolving any issues they encounter. By leveraging technology, EKVI aims to modernize agricultural practices, enhance market access, and improve the livelihoods of farmers in Madhya Pradesh.

f) Technology Description

The technology behind the E-Agricultural Marketing ("EKVI") initiative by the Madhya Pradesh Government involves the development of robust online platforms and mobile applications. These digital tools are designed to modernize agricultural marketing practices by integrating traditional mandis (agricultural markets) into a unified digital ecosystem. The platforms provide farmers with real-time market information, including prices and demand trends, enabling them to make informed decisions. Buyers can directly connect with farmers through these digital channels, facilitating transparent and efficient transactions. The technology also supports features like online bidding, payment gateways, and digital documentation, simplifying the trading process and reducing administrative overhead. By leveraging advanced technology, EKVI aims to enhance market accessibility, promote fair pricing, and improve overall efficiency in agricultural marketing across Madhya Pradesh.

g) Benefits to stakeholders

The E-Agricultural Marketing ("EKVI") initiative by the Madhya Pradesh Government offers substantial benefits to stakeholders across the agricultural value chain. For farmers, it provides direct access to a wider market, enabling them to obtain fair prices for their produce and reducing reliance on intermediaries. Real-time market information through digital platforms helps farmers make informed decisions, enhancing their profitability and competitiveness. Buyers benefit from a transparent marketplace where they can access a diverse range of agricultural products efficiently. Additionally, the initiative promotes efficiency in agricultural trading processes, reduces transaction costs, and supports sustainable economic growth in Madhya Pradesh. By leveraging digital technology, EKVI aims to empower farmers, improve market accessibility, and foster a more inclusive and resilient agricultural sector.

h) Highlights of the System

- *Digital Mandi Integration:* Traditional mandis are digitized for transparent trading.
- *Real-time Market Information:* Farmers access current prices and demand trends.
- *Direct Farmer-Buyer Interaction:* Facilitates seamless transactions without intermediaries.
- *User-friendly Online Platforms:* Easy-to-use portals and mobile apps for efficient trading.
- *Support for Farmers:* Training programs and support centers enhance digital literacy.

Conclusion:

In conclusion, the E-Agricultural Marketing ("EKVI") initiative by the Madhya Pradesh Government marks a significant leap towards modernizing agricultural practices and enhancing market efficiency. By leveraging digital technology to integrate traditional mandis into a unified online platform, EKVI promotes transparency, efficiency, and fair pricing in agricultural transactions. Farmers benefit from direct access to market information and buyers, reducing dependence on intermediaries and improving income opportunities. The initiative's user-friendly interfaces and support mechanisms ensure widespread adoption and effective utilization of digital tools among stakeholders. Overall, EKVI not only aims to boost agricultural productivity and farmer incomes but also sets a precedent for sustainable economic growth and inclusive development in Madhya Pradesh's agricultural sector.

4.2.6 Lokvani-An effort to empower citizens - An Initiative of the UP Government

a) Background

Lokvani, an initiative by the Uttar Pradesh Government, was launched in the early 2000s to empower citizens by enhancing transparency, accountability, and efficiency in government services. Aimed at addressing the challenges of accessing government services, Lokvani established internet kiosks across rural and semi-urban areas, providing a single point of contact for lodging complaints, tracking applications, and obtaining essential certificates. This initiative sought to reduce corruption, foster greater engagement between the government and citizens, and ensure that government services were accessible to all, regardless of location or socio-economic status, thus promoting a more responsive and accountable governance model.

Overall, Lokvani stands as a pioneering effort by the Uttar Pradesh Government to harness the power of technology for the benefit of its citizens, driving significant improvements in service delivery and governance.

b) New Initiative in Sitapur District, Uttar Pradesh

Lokvani is a step in this direction, meaning "voice of the people" in Hindi. It is a public-private partnership project designed to offer a single-window, self-sustainable e-Governance solution that ensures transparent, accountable, and responsive administration for grievance handling, land record maintenance, and a diverse range of essential services. The project was conceived by Mr. Amod Kumar, the District Magistrate, who developed a governance model using ICT to manage the delivery of services to all citizens.

c) e-Accountability

The e-Accountability component of the Lokvani initiative by the Uttar Pradesh Government is essential in enhancing transparency and accountability within public administration. Through the use of digital platforms, Lokvani enables citizens to lodge grievances, track their status in real-time, and access various government services online. This system significantly reduces the potential for corruption and bureaucratic delays by eliminating intermediaries and providing a direct interface between the government and citizens.

Furthermore, it allows for continuous monitoring and feedback, ensuring that government officials are responsive and accountable to the needs and concerns of the public. By fostering an environment of openness and accountability, Lokvani not only improves the efficiency of service delivery but also builds trust and confidence among citizens in the governance process. This digital transformation represents a major step towards a more transparent, accountable, and citizen-centric administration in Uttar Pradesh.

d) Management and Conceptualisation of The Lokvani Model

The Lokvani model, conceptualized and managed by the Uttar Pradesh Government under the guidance of Mr. Amod Kumar, District Magistrate, aimed to empower citizens through e-Governance. This initiative utilized Information and Communication Technology (ICT) to establish a single-window system, providing easy access to government services, grievance redressal, and essential information via internet kiosks in rural and semi-urban areas. As a public-private partnership, Lokvani focused on transparency, accountability, and responsiveness, continuously improving based on user feedback. This innovative approach not only streamlined administrative processes but also built trust and engagement between the government and its citizens, setting a benchmark for digital governance.

e) Project Objectives

The objectives of the Lokvani model, an initiative by the Uttar Pradesh Government, are centered around empowering citizens through enhanced access to government services and fostering a more transparent, accountable, and efficient administration. Primarily, Lokvani aims to provide a single-window platform where citizens can easily lodge grievances, access land records, and obtain essential government services without the need for intermediaries. By leveraging Information and Communication Technology (ICT), the initiative seeks to reduce bureaucratic delays and corruption, ensuring that government services are delivered more efficiently and equitably. Additionally, Lokvani aims to bridge the digital divide by establishing internet kiosks in rural and semi-urban areas, making digital services accessible to all, especially the underserved populations. Ultimately, the Lokvani model strives to build a more responsive and citizen-centric governance structure, fostering trust and engagement between the government and its citizens.

f) Service Delivery Range

Lokvani is an initiative by the Uttar Pradesh Government aimed at empowering citizens by improving service delivery through digital means. This program provides a platform for the public to access various government services and information online, thereby enhancing transparency, reducing corruption, and facilitating efficient grievance redressal. Lokvani enables citizens to check the status of applications, register complaints, and obtain essential documents without the need for intermediaries, thus making governance more accessible and citizen-centric.

g) Lokvani business model

The business model of Lokvani, an initiative by the Uttar Pradesh Government, focuses on a public-private partnership to deliver government services to citizens through digital platform. These kiosks, operated by private entrepreneurs, serve as access points where citizens can avail various e-governance services such as obtaining certificates, paying utility bills, and lodging grievances. The government provides the necessary digital infrastructure and support, while the entrepreneurs earn a commission for each transaction. This model ensures widespread reach and accessibility, promoting transparency, efficiency, and citizen empowerment.

h) Sustainability

The sustainability of Lokvani, an initiative by the Uttar Pradesh Government, is ensured through its effective public-private partnership model. By empowering private entrepreneurs to operate digital platforms, Lokvani guarantees ongoing service delivery and financial incentives for operators through transaction commissions. The government's continuous investment in digital infrastructure and support ensures system robustness and efficiency. This model not only enhances transparency and accessibility but also builds citizen trust and engagement, thereby securing the long-term viability and impact of the initiative.

i) Lokvani Success

The success of Lokvani, an initiative by the Uttar Pradesh Government to empower citizens, is evident in its efficient delivery of government services through digital platforms. By enabling easy access to services like document issuance, bill payments, and grievance redressal, Lokvani enhances transparency and reduces bureaucratic hurdles. The initiative's impact is strengthened by its ability to streamline processes, improve citizen satisfaction, and foster greater accountability in governance. Through these efforts, Lokvani not only empowers citizens but also sets a example for effective e-governance models across the region.

j) Implementation details

Lokvani, an initiative of the Uttar Pradesh Government, is implemented through a network of digital platforms operated by private entrepreneurs across the state. These platforms serve as access points where citizens can avail various government services such as applying for certificates, paying bills, and registering complaints online. The government provides the necessary digital infrastructure, training, and support to ensure smooth operations and service delivery. This decentralized approach enhances accessibility, reduces bureaucratic delays, and promotes transparency in governance, thereby empowering citizens to engage more effectively with administrative processes.

k) Achievements and challenges

Lokvani, a digital initiative by the Uttar Pradesh Government, has made considerable progress in allowing citizens by providing improved access to government services online. The program has effectively simplified administrative processes, minimized corruption, and increased transparency in service delivery. Nevertheless, challenges persist, including ensuring equal access for all demographic groups, overcoming technological hurdles in rural regions, and sustaining ongoing citizen engagement. Despite these obstacles, Lokvani continues to advance digital inclusion and empower citizens throughout Uttar Pradesh.

Conclusion:

Lokvani, an initiative by the Uttar Pradesh Government, has achieved significant milestones in empowering citizens through enhanced access to government services via digital platforms. It has successfully streamlined processes, reduced corruption, and improved transparency in service delivery. However, challenges such as ensuring equitable access across all demographics, addressing technological barriers in rural areas, and maintaining sustained citizen engagement remain. Despite these challenges, Lokvani continues to make strides in fostering digital inclusion and citizen empowerment across Uttar Pradesh.

4.2.7 Tamilnilam - The Land Records Computerization Project of Tamil Nadu

a) Background

Tamilnilam, the Land Records Computerization Project of Tamil Nadu, represents a significant initiative aimed at modernizing the land administration system in the state. Launched in the early 2000s, this project sought to digitize and streamline land records, addressing longstanding issues of inefficiency, inaccuracy, and lack of transparency in land management. Tamilnilam aimed to create a comprehensive, easily accessible digital database of land records, facilitating better governance and reducing disputes related to land ownership. The project involved extensive data collection, verification, and integration processes, leveraging advanced information technology to ensure the accuracy and reliability of land records. By enhancing the accessibility and accuracy of land information, Tamilnilam aimed to empower landowners, improve revenue collection, and support overall economic development in Tamil Nadu.

b) Objective of the Project

The objective of Tamilnilam - The Land Records Computerization Project of Tamil Nadu was to modernize the state's land administration by digitizing land records. This initiative aimed to create a unified and accurate digital database, enhancing transparency, reducing disputes, and improving the efficiency of land management. By leveraging advanced technology, Tamilnilam sought to empower landowners with clear records, streamline administrative processes, boost revenue collection, and support economic development through a more reliable and transparent land market.

c) Tamilnilam services

Tamilnilam - The Land Records Computerization Project of Tamil Nadu provides several essential services aimed at improving the management and accessibility of land records. These services include:

- *Digitization of Land Records:* Conversion of traditional paper-based land records into a digital format, creating a comprehensive and easily searchable database.
- *Online Access to Land Records*: Enabling landowners, government officials, and other stakeholders to access land records online, allowing them to view, download, and print copies of land documents.
- *Verification of Land Ownership:* Providing tools for users to verify land ownership details, ensuring the accuracy and reliability of land records.
- *Status Checks:* Allowing users to check the status of their land holdings, including any pending applications or updates.
- *Grievance Redressal:* Implementing an efficient system for addressing and resolving land-related disputes and errors, helping to maintain the integrity of land records.
- *Integration with other Government Databases:* Facilitating the sharing of land record data with other governmental departments to improve coordination and streamline administrative processes.
- *Transparency and Reduction of Corruption:* Enhancing transparency in land transactions and reducing opportunities for corruption by making land records easily accessible and verifiable.

Through these services, Tamilnilam aims to modernize land administration in Tamil Nadu, making it more efficient, transparent, and user-friendly.

d) Revenue model of Tamilnilam Project

The revenue model of Tamilnilam - The Land Records Computerization Project of Tamil Nadu is primarily based on service fees charged for accessing and processing land records and related documentation. These fees include charges for obtaining certified copies of land documents, verifying land ownership, and other administrative services. Additionally, the project may receive funding from government budgets allocated for modernization and digital infrastructure initiatives. By streamlining land administration and enhancing service delivery, Tamilnilam aims to improve efficiency and generate revenue to sustain its operations while contributing to the broader goal of economic development and transparency in land management.

e) Implementation details

The implementation of Tamilnilam - The Land Records Computerization Project of Tamil Nadu involved several critical steps:

- *Digitization of Records:* Existing paper-based land records were collected, scanned, and digitized to create a centralized digital database.
- *Data Verification*: Extensive verification processes were conducted to ensure accuracy, including cross-checking with physical records and resolving discrepancies.
- *IT Infrastructure:* Development of robust IT infrastructure, including specialized software, secure servers, and high-speed internet connectivity, to support the digital system.
- *Training:* Government officials and staff received training to effectively use the new digital tools and processes.

- *Online Access:* An online portal was launched to provide stakeholders with easy access to land records and related services.
- *Grievance Redressal:* An efficient system was established to handle errors and disputes related to land records.
- *Integration:* The digital land records database was integrated with other government databases to enhance coordination and streamline processes.
- *Public Awareness:* Campaigns were conducted to inform the public about the project's benefits and how to use the new services.

These steps aimed to modernize land administration, improve service delivery, and increase transparency in land transactions.

f) Software Features of Tamilnilam

The Land Records Computerization Project of Tamil Nadu include a robust digitization platform for converting paper-based records into a centralized digital database. It offers an intuitive online portal where stakeholders can access and manage land records, facilitating tasks such as verifying ownership, retrieving documents, and initiating transactions. Advanced search capabilities enable quick retrieval of specific records, while integrated validation tools ensure data accuracy. Secure authentication and encryption protocols safeguard sensitive information, while seamless integration with other governmental databases enhances coordination and improves overall administrative efficiency. These features collectively support the project's goals of modernizing land administration, promoting transparency, and enhancing service delivery across Tamil Nadu.

g) Hardware infrastructure in Talukas

The hardware infrastructure at the talukas (administrative subdivisions) of Tamilnilam - The land records computerization project of Tamil Nadu comprises essential components to support its digitization efforts. This includes installation of high-performance servers at each taluka office to store and manage the digital land records securely. Additionally, the project deploys computer terminals equipped with necessary software for accessing and updating the database. High-speed internet connectivity is essential to ensure seamless online access to land records through the project's portal. These hardware provisions enable efficient digitization, storage, retrieval, and management of land records at the local level, enhancing accessibility and service delivery to stakeholders across Tamil Nadu.

h) Business Process Reengineering and Training of Tamilnilam Project

The business process reengineering of Tamilnilam - The Land Records Computerization Project of Tamil Nadu involved transforming traditional land administration practices through digital technology and streamlined workflows. This initiative aimed to simplify and optimize processes such as data collection, verification, and retrieval of land records. It introduced new methodologies for digitizing and storing records centrally, reducing dependence on paper-based systems and minimizing errors. By implementing an online portal for easy access to land records and integrating with other governmental databases, the project enhanced transparency and efficiency in land transactions. Training programs were also conducted to equip staff with the skills needed to operate and maintain the new digital systems effectively. Overall, the reengineering efforts aimed to modernize land administration, improve service delivery, and foster a more transparent and accountable governance framework in Tamil Nadu.

i) Achievements of Tamilnilam

The achievements of Tamilnilam - The land records computerization project of Tamil Nadu is profound. It successfully digitized and centralized land records, improving accessibility and transparency in land administration. By eliminating paper-based inefficiencies and reducing errors, the project streamlined processes for verifying land ownership, accessing records online, and resolving disputes efficiently. It enhanced service delivery to stakeholders, including landowners and government officials, through an intuitive online portal and integrated data systems. The implementation of Tamilnilam significantly reduced corruption opportunities, fostered public trust, and contributed to economic development by creating a more reliable and accountable land governance framework in Tamil Nadu.

Conclusion:

In conclusion, Tamilnilam - The land records computerization project of Tamil Nadu stands as a testament to successful modernization in land administration. Through comprehensive digitization and integration of land records, the project has significantly improved efficiency, transparency, and accessibility for stakeholders. By leveraging advanced technology and streamlined processes, Tamilnilam has not only reduced bureaucratic hurdles but also enhanced public trust in the governance of land transactions. Moving forward, its achievements pave the way for continued advancements in administrative effectiveness and economic development across Tamil Nadu, setting a benchmark for other states to follow in upgrading their land management systems.

4.2.8 e-Kosh- Computerization of the Treasury Department an initiative of the Chattisgarh Government

a) Background

The e-Kosh project, initiated by the Chattisgarh Government, aims to modernize and digitize the treasury department's operations. Launched to streamline financial transactions and enhance transparency, e-Kosh focuses on automating processes related to budget allocation, expenditure management, and revenue collection. By implementing robust IT infrastructure and software solutions, the project aims to improve efficiency in fund management and reduce administrative delays. Through its online portal and integrated systems, e-Kosh facilitates real-time monitoring and reporting, enabling faster decision-making and accountability in financial operations across Chattisgarh.

b) Objective of e-Kosh project

The e-Kosh initiative by the Chattisgarh Government aims to modernize the treasury department through comprehensive computerization. Its primary objectives include automating financial transactions, improving budget management efficiency, enhancing transparency in revenue collection, and facilitating real-time monitoring and reporting of financial data. By digitizing processes and implementing advanced IT infrastructure, e-Kosh seeks to streamline operations, reduce paperwork, minimize errors, and strengthen accountability in financial management across Chattisgarh.

c) Implementation strategies of e-Kosh

The implementation strategies of the e-Kosh computerization of the treasury department project in Chattisgarh include deploying advanced IT infrastructure and software to automate financial processes such as budget allocation, expenditure tracking, and revenue collection. The project emphasizes training and capacity building for treasury department personnel to effectively utilize the new digital systems. Integration of financial modules and databases ensures seamless data flow and interoperability, while robust monitoring mechanisms facilitate real-time oversight and reporting. Stakeholder engagement and public outreach efforts are integral to promoting transparency and gaining acceptance of the digital transformation. These strategies collectively aim to enhance efficiency, reduce delays, and improve accountability in financial management across Chattisgarh.

d) Benefits of e-Kosh

The e-Kosh computerization of the treasury department project in Chattisgarh offers several key benefits. It enhances operational efficiency by automating financial processes, thereby reducing paperwork and administrative delays. Real-time monitoring and reporting capabilities improve transparency and accountability in budget allocation and expenditure management. The project also strengthens revenue collection through streamlined systems, minimizing errors and enhancing fiscal discipline. Additionally, e-Kosh facilitates easier access to financial information and promotes better decision-making, ultimately supporting economic growth and effective governance in Chattisgarh.

e) Current status

As of the current status, the e-Kosh computerization of the treasury department project by the Chattisgarh Government has significantly advanced financial management capabilities with the state. The project has successfully implemented automated systems for budget allocation, expenditure tracking, and revenue collection, enhancing efficiency and transparency. Real-time monitoring and reporting functionalities are operational, providing officials with timely financial data for decision-making. Stakeholder engagement efforts continue to promote acceptance and utilization of the digital platform across various departments. Overall, e-Kosh continues to play a pivotal role in modernizing financial governance and promoting accountability in Chattisgarh.

f) Future Plans

The future plans for the e-Kosh computerization of the treasury department project by the Chattisgarh government include further enhancement of digital infrastructure and capabilities. This involves expanding the scope of automated financial processes to cover more departments and transactions. Additionally, there are plans to integrate advanced analytics and data visualization tools to enhance decision-making and policy formulation based on real-time financial insights. The project aims to continue improving transparency and accountability in financial management across Chattisgarh while adapting to evolving technological advancements and user needs.

Conclusion: In conclusion, the e-Kosh computerization of the treasury department project initiated by the Chattisgarh government marks a significant leap towards modernizing financial governance. By automating processes, enhancing transparency, and improving efficiency in budget management and revenue collection, the project has strengthened accountability and facilitated better decision-making. Moving forward, e-Kosh is poised to continue its pivotal role in transforming financial administration across Chattisgarh, contributing to sustainable development and effective governance in the state.

4.3 Visits to local e-governance sites (CSC, eSeva, Post Office, Passport Seva Kendra, etc) as part of Tutorials.

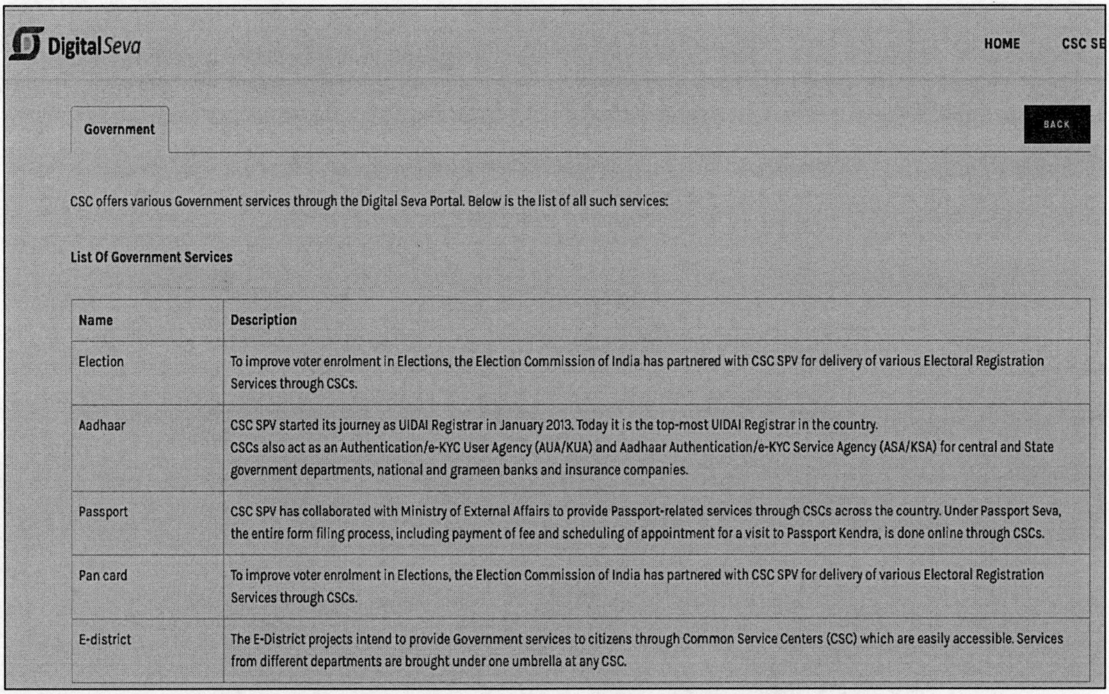
DigitalSeva HOME CSC SE

Government BACK

CSC offers various Government services through the Digital Seva Portal. Below is the list of all such services:

List Of Government Services

Name	Description
Election	To improve voter enrolment in Elections, the Election Commission of India has partnered with CSC SPV for delivery of various Electoral Registration Services through CSCs.
Aadhaar	CSC SPV started its journey as UIDAI Registrar in January 2013. Today it is the top-most UIDAI Registrar in the country. CSCs also act as an Authentication/e-KYC User Agency (AUA/KUA) and Aadhaar Authentication/e-KYC Service Agency (ASA/KSA) for central and State government departments, national and grameen banks and insurance companies.
Passport	CSC SPV has collaborated with Ministry of External Affairs to provide Passport-related services through CSCs across the country. Under Passport Seva, the entire form filing process, including payment of fee and scheduling of appointment for a visit to Passport Kendra, is done online through CSCs.
Pan card	To improve voter enrolment in Elections, the Election Commission of India has partnered with CSC SPV for delivery of various Electoral Registration Services through CSCs.
E-district	The E-District projects intend to provide Government services to citizens through Common Service Centers (CSC) which are easily accessible. Services from different departments are brought under one umbrella at any CSC.

Figure 4.2 List of government services provided by government to citizens

E-governance sites such as Common Service Centers (CSC), eSeva centers, post offices, and Passport Seva Kendras are vital digital platforms designed to streamline the interaction between the government and its citizens. These platforms provide a wide range of services aimed at enhancing accessibility, transparency, and efficiency in public administration. As part of educational tutorials, visiting these sites can offer valuable insights into how modern technology is leveraged to improve governance and service delivery. Here the services provided by these websites are discussed one by one along with pictorial representation as a part of tutorial visits.

4.3.1 Common Service Center (CSC)

The Digital Seva Portal, accessible via https://digitalseva.csc.gov.in,serves as the online platform for the Common Service Centers (CSCs) initiative. CSCs are crucial components of the Digital India program, aimed at providing essential public services to citizens, especially in rural and remote areas. Here's a general description of the services provided by CSCs through the Digital Seva Portal.

a) Government services

The following are the government services provided to citizens through CSC portal. It includes election, Aadhaar, Passport, Pan Card and e-district. The pictorial representation of these services is given in the above figure 4.2.

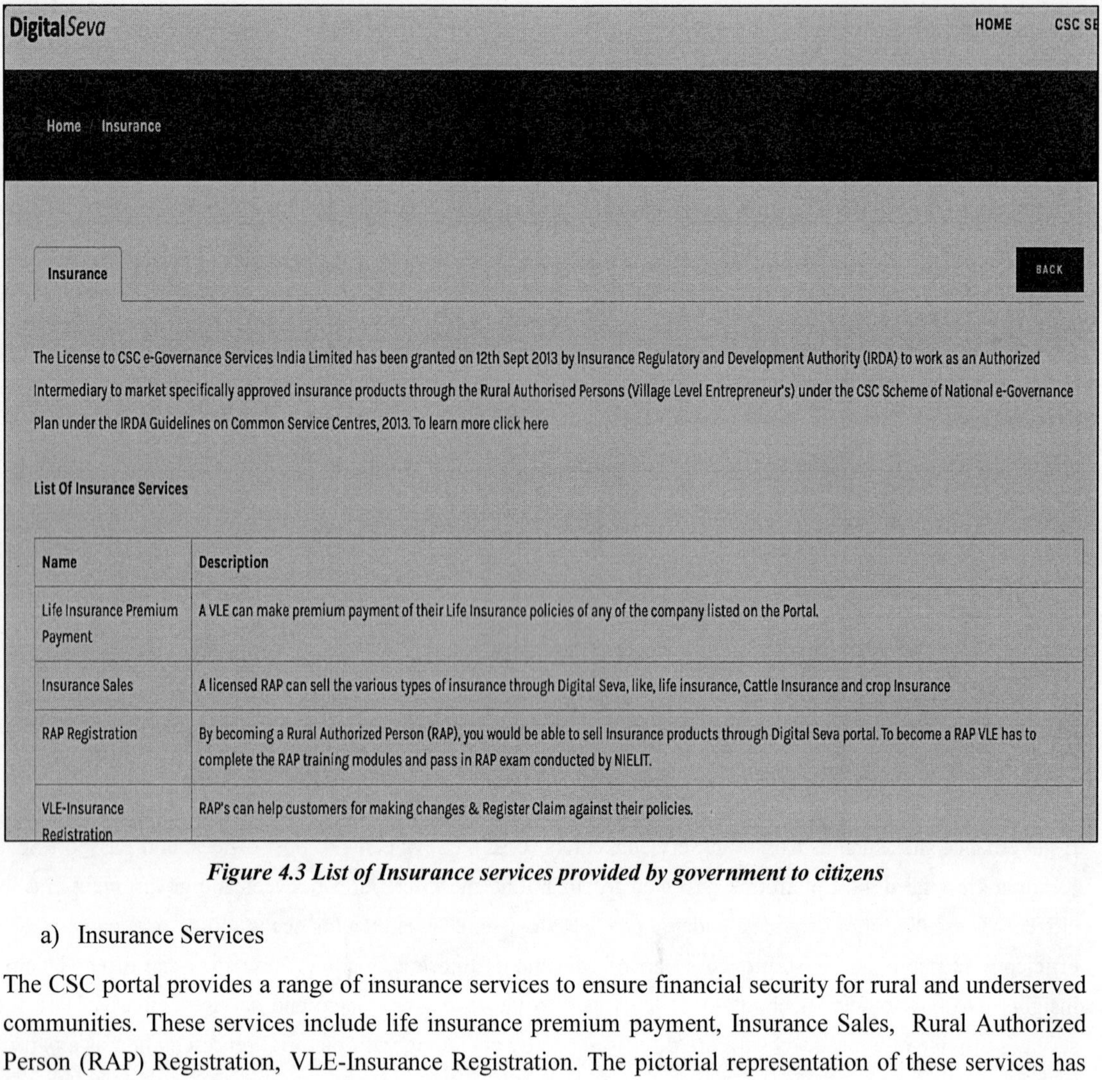

DigitalSeva HOME CSC SE

Home / Insurance

Insurance BACK

The License to CSC e-Governance Services India Limited has been granted on 12th Sept 2013 by Insurance Regulatory and Development Authority (IRDA) to work as an Authorized Intermediary to market specifically approved insurance products through the Rural Authorised Persons (Village Level Entrepreneur's) under the CSC Scheme of National e-Governance Plan under the IRDA Guidelines on Common Service Centres, 2013. To learn more click here

List Of Insurance Services

Name	Description
Life Insurance Premium Payment	A VLE can make premium payment of their Life Insurance policies of any of the company listed on the Portal.
Insurance Sales	A licensed RAP can sell the various types of insurance through Digital Seva, like, life insurance, Cattle Insurance and crop Insurance
RAP Registration	By becoming a Rural Authorized Person (RAP), you would be able to sell Insurance products through Digital Seva portal. To become a RAP VLE has to complete the RAP training modules and pass in RAP exam conducted by NIELIT.
VLE-Insurance Registration	RAP's can help customers for making changes & Register Claim against their policies.

Figure 4.3 List of Insurance services provided by government to citizens

a) Insurance Services

The CSC portal provides a range of insurance services to ensure financial security for rural and underserved communities. These services include life insurance premium payment, Insurance Sales, Rural Authorized Person (RAP) Registration, VLE-Insurance Registration. The pictorial representation of these services has been shown in the above figure 4.3.

Education

BACK

CSC offers various Education services through the Digital Seva Portal. Below is the list of all such services:

List Of Government Services

Name	Description
Cyber gram Yojana	Cyber Gram Yojana aims to provide hands-on training in computers for the students of Minority Community and enable them to acquire basic ICT skills that would empower them.
Women Digital Literacy Programme	Today, computing skills are essential for empowerment and digital literacy for women can contribute and be a change agent especially in rural areas leading to overall societal development. Digital media has extraordinary potential for the empowerment of women in terms of disseminating information and knowledge. Yet, overall use of digital media by women is still very low in rural India. The objective of the project is to train and empower 25,000 rural women on Basic Computer Course (BCC).
E-Swavlambika	CSC SPV is implementing a project named 'Information & Communication Technology (ICT) for Capacity Building and Livelihood Generation for Women' (e-Swavlambika),supported by Telecom Regulatory Authority of India (TRAI) with the objective of enabling the rural women to acquire skills and knowledge which will lead to their empowerment and transformation into self employed home makers
Apply for Mandatory Free VLE CCC Examination	In order to impart basic IT training to the VLEs, the Ministry of Electronics and Information Technology (MeitY) started the Course on Computer Concepts (CCC) through the National Institute of Electronics & Information Technology (NIELIT) in 2010.
Legal Literacy Project	Legal literacy is seen as a tool to bring change at the grassroots level. The project aims to spread legal literacy and awareness related to rights by conducting sessions by gathering40 participants from neighboring areas. It also strengthens rural people so that they know and understand the primary levels of laws recognize them and challenge injustices much more forcefully.
NIELIT Services	National Institute of Electronics and Information Technology (NIELIT) is an autonomous scientific society that provides higher and professional education through non-formal sector. CSCs can provide facilitation services to the students for various courses offered by NIELIT.
NIOS Services	The National Institute of Open Schooling (NIOS) and CSC SPV joined hands to make CSCs as NIOS Facilitation Centers. Under this partnership, CSCs can promote the Open Schooling in Rural India, Register Students, Pay Registration and Examination Fee; Know the Status of Admission, and Declare Results.
Online English Speaking Course	Online English Speaking Course provides higher and professional education, skill development and vocational education to the rural community. An important component of this is the English Learning course titled 'English for Aam Aadmi', targeted for the rural youth to teach them the language in a very simple and interactive way.
Cricket Strokes (Learn Cricket Online)	Cricket Strokes helps to learn cricket online, under the mentorship of Kris Srikkanth, an ace cricketer known for his swashbuckling and aggressive batting style. This program will help budding cricketers to learn the nuances of cricket and understand the game of cricket in a structured way.
Basic Computer Course	CSC SPV has launched a new programme, "Basic Computer Course (BCC)". The programme offers basic computer training to equip a person to use computers in day-to-day life for professional and personal use.
Tally Certified Program	Tally Certified Program is a transaction service CSC has launched through Digital Seva Portal. It will be an online process, where candidate have to choose one correct answer from the given options.
Tally Kaushal Praman Patra	Candidate who is interested in Tally and wants to pursue it as career choice can opt for this course. Candidate from any background can register themselves for this course. Course Portal: csctally.in
Learn English: Certificate from British Council	AA Edutech had developed a digital learning program for learning spoken English through Cricket, jointly with the British Council. British Council will provide course completion certificate upon the candidate completing the course and scoring the minimum required marks.
ePashu Chikitsha	CSC eGovernance Services India Limited is the first entity in India to offer Animal Telemedicine facility (ePashu Chikitsa) through its vast CSC network across the country. CSC centres can now extend their helping hands to pet owners (Pashu Palak) by providing tele veterinary doctors facility in their communities.
CSC School -Multimedia Content (6th to 10th)	The objective of the project is to make CSC centers a hub for providing e-Learning Content in Video Lectures, Chapter Notes format in Hindi & English medium for the students of Class 6th-12th. www.bhagatsir.com is providing scientific learning based quality education to all students anywhere, anytime and has emerged as the first education portal providing content in Hindi & English Medium.

KHAN Academy	Khan Academy is an NGO working to provide world-class education absolutely free of cost. Anyone can visit their website and register as a student, parent or teacher and begin their learning journey.
CSC NIELIT Center	National Institute of Electronics and Information Technology (NIELIT) is an autonomous scientific society that provides higher and professional education through non-formal sector. CSCs can provide Facilitation Center for ACC, BCC, CCC, CCC+ and ECC offered by NIELIT.
NIELIT-Accreditation Center	National Institute of Electronics and Information Technology (NIELIT) is an autonomous scientific society that provides higher and professional education through non-formal sector. CSCs can provide Accreditation Centre for 'O/A/B/C' level offered by NIELIT.

E-LEGAL SERVICES	Citizens particularly in rural locations are not aware about legal entitlements which the constitution has provided. As a result of this they are trapped in various legal cases and they are also not aware with whom to discuss the matter. In order to reduce the gap and provide legal help, CSC SPV collaborated with National University of Juridical Sciences (NUJS) to provide e legal consultancy through pool of lawyers using the platform of CSCs spread across India. The service seeks to provide legal consultancy to citizens though the CSCs present in rural locations at their doorsteps.
iScholar i30 IIT-JEE 2017 1yr Online Course	CSC SPV has collaborated with iScholar i30 for providing the IIT-JEE and engineering entrance exam coaching through Apna CSC. Considered one of the toughest exams, less than 1% succeeds due to the enormous syllabus, constantly evolving paper setting patterns and ever increasing cut-off percentages.
Competitive Exam Prep-IIT/PMT/Banking (Embibe)	CSC VLEs have the chance of a lifetime to participate in selling India's best product for IIT and Medical entrance exams. This product will be available for all exams across India including Board exams. This product is the best in the country. It guarantees score improvement without study by pointing out careless mistakes and other reasons why students lose marks. This is without even increasing knowledge.

Figure 4.4 List of education services provided by government to citizens

a) Education Services

The CSC portal offers a variety of education services aimed at improving digital literacy and skill development in rural and underserved areas. Key services include Cyber gram Yojana, Women Digital Literacy Programme, E-Swavlambika, Apply for Mandatory Free VLE CCC Examination, Legal Literacy Project, NIELIT Services, NIOS Services, Online English-Speaking Course, Cricket Strokes (Learn Cricket Online), Basic Computer Course, Tally Certified Program etc. The pictorial representation of these services is given in the above figure 4.4.

b) Banking Services

The CSC portal provides an array of banking services to enhance financial inclusion, particularly in rural and underserved areas. These services include DigiPay, Pradhan Mantri Jan Dhan Yojana(PMJDY), Digital Financial Inclusion. The pictorial representation of these services is shown in the below figure 4.5.

DigitalSeva HOME CSC S

Under Reserve Bank of India guidelines for delivery of financial services through the CSCs, CSC SPV has partnered with 42 public, private sector and regional rural banks to provide banking facilities to the unbanked. To learn more, click here

List Of Banking Services

Name	Description
DigiPay	CSC-SPV has collaborated with National Payment Corporation of India (NPCI) to launch Aadhaar Enabled payment System (AePS) at all CSC locations across the country. This system is based on demographic and biometric/iris information of an individual, which eliminates the threat of any fraud and non-genuine activity
Pradhan Mantri Jan Dhan Yojana(PMJDY)	PMJDY is a National Mission on Financial Inclusion encompassing an integrated approach to bring about comprehensive financial inclusion of all the households in the country. The plan envisages universal access to banking facilities with at least one basic banking account for every household, financial literacy, access to credit, insurance and pension facility.
Digital Financial Inclusion	The project titled "Digital Finance for Rural India: Creating Awareness and Access through CSC's aims to enable the CSCs to become Digital Financial hubs, by hosting awareness sessions on government policies and digital finance options available for rural citizens as well as enabling various mechanisms of digital financial services such as such as IMPS, UPI, Bank PoS machines etc.

Figure 4.5 List of banking services provided by government to citizens

c) Business to consumer (B2C) services

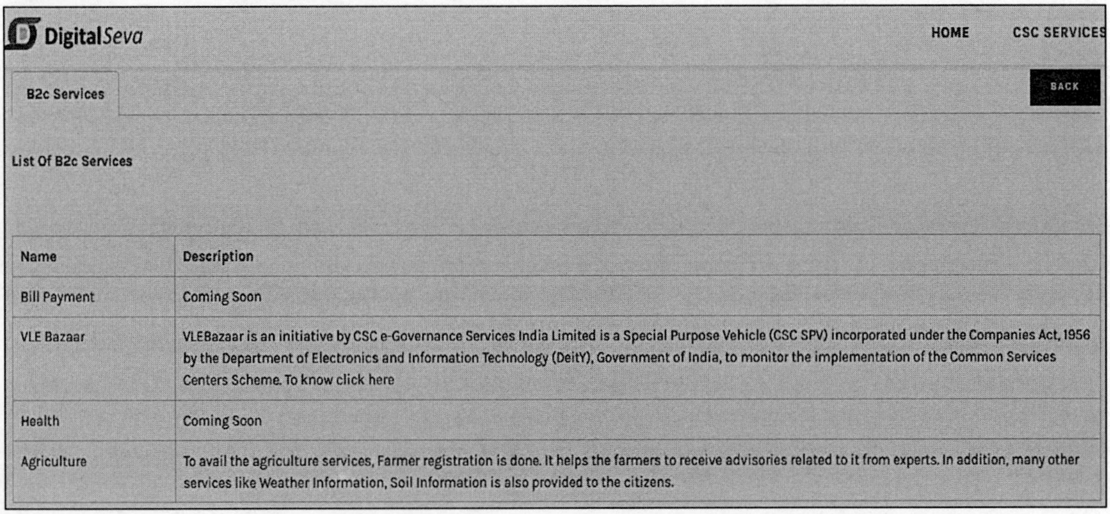

DigitalSeva HOME CSC SERVICES

B2c Services BACK

List Of B2c Services

Name	Description
Bill Payment	Coming Soon
VLE Bazaar	VLEBazaar is an initiative by CSC e-Governance Services India Limited is a Special Purpose Vehicle (CSC SPV) incorporated under the Companies Act, 1956 by the Department of Electronics and Information Technology (DeitY), Government of India, to monitor the implementation of the Common Services Centers Scheme. To know click here
Health	Coming Soon
Agriculture	To avail the agriculture services, Farmer registration is done. It helps the farmers to receive advisories related to it from experts. In addition, many other services like Weather Information, Soil Information is also provided to the citizens.

Figure 4.6 List of B2C services provided by government to citizens

The CSC (Common Service Center) portal offers a range of B2C (Business to Consumer) services designed to facilitate convenient access to various governmental and private sector services for citizens. These services include Bill Payment, VLE Bazaar, Health and Agriculture. The pictorial representation of B2C services provided by government to citizens are show in the above figure 4.6.

d) Travel services

The CSC (Common Service Center) portal offers a variety of travel-related services to cater to the needs of consumers. These include booking tickets for various modes of transport such as bus, airlines, Irctc and Hotels etc. The pictorial representation of various travel services are shown in the below figure 4.7.

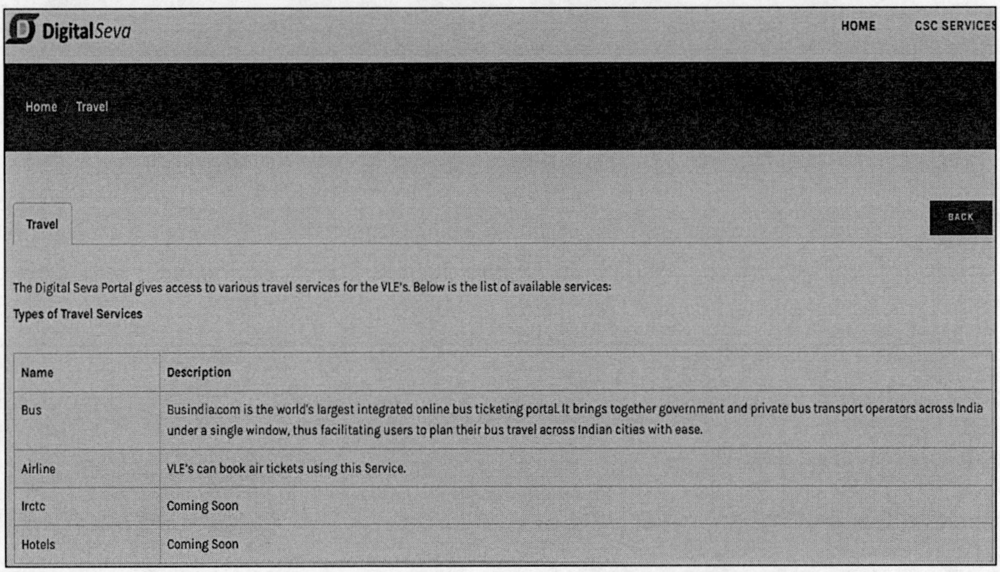

DigitalSeva HOME CSC SERVICES

Home / Travel

Travel BACK

The Digital Seva Portal gives access to various travel services for the VLE's. Below is the list of available services:

Types of Travel Services

Name	Description
Bus	Busindia.com is the world's largest integrated online bus ticketing portal. It brings together government and private bus transport operators across India under a single window, thus facilitating users to plan their bus travel across Indian cities with ease.
Airline	VLE's can book air tickets using this Service.
Irctc	Coming Soon
Hotels	Coming Soon

Figure 4.7 List of various travel services provided by government to citizens

4.3.2 eSeva

Then eSeva services accessible via https://www.e-seva.in/services.php#AEPS-Services

encompass a wide range of government-to-citizen (G2C) services aimed at streamlining access to essential public services. These include the Aadhaar Enabled Payment Service (AEPS), Money Transfer Services, Micro ATM Services, Bill Payment Services, Cash Management Solution (CMS) Services, Recharge Services, Loan Services, PAN Card Services, Fastag Services, Digital Signature Services, Travel Services, Courier Services, e-Learning Services, GST Registration & Filing Services, ITR & TDS Return Filing Services and Business License Services. The portal facilitates online submission of forms and documents for various government schemes and services, thereby reducing the need for physical visits to government offices. eSeva services aim to enhance transparency, efficiency, and convenience for citizens in their interactions with the government. The figure 4.8 given below shows various services provided through e-seva portal. Further, every services are described in brief along with its service portal screenshots.

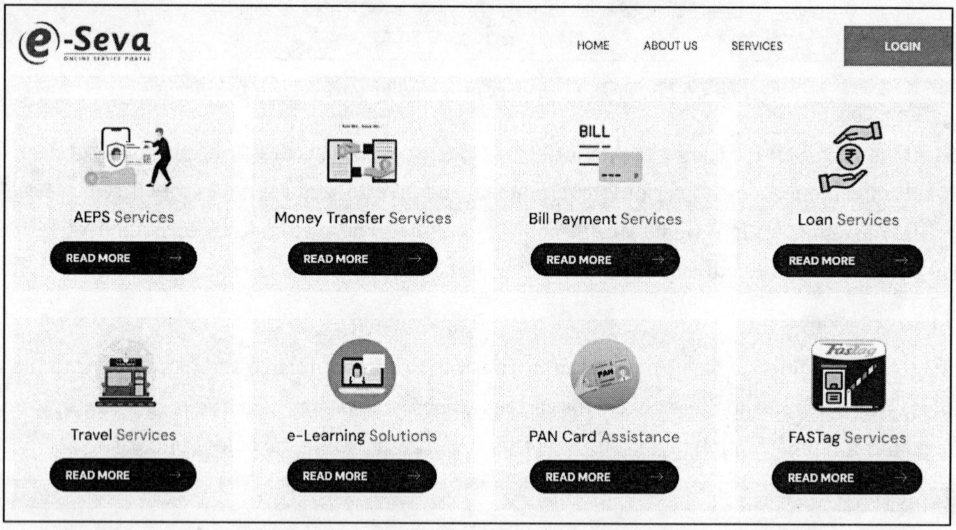

Figure 4.8 List of various services provided through eseva portal

a) Aadhar Enabled Payment Service (AEPS)

eSeva portal, provides Aadhaar Enabled Payment System (AEPS) services, which enhance financial inclusion by enabling basic banking transactions using Aadhaar authentication. The AEPS services available through eSeva include Cash Withdrawal, Cash Deposit, Balance Inquiry, Mini Statement and Fund Transfer. The APES services on eSeva portal is shown in the below figure 4.9.

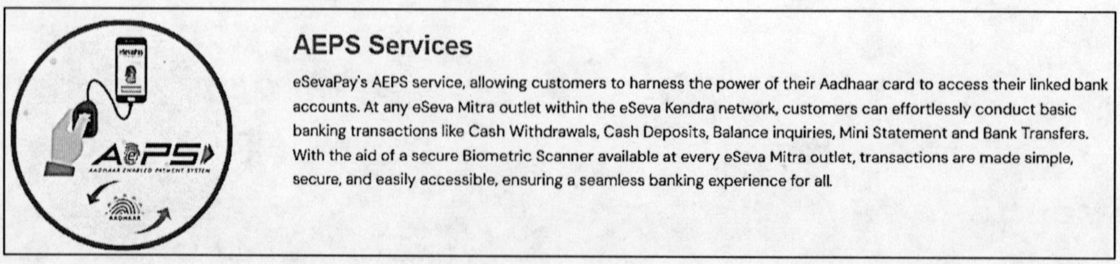

Figure 4.9 Various APES Services available on eSeva portal

b) Money Transfer Services

Money Transfer Service (MTS) offers a convenient money transfer service aimed at facilitating easy and secure financial transactions. This service allows users to transfer money between bank accounts, providing a quick and efficient way to send funds to family members, friends, or business partners. The Money Transfer service supports domestic transfers, ensuring that users can send money to various destinations with ease. The money transfer services on eSeva portal is shown below in figure 4.10.

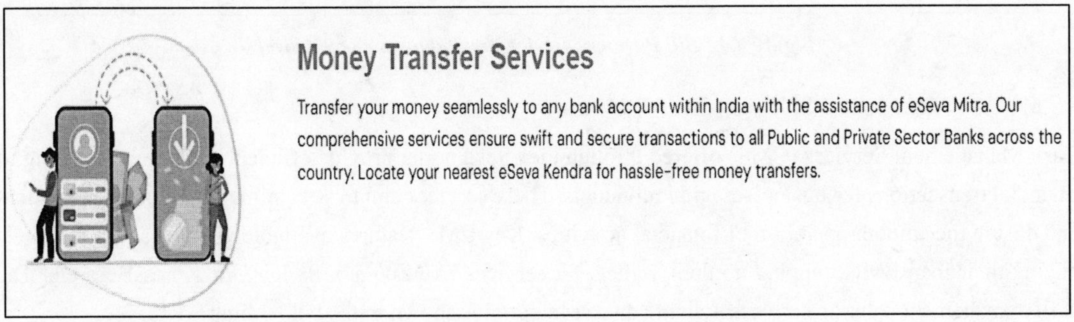

Figure 4.10 Money Transfer Services available on eSeva portal

c) Micro ATM Service

Micro ATM services offers essential banking facilities to underserved and rural areas. These services aim to enhance financial inclusion by bringing basic banking operations closer to communities with limited access to traditional bank branches. The key Micro ATM services available through the eSeva portal include Cash Withdrawal, Cash Deposit, Balance Inquiry, Mini Statement and Fund Transfer. The micro ATM services on eSeva portal is shown in the below figure 4.11.

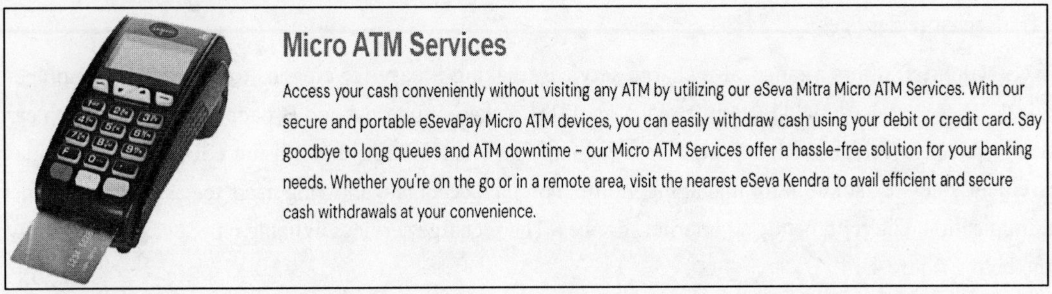

Figure 4.11 Micro ATM services available on eSeva portal

d) Bill Payment Services

Bill payment services offers comprehensive bill payment services, making it easier for citizens to manage their utility and service payments. These services provide a convenient and centralized platform for handling various types of bills, including electricity, Gas, telecom, water, credit card and FASTag recharge also. It is not only limited to these services but also provides other services such as loan repayment municipal corporation tax, insurance premium, school fee and beyond. The money transfer services on eSeva portal is shown in the below figure 4.12.

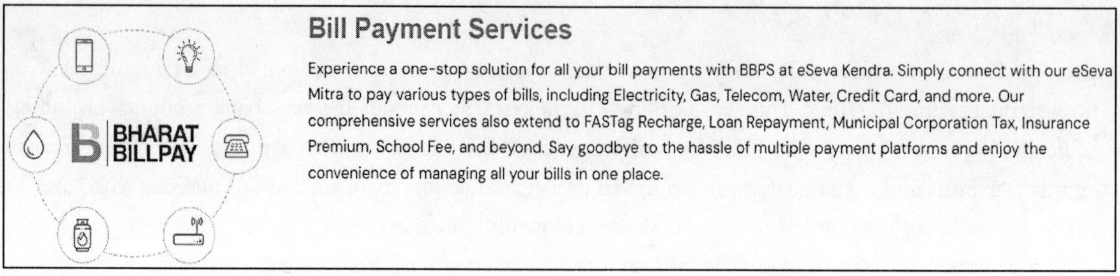

Figure 4.12 Bill Payment services available on eSeva portal

e) Cash Management Solution (CMS) Services

Cash Management Services (CMS) offered through the eSeva portal provide efficient and secure handling of financial transactions for businesses and individuals. These services aim to streamline cash flow management and ensure the smooth operation of financial activities. Key CMS features available via eSeva portal include paying their loan EMIs, topping up their wallets for services like Zomato, Swiggy, or XpressBees etc. The cash management solution serivces avilable on eSeva portal is shown in the below figure 4.13.

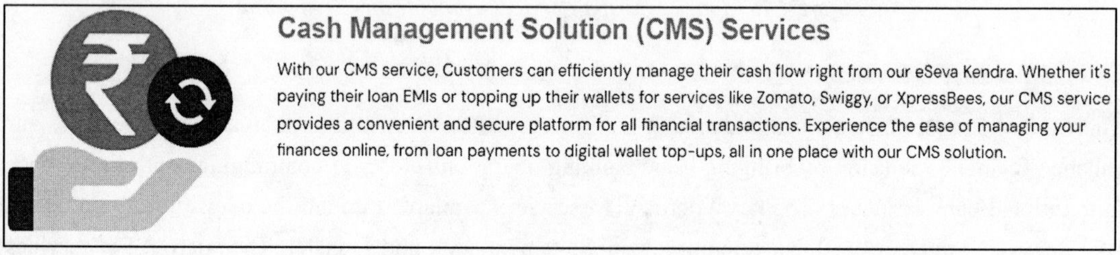

Figure 4.13 Cash management solution services available on eSeva portal

f) Recharge Services

The eSeva portal, offers a range of recharge services, making it easy for citizens to top up various prepaid services. These services include mobile recharge, DTH recharge, Internet and Broadband recharge, data card recharge, electric vehicle recharge etc.These recharge services offered through the eSeva portal provide a convenient, one-stop solution for managing multiple prepaid accounts, allowing users to easily maintain their communication, entertainment, and internet services. The recharge services avilable on eSeva portal is shown in the below figure 4.14.

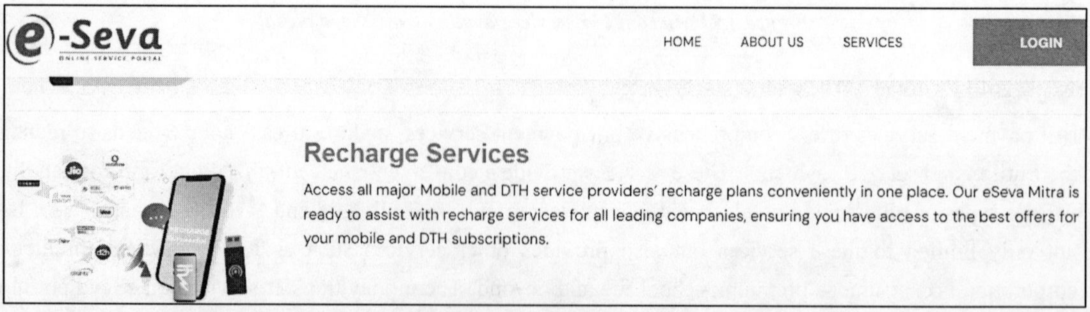

Figure 4.14 Recharge services available on eSeva portal

g) Loan services

The eSeva portal, provides access to various loan services to help individuals and businesses meet their financial needs. The loan services available on the eSeva portal include Personal Loans, Home Loans, Business Loans, Agriculture Loans, Education Loans, Vehicle Loans and Gold Loans. These loan services are facilitated through partnerships with various reputable banks/NBFCs and financial institutions, making it easier for citizens to access credit and financial support through a single, convenient platform. The loan services avilable on eSeva portal is shown in below figure 4.15.

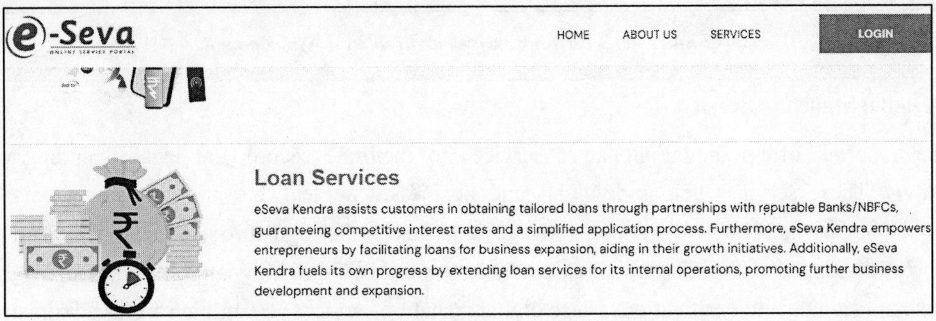

Figure 4.15 shows loan services available at eSeva portal

h) PAN Card Services

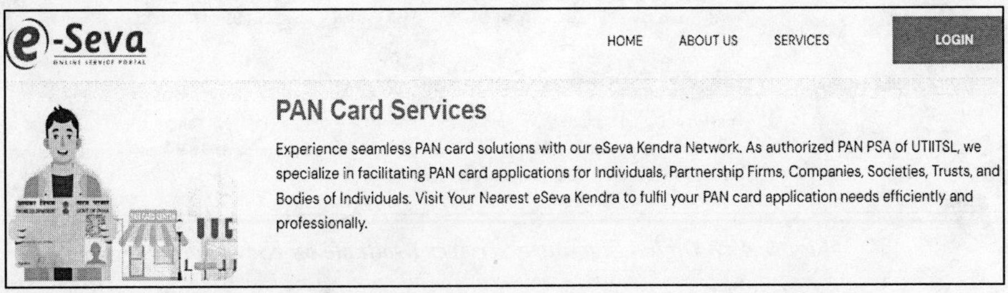

Figure 4.16 PAN card services available on eSeva portal

The eSeva portal, provides comprehensive PAN card services to facilitate the application and management of Permanent Account Numbers (PAN) for individuals and entities. The PAN card services available on the eSeva portal include new PAN card application, PAN card correction/update, duplicate PAN card, reprint of PAN card, status check and linking PAN with Aadhaar. These services simplify the process of obtaining and managing PAN cards, making it more convenient for citizens through the eSeva portal. The PAN card services is avilable on eSeva portal is shown in the above figure 4.16.

i) Fastag Services

The eSeva portal, offers a variety of FASTag services to facilitate electronic toll collection and streamline the process for vehicle owners. The FASTag services available on the eSeva portal include new Fastag issuance, Fastag recharge, replacement of Fastag, linking Fastag to bank account and customer support services related to Fastag usage. These services make it convenient for vehicle owners to obtain and manage their FASTag, ensuring a seamless and efficient toll payment experience through the eSeva portal. The below figure 4.17 shows the Fastag services available on eSeva protal.

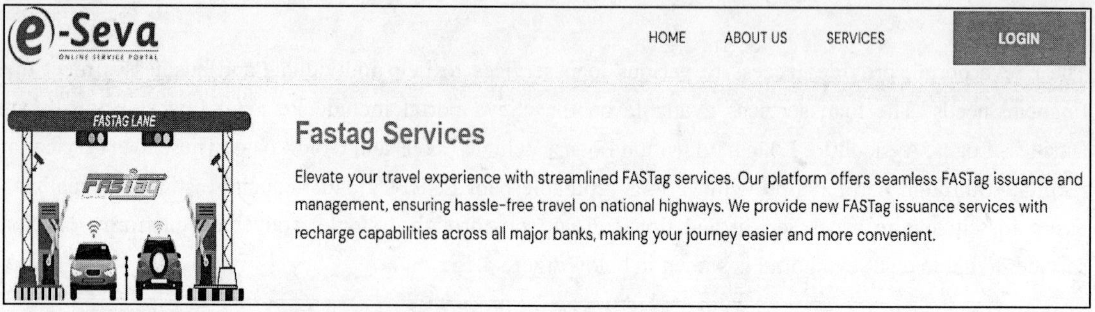

Figure 4.17 Fastag services available on eSeva portal

j) Digital Signature Service

The eSeva portal, offers digital signature services to facilitate secure and legally binding electronic transactions. These services help individuals and businesses authenticate and sign documents digitally, ensuring the integrity and authenticity of the transactions. The digital signature services available on the eSeva portal include issuance of Digital Signature Certifiate, renewal of Digital Signature Certificate, eSign services and document signing and verification. These digital signature services streamline various administrative and legal processes, enabling secure, efficient, and paperless transactions through the eSeva portal. The digital signature services available on eSeva portal is shown in the below figure 4.18.

Figure 4.18 Digital Signature Services available on eSeva portal

k) Travel Services

The eSeva portal offers a range of travel services designed to facilitate convenient travel planning and booking for citizens. The travel services available on the eSeva portal include train ticket booking, bus ticket booking, flight ticket booking, hotel booking, tour package and car rentals services. These comprehensive travel services make the eSeva portal a one-stop platform for all travel-related needs, simplifying the process of planning and booking trips for users. The travel services available on eSeva portal is shown in the below figure 4.19.

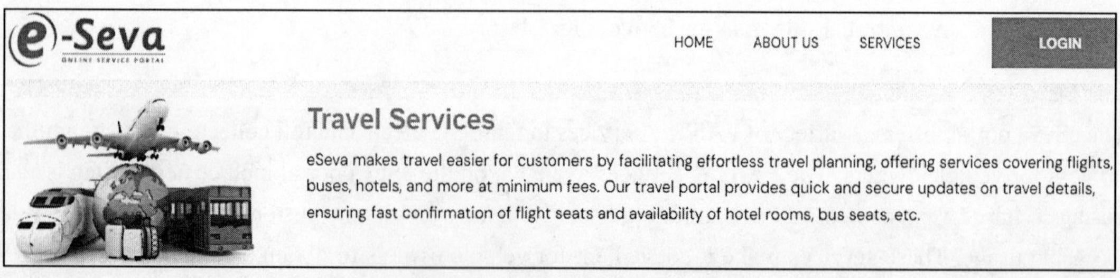

Figure 4.19 Travel services available on eSeva portal

l) Courier Services

The eSeva portal offers a variety of services, including those related to government and private sectors. However, the specific availability of courier services may vary depending on the region and the portal's updates. As of the latest information, eSeva typically provides services to the customers ensuring the timely and secure delivery of their parcels. By forming collaborations with reliable courier services, our eSeva Kendra establishes itself as the premier location for effective logistics solutions, offering satisfaction and peace of mind to both senders and recipients. The courier services available on eSeva portal is shown in the below figure 4.20.

Figure 4.20 Courier services available on eSeva portal

m) e-Learning Services

The eSeva portal offers a variety of e-learning services to support education and skill development. These services may include access to online courses and tutorials across various subjects, Digital libraries and e-books, diploma and certificate courses on web designing, entrepreneur development, online examinations, e-learning modules for comepetitive exam preparation and many more. The e-learning services available on eSeva portal is shown in the below figure 4.21.

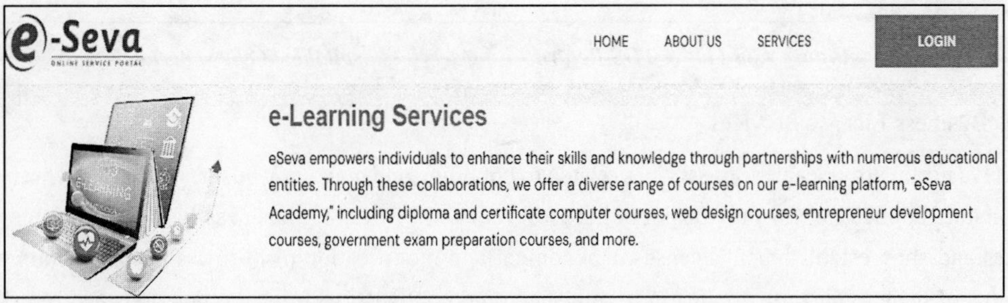

Figure 4.21 E-learning services available on eSeva portal

n) GST Registration & Filing Services

The eSeva portal provides various GST (Goods and Services Tax) related services to assist businesses and individuals in complying with tax regulations. These services may include GST registration for new businesses, filing of GST returns (monthly, quarterly, and annual), amendment and cancellation of GST registration, assistance with GST payments, generation of e-way bills, GST compliance and advisory services and access to GST-related forms and documents. The GST registration & filing services available on eSeva protal is shown in the below figure 4.22.

Figure 4.22 GST Registration Filing Services available on eSeva portal

o) ITR & TDS Return Filing Services

The eSeva portal offers various services related to Income Tax Return (ITR) and Tax Deducted at Source (TDS) filing to assist individuals and businesses in meeting their tax obligations. These services may include filing of Income Tax Returns (ITR) for individuals, businesses, and other entities, assistance with TDS return filing, generation and submission of TDS certificates (Form 16/16A), correction of TDS returns, calculation of tax liabilities, tax planning and advisory services, access to relevant tax forms and documentation. The ITR & TDS return filing services available on eSeva protal is shown in the below figure 4.23.

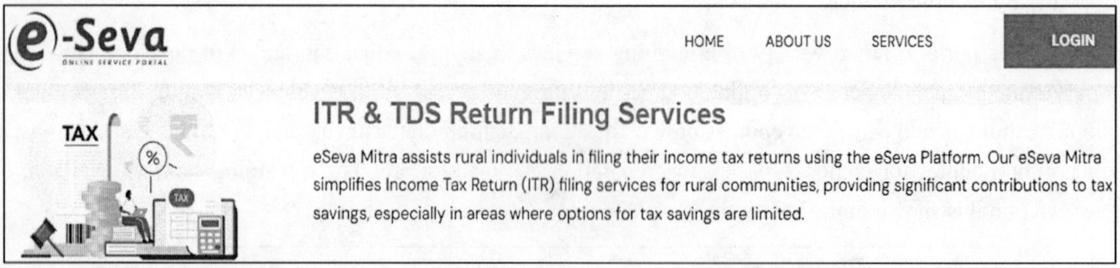

Figure 4.23 ITR & TDS Return Filing services available at eSeva portal

p) Business License Services

The eSeva portal provides various services related to obtaining and managing business licenses. These services may include application for new business licenses, renewal of existing business licenses, issuance of trade licenses and shop establishment licenses, amendment and modification of business license details, tracking the status of business license applications, guidance on compliance with local regulations and requirements, access to relevant forms and documentation. The business license services available at eSeva protal is shown in the below figure 4.24.

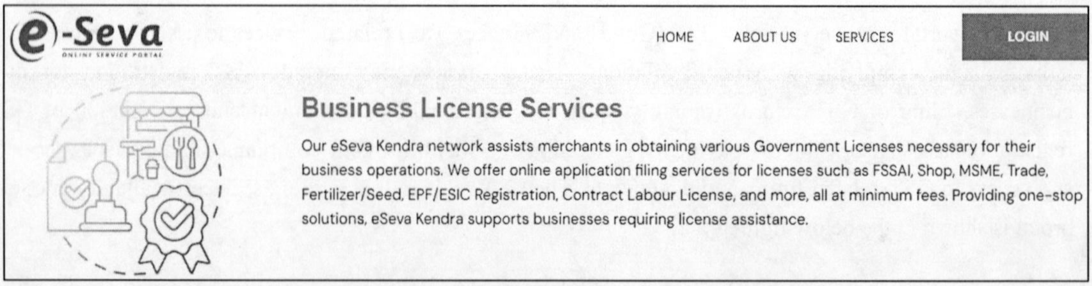

Figure 4.24 shows Business License Services available at eSeva portal

4.3.3 Post office

Post offices offer a variety of services beyond just mailing letters and packages. Here are some common services provided by post offices.

a) Mail Services

- *Standard Mail:* Sending letters, postcards, and parcels domestically and internationally.
- *Registered Mail:* Provides proof of mailing and delivery.
- *Speed Post:* Fast and reliable express delivery service.
- *Parcel Services:* Sending large packages, with options for both domestic and international shipping.
- *Bulk Mail:* For businesses sending large volumes of mail.

The mail services provided by post office is shown in the below figure 4.25

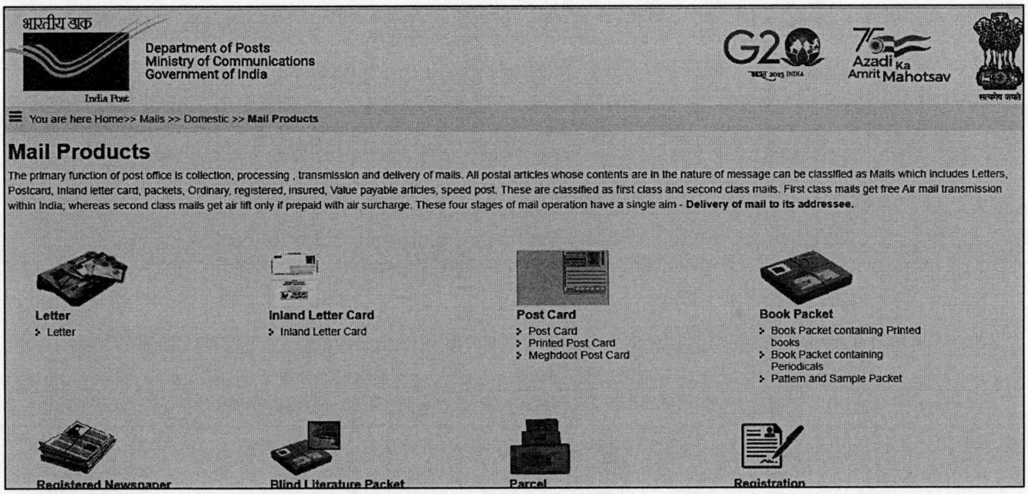

Figure 4.25 Mail services provided on post office portal

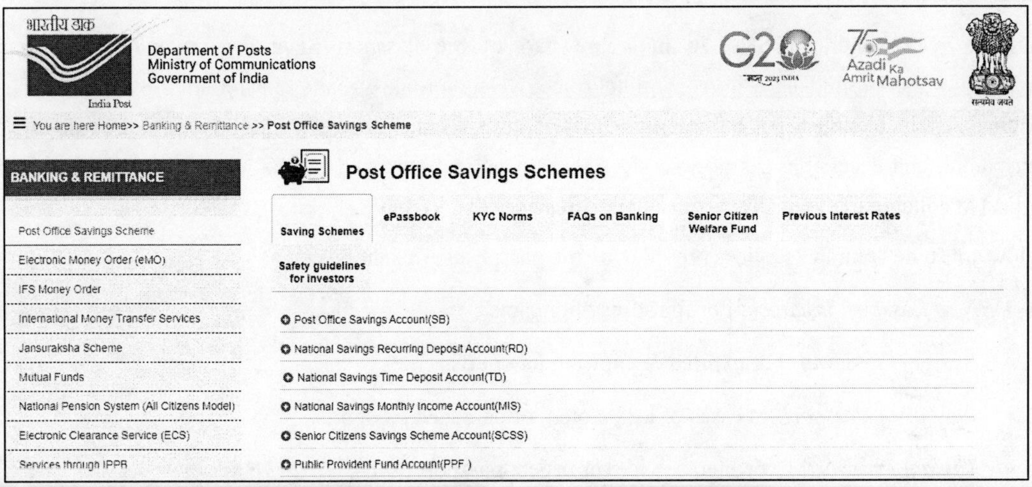

Figure 4.26 (a) Various financial services provided on post office portal

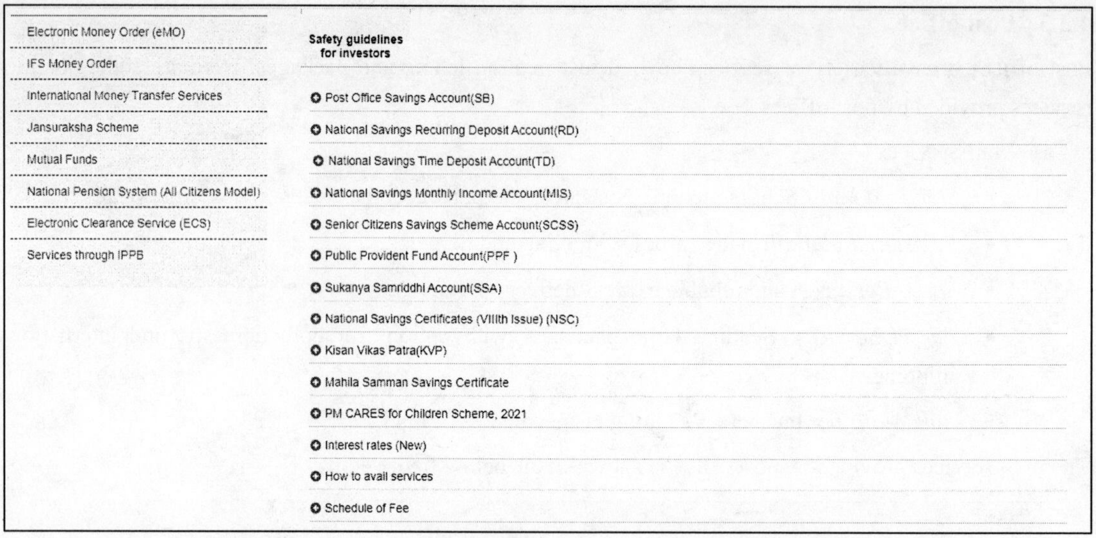

Figure 4.26 (b) Various financial services provided on post office portal

b) Financial Services

- *Savings Accounts:* Various types of savings accounts with different interest rates and terms.
- *Recurring Deposits:* Fixed monthly deposits for a specified period.
- *Fixed Deposits:* Lump sum deposits for a fixed period with higher interest rates.
- *Money Orders:* Sending money securely to individuals domestically and internationally.
- *Postal Life Insurance:* Insurance policies offering life coverage.

The various financial services proided by post office have been shown in the figure 4.26(a) and 4.26(b) respectively.

4.3.4 Passport Seva Kendra

Passport Seva Kendras (PSKs) in India are part of the Passport Seva Project and accessed using https://www.passportindia.gov.in/AppOnlineProject/welcomeLink website, an initiative by the Ministry of External Affairs to streamline and improve the passport issuance process. Its purpose is to provide efficient, transparent, and accessible passport services to citizens and managed by the Ministry of External Affairs (MEA) in collaboration with Tata Consultancy Services (TCS), India.

Below are some common services provided by the passport seva kendra.

- *New Passport Issuance:* For first-time applicants.
- *Passport Renewal:* For expired or expiring passports.
- *Reissue of Passport:* In cases of lost, stolen, or damaged passports.
- *Tatkaal Passport:* Expedited service for urgent passport needs.

- *Miscellaneous Services:* Including name change, address change, addition of spouse name, and others.

a) *New Passport Issuance:* The new passport issuance service by Passport Seva Kendras (PSKs) in India is designed to facilitate the application and issuance of passports for first-time applicants. Here's a detailed guide on how to apply for a new passport. Figure 4.27 shows the passport seva portal.

Step-by-Step Process for new passport issuance are as follows:

Online Registration

- *Visit the Passport Seva Portal:* Go to Passport Seva Portal.
- *Create an Account:* Register as a new user by providing your details and creating a username and password.
- *Login:* Use your credentials to log in to the portal.

Filling the Application Form

- *Apply for Fresh Passport:* Select the option to apply for a new passport.
- *Fill Out the Form:* Complete the application form with accurate personal details, address, and other required information.
- *Save and Review:* Save your progress and review the information for any errors.

Payment of Fees

- *Calculate Fees:* The fees for a new passport depend on the type of passport (e.g., normal or Tatkaal) and the number of pages (36 or 60).
- *Online Payment:* Pay the fees online using a credit/debit card, internet banking, or SBI bank challan.

Booking an Appointment

- *Schedule an Appointment:* Select a convenient date and time for your visit to the nearest PSK or Post Office Passport Seva Kendra (POPSK).
- *Appointment Confirmation:* You will receive a confirmation of your appointment along with an appointment number.

Figure 4.27 Passport Seva Portal

Visiting the Passport Seva Kendra

- *Documents Preparation:* Prepare a set of required documents along with their photocopies. Common documents include:
- *Proof of Address* (e.g., Aadhar card, voter ID, utility bills)
- *Proof of Date of Birth* (e.g., birth certificate, school leaving certificate)
- *Identity Proof* (e.g., Aadhar card, PAN card, voter ID)
- *Appointment Receipt:* Bring the printout of your appointment receipt.
- *Arrival:* Arrive at the PSK/POPSK at least 15-30 minutes before your appointment time at the Passport Seva Kendra
- *Token Issuance:* On arrival, you will receive a token.
- *Verification:* Proceed to the verification counters where your documents will be checked.
- *Biometric Data:* Your photograph and fingerprints will be captured.
- Application Submission: Submit your application form along with the verified documents.

Police Verification

- *Initiation:* After submission, the police verification process is initiated.

- *Verification Process:* A police officer will visit your residence to verify your address and other details.
- *Completion:* Ensure you provide accurate information to expedite the verification.

Passport Issuance

- *Processing:* Once verification is complete, your application will be processed.
- *Dispatch:* The passport is printed and dispatched to your address via registered post.
- *Tracking:* You can track the status of your application on the Passport Seva Portal.

b) Passport Renewal: The Passport Seva Kendra (PSK) in India also offers passport renewal services. Here is a general steps for passport renewal process.

Register and Login:

- Visit the Passport Seva website.
- Register using a valid email ID.
- Login to the portal with your credentials.

Application Form:

- Select the "Apply for Fresh Passport/Re-issue of Passport" option.
- Fill out the application form with accurate details.
- Select the type of passport (ordinary, diplomatic, official) and the type of application (normal, tatkal).

Pay the Fee:

- Calculate the fee based on the passport type and application type.
- Pay the fee online using the available payment options (credit/debit card, internet banking).

Schedule an Appointment:

- Schedule an appointment at your nearest PSK.
- Choose a convenient date and time from the available slots.

Visit PSK:

- Visit the PSK at the scheduled appointment time.
- Carry the printout of the appointment confirmation, original passport, and other required documents (such as address proof, identity proof, etc.).

Document Verification:

- At the PSK, your documents will be verified.
- Biometric data (fingerprints and photograph) will be captured.

Police Verification:

- For most renewals, police verification may be required.
- The police will visit your residence to verify your details.

Passport Issuance:

- Once the verification is complete, the renewed passport will be printed and dispatched.
- You can track the status of your application online through the Passport Seva portal.

Documents Required for renewal of passport

- Original passport and a self-attested photocopy.
- Address proof (Aadhar card, utility bills, etc.).
- Proof of date of birth.
- Marriage certificate (if applicable).
- Other relevant documents as specified during the application process.

c) Re-issue of passport: The passport reissue service provided by Passport Seva Kendra (PSK) in India covers the renewal of passports that are about to expire or have expired, as well as the reissue of passports for various other reasons such as change in personal details, exhaustion of pages, etc. The below figure 4.28 shows the re-issue of passport on passport seva portal.

Here are the steps for Passport reissue.

Register and Login:

- Visit the Passport Seva website.
- Register using a valid email ID and create a login.
- Log in to the portal with your credentials.

Application Form:

- Click on "Apply for Fresh Passport/Re-issue of Passport".
- Fill out the application form with accurate details.
- Select the type of passport (ordinary, diplomatic, official) and the reason for reissue (e.g., expiry, change in details, etc.).

Pay the Fee:

- Calculate the fee based on the type of passport and application.
- Pay the fee online using the available payment options (credit/debit card, internet banking).

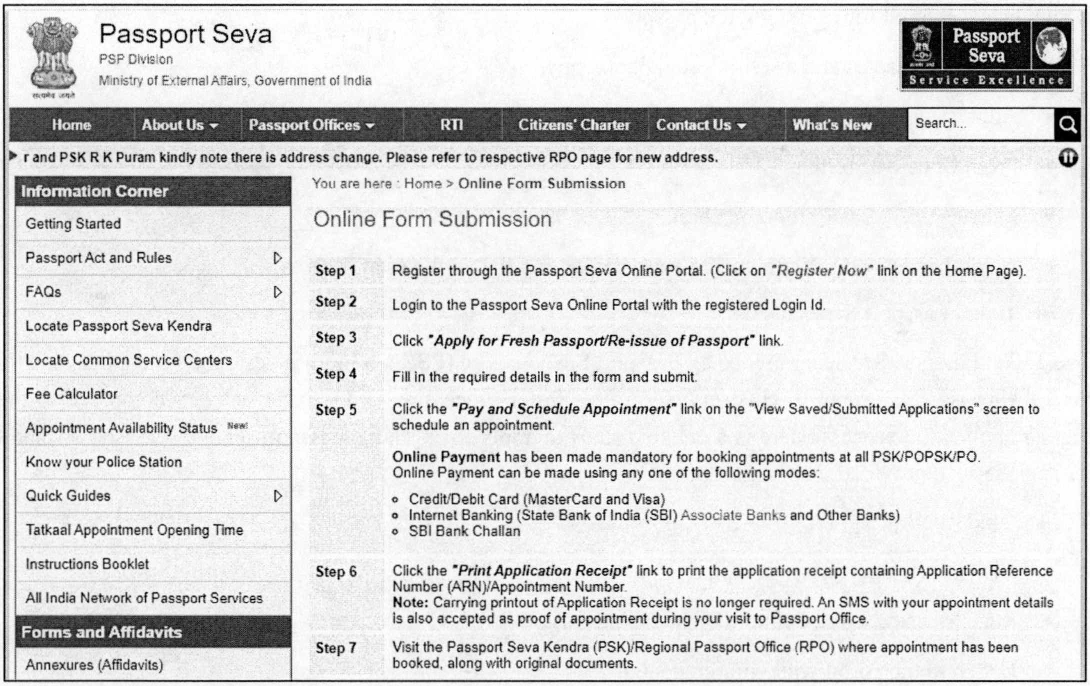

Figure 4.28 Re-issue of passport on passport seva portal

Schedule an Appointment:

- Schedule an appointment at your nearest PSK.
- Choose a convenient date and time from the available slots.

Visit PSK:

- Visit the PSK at the scheduled appointment time.
- Carry the printout of the appointment confirmation, your current passport, and other required documents (such as address proof, identity proof, etc.).

Document Verification:

- At the PSK, your documents will be verified.
- Biometric data (fingerprints and photograph) will be captured.

Police Verification:

- For most reissue applications, police verification may be required.
- The police will visit your residence to verify your details.

Passport Issuance:

- Once the verification is complete, the reissued passport will be printed and dispatched.
- You can track the status of your application online through the Passport Seva portal.

Documents Required for re-issuing the passport

- Original passport and a self-attested photocopy.
- Address proof (Aadhar card, utility bills, etc.).
- Proof of date of birth.
- Marriage certificate (if applicable).
- Any other relevant documents as specified during the application process.

d) Tatkal Passport Service

The Tatkal Passport Service provided by Passport Seva Kendra (PSK) in India is designed for applicants who need their passports urgently. This service ensures faster processing and quicker delivery compared to the regular application process. Here is a detailed steps to apply for a Tatkal passport. Figure 4.29 shows tatkal passport service provided on passport portal.

Register and Login:

- Visit the Passport Seva website.
- Register using a valid email ID and create a login.
- Log in to the portal with your credentials.

Application Form:

- Click on "Apply for Fresh Passport/Re-issue of Passport".
- Fill out the application form with accurate details.
- Select the type of passport (ordinary) and choose the "Tatkal" option under the type of application.

Pay the Fee:

- Calculate the fee for the Tatkal application, which is higher than the normal application.
- Pay the fee online using the available payment options (credit/debit card, internet banking).

Schedule an Appointment:

- Schedule an appointment at your nearest PSK.
- Choose a convenient date and time from the available slots. Tatkal appointments are given priority, and you might get an earlier slot.

Visit PSK:

- Visit the PSK at the scheduled appointment time.
- Carry the printout of the appointment confirmation, your current passport (if reissuing), and other required documents (such as address proof, identity proof, etc.).

Document Verification:

- At the PSK, your documents will be verified.
- Biometric data (fingerprints and photograph) will be captured.

Police Verification:

- For Tatkal applications, police verification may be done before or after passport issuance. In some cases, the verification is expedited.
- The police may visit your residence to verify your details.

Passport Issuance:

- Once the verification is complete, the Tatkal passport will be printed and dispatched.
- You can track the status of your application online through the Passport Seva portal.

Documents Required for Tatkal Passport

- Original passport and a self-attested photocopy (for reissue).
- Address proof (Aadhar card, utility bills, etc.).
- Proof of date of birth.
- Identity proof (Aadhar card, PAN card, etc.).
- Annexure E (an affidavit as per the prescribed format).
- Additional documents (as specified during the application process).

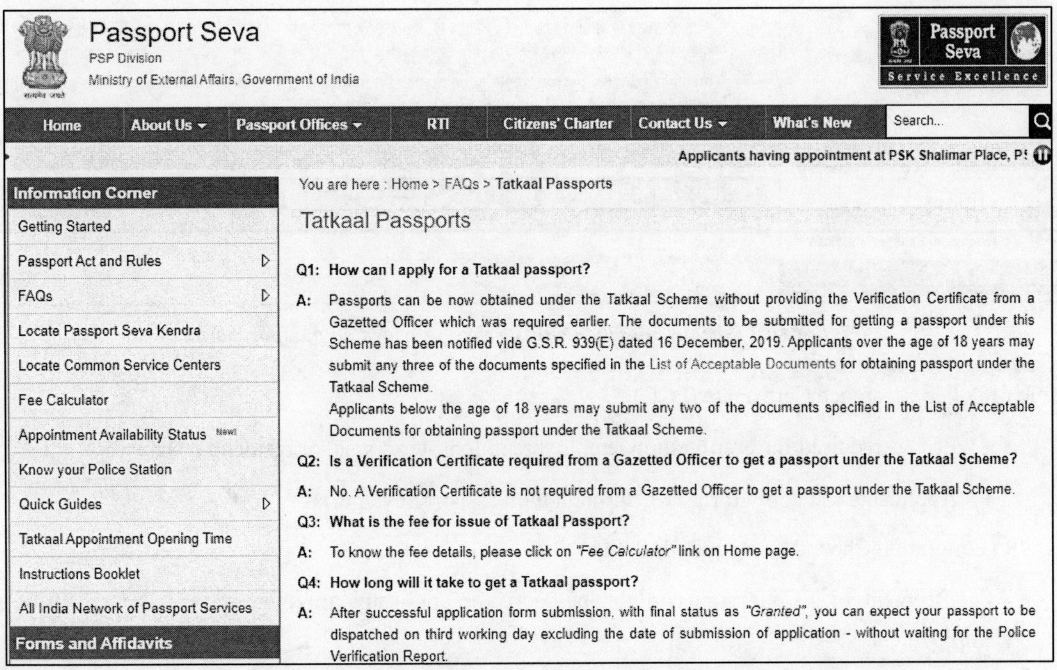

Figure 4.29 Tatkal passport service on passport portal

e) Miscellaneous Services

Passport Seva Kendras (PSKs) in India offer a variety of miscellaneous services apart from issuing and renewing passports. These services cater to different needs of passport holders and applicants. Here is an overview of the miscellaneous services provided by PSKs. Figure 4.29 shows the various miscellaneous services provided on passport seva kendra portal.

Change in existing Personal Particulars

- Change or correction in name, date of birth, address, or other personal details.
- Adding spouse's name or child's name in the passport.
- Change in appearance.

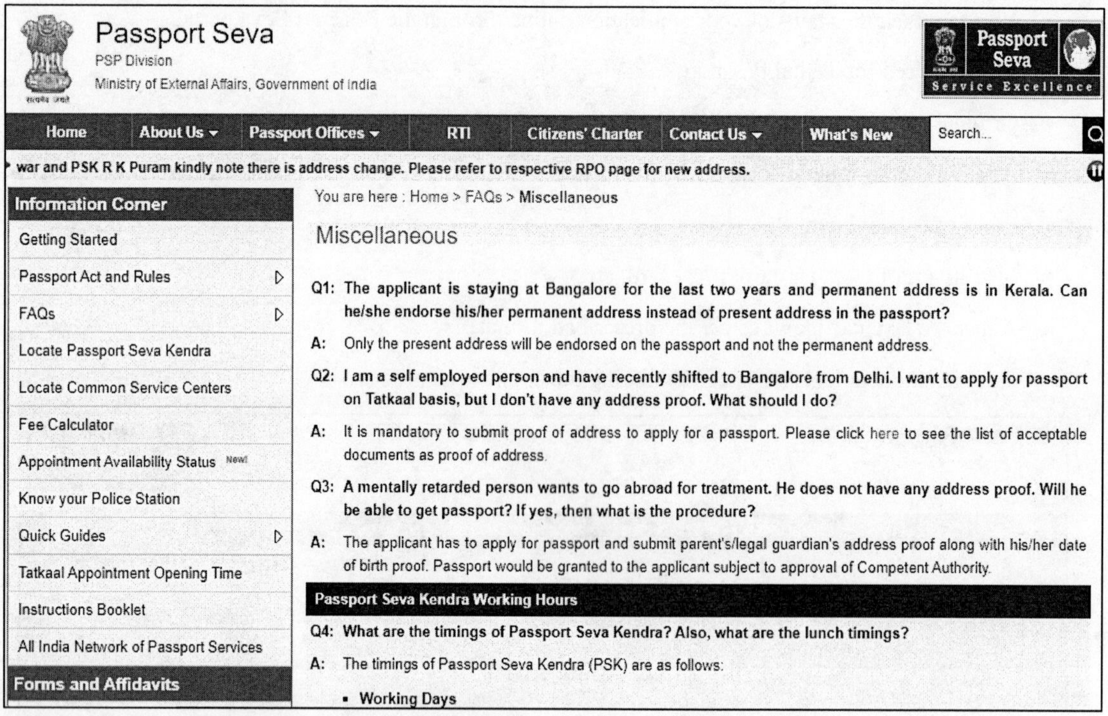

Figure 4.30 Various miscellaneous services provided on passport portal

Issue of Police Clearance Certificate (PCC)

- PCC is required for immigration, employment, long-term visa, or residential status.
- Applicants can apply for a PCC through the Passport Seva portal.

ECNR (Emigration Check Not Required) Status

- Endorsement of ECNR status in the passport for applicants traveling to specific countries for employment.
- Removing ECR (Emigration Check Required) status from the passport.

Lost/Damaged Passport:

- Reissue of passport in case it is lost or damaged.
- Necessary documents and police report might be required.

Passport for Minors:

- Issuance or renewal of passports for children below 18 years of age.
- Special procedures and documents are required for minor applicants.

Additional Booklet:

- Issuance of an additional booklet if the pages in the current passport are exhausted. A separate application is needed for the additional booklet.

Cancellation of Passport:

- Cancellation of passport for various reasons such as acquiring foreign nationality, surrendering Indian citizenship, etc.

UNIT SUMMARY

This chapter delves into India's e-Governance initiatives and their impact on citizens, focusing on various projects that have significantly transformed public service delivery. It begins by examining the National e-Governance Plan (NeGP), which laid the foundation for digitizing governmental processes. Key initiatives such as Government to Citizen (G2C), Government to Business (G2B), and Government to Government (G2G) are highlighted, showcasing how these efforts have streamlined interactions between the government and its stakeholders. The chapter also discusses Mission Mode Projects (MMPs), both at the central and state levels, and how they contribute to India's e-Governance landscape. It further explores recent initiatives, including the government's push towards m-Governance, which leverages mobile technology to reach a broader audience. Through case studies like Akshaya (Kerala), KAVERI (Karnataka), and Lokvani (Uttar Pradesh), the chapter illustrates best practices in managing e-Governance projects across different states. These examples provide valuable insights into the challenges and successes of implementing e-Governance in diverse contexts. Finally, the chapter emphasizes the importance of practical exposure through visits to local e-Governance sites such as Common Service Centers (CSC), eSeva, Post Offices, and Passport Seva Kendras. These visits help students and practitioners understand the on-ground realities and the impact of these initiatives on daily life.

EXERCISES

Q1 What is the primary objective of the National e-Governance Plan (NeGP)?

1) Improve infrastructure in rural areas
2) Promote e-commerce in India
3) Make all government services accessible to the common man through electronic media
4) Enhance private sector participation in governance

Q2 Which of the following is an example of a Government to Citizen (G2C) initiative?

1) GST Network
2) e-Procurement Exchange
3) Passport Seva Kendra
4) e-Biz portal

Q3 What is the focus of Government to Business (G2B) initiatives?

1) Providing subsidies to businesses
2) Facilitating interactions between the government and businesses
3) Training employees in government offices
4) Promoting exports through government channels

Q4 Which initiative is primarily targeted towards improving inter-governmental processes?

1) G2C initiatives
2) G2B initiatives
3) G2G initiatives
4) m-Governance initiatives

Q5 What are Mission Mode Projects (MMPs)?

1) Projects aimed at reducing government expenditure
2) Specific e-Governance projects focused on a particular sector or department
3) Projects to promote digital literacy
4) Initiatives to increase foreign investment in India

Q6 Which state government initiative is known as Akshaya?

1) Andhra Pradesh
2) Kerala
3) Gujarat
4) Karnataka

Q7 The KAVERI initiative by the Karnataka Government focuses on which area?

1) Education
2) Land records management
3) IT dissemination
4) Healthcare

Q8 Which state government launched the e-Procurement Exchange initiative?

1) Tamil Nadu
2) Madhya Pradesh

3) Andhra Pradesh

4) Uttar Pradesh

Q9 What is the focus of the Nagarpalika initiative by the Gujarat Government?

1) Rural development

2) Urban governance

3) Agricultural marketing

4) Citizen empowerment

Q10 Which initiative in Madhya Pradesh is aimed at e-Agricultural Marketing?

1) Lokvani

2) Tamilnilam

3) e-Kosh

4) EKVI

Q11 The Lokvani initiative by the Uttar Pradesh Government is focused on:

1) Empowering government employees

2) Empowering citizens

3) Enhancing business relations

4) Improving inter-governmental communication

Q12 Which state's government launched the Tamilnilam project?

1) Karnataka

2) Tamil Nadu

3) Kerala

4) Maharashtra

Q13 What is the main purpose of the e-Kosh initiative in Chhattisgarh?

1) Education management

2) Treasury department computerization

3) Healthcare services

4) Land records digitization

Q14 Which of the following is an example of m-Governance?

1) Digital India portal

2) Common Service Centers (CSC)

3) Mobile-based services provided by the government

4) Passport Seva Kendra

Q15 What is the primary function of a Common Service Center (CSC)?

1) Provide healthcare services
2) Facilitate access to various e-Governance services for citizens
3) Act as a postal office
4) Manage land records

Answers

Q.N.	1	2	3	4	5	6	7	8	9	10	11	12	13	14	15
Option	C	C	B	C	B	B	B	C	B	D	B	B	B	C	B

Short Answer Type Questions

1. What is the National e-Governance Plan (NeGP)?
2. What are Government to Citizen (G2C) initiatives?
3. How do Government to Business (G2B) initiatives benefit the business community?
4. What are Mission Mode Projects (MMPs) under NeGP?
5. What are State Mission Mode Projects (State MMPs)?
6. What is the significance of Integrated Mission Mode Projects (IMMPs)?
7. What role does m-Governance play in the Indian context?
8. What is the Akshaya project, and how does it impact citizens?
9. How has the KAVERI project in Karnataka improved government services?
10. What is the Lokvani initiative, and how does it empower citizens?
11. What is the e-Kosh project in Chhattisgarh?
12. What are Common Service Centers (CSCs), and what role do they play in e-Governance?
13. How does the Passport Seva Kendra (PSK) enhance e-Governance?
14. What is the significance of the Nagarpalika project in Gujarat?
15. What is the focus of the Tamilnilam project in Tamil Nadu?

Long Answer Type Questions

1. Describe the objectives and key components of the National e-Governance Plan (NeGP). How has NeGP contributed to the transformation of public services in India?
2. Discuss various Government to Citizen (G2C) initiatives implemented under the NeGP. How have these initiatives improved the accessibility and efficiency of government services for citizens?

3. Analyze the role of Government to Business (G2B) initiatives in enhancing the business environment in India. How do these initiatives streamline interactions between businesses and the government?
4. Examine the concept of Government to Government (G2G) initiatives within the framework of e-Governance in India. How do G2G initiatives facilitate better coordination and efficiency among various government departments?
5. Evaluate the significance of Central Government initiatives as Mission Mode Projects (MMPs) under the NeGP. How do these projects aim to achieve the goals of e-Governance?
6. Discuss the importance of State Mission Mode Projects in the context of the NeGP. How do these projects address state-specific needs, and what challenges do they face in implementation?
7. What are Integrated Mission Mode Projects, and how do they differ from other MMPs? Discuss their role in achieving cross-sectoral objectives in e-Governance.
8. Review recent initiatives in e-Governance by the Government of India, particularly in the area of m-Governance. How do these initiatives leverage mobile technology to improve service delivery?
9. Provide a detailed analysis of the Akshaya Project in Kerala as a case study of successful e-Governance implementation. What were the objectives, challenges, and outcomes of this project?
10. Describe the KAVERI project in Karnataka and its significance in land registration and property management. How has e-Governance improved these processes?
11. Discuss the implementation of the e-Procurement Exchange for the Government of Andhra Pradesh. How has this project streamlined procurement processes? What challenges were faced, and how were they overcome?
12. Analyze the role of the Nagarpalika initiative in Gujarat in improving urban governance. How has this project leveraged e-Governance to enhance service delivery at the municipal level?
13. Examine the e-Agricultural Marketing (EKVI) initiative by the Madhya Pradesh Government. How has it transformed agricultural marketing and benefited farmers? Discuss the challenges and successes of this project.
14. Describe the Lokvani project in Uttar Pradesh and its efforts to empower citizens through e-Governance. What services does it provide, and how has it improved transparency and accountability in governance?
15. Evaluate the Tamilnilam project in Tamil Nadu, focusing on the computerization of land records. How has this initiative improved the accuracy and accessibility of land records for citizens?
16. Discuss the e-Kosh project in Chhattisgarh, focusing on the computerization of the treasury department. How has this project enhanced financial management and transparency in the state government?
17. Explain the role of Common Service Centers (CSC) in promoting e-Governance at the grassroots level. How do CSCs contribute to bridging the digital divide and providing essential services to rural areas?

18. Analyze the impact of the eSeva initiative in enhancing service delivery in various states. How does it integrate different government services into a single platform?
19. Discuss the role of Post Offices in India's e-Governance framework. How are traditional postal services being modernized to include digital services? What is the significance of this transformation for rural and remote areas?
20. Examine the Passport Seva Kendra initiative as a model of efficient service delivery through e-Governance. How has it improved the passport application and issuance process? Discuss the key features and outcomes of this initiative.

Dynamic QR code for futher readings

REFERENCES AND SUGGESTED READING

1. Gupta, R. K. (2023), "E-Governance in India: A Comprehensive Guide", Sage Publications India
2. Yadav, S. N. (2023), "Digital Governance and Development: Indian Perspectives", Routledge India
3. Rao, M. P. and Kumar, V. S. (2022), "Case Studies in Indian E-Governance: Lessons and Best Practices", Springer
4. Sharma, A. R. (2022), "Managing E-Governance Projects in India: Success Stories and Challenges", Cambridge University Press.
5. Desai, P. B. and Patel, N. S. (2021), "Local E-Governance Models in India: An Analytical Study", Oxford University Press
6. Metha, R. A. (2023), "Digital India: Innovations and Impact on Governance", Sage Publications.
7. Prasad, S. K. (2022), "E-Governance and Citizen Engagement in India: A Study", Routledge India
8. Singh A. J. and Verma M. N. (2023), "Transforming Public Services: E-Governance Initiatives in Indian States", Springer
9. Sharma, K. R. (2022), "E-Governance in India: From Concept to Practice", Cambridge University Press

5 Evaluation of e-governance Projects

UNIT SPECIFIES

Through this unit we discuss the following aspects:

- *Primarily evaluation of e-governance projects*
- *Preparing mini project report by students*

RATIONALE

The unit focuses on evaluating diverse e-governance projects to assess their effectiveness in improving government services and citizen engagement. By examining national initiatives like Aadhaar and Digital India, and state-level projects such as Bhoomi and e-District, students can analyze the impact of digital transformation on service delivery, transparency, and efficiency. This evaluation helps identify best practices and challenges, offering insights into enhancing e-governance systems and fostering better public administration.

PRE-REQUESITE

None

UNIT OUTCOMES

After the completion of this unit the students will be able to:

U5-O1: Evaluate the various national and state level e-governance project's success

U5-O2: Understand the practical experience of project evaluation

U5-O3: Perform report writing and presentation skills.

U5-O4: Prepare the project report on the various e-government projects as per stated guidelines.

Unit-5 Outcomes	Expected Mapping with Programme Outcomes *(1- Weak Correlation; 2- Medium correlation; 3- Strong Correlation)*					
	CO-1	**CO-2**	**CO-3**	**CO-4**	**CO-5**	**CO-6**
U5-O1	2	1	2	1	2	1
U5-O2	1	1	1	1	1	2
U5-O3	1	1	1	1	1	2
U5-O4	1	1	1	1	1	3

5.1 Primarily evaluation of various e-governance projects

Evaluating e-governance projects is essential for understanding their effectiveness, efficiency, and overall impact on governance and public services. There are various factors, including usability, effectiveness, accountability, transparency, impact assessment, user satisfaction, and sustainability, can be taken into consideration while evaluating a project. Let's examine each of these characteristics individually in this section.

One of the primary criteria for evaluation is usability. This encompasses how user-friendly the interface is and how easily users can navigate the system. A well-designed user interface is crucial for encouraging adoption and frequent use among citizens. Evaluators often conduct user satisfaction surveys and usability testing to gauge how intuitive and accessible the system is. High usability can significantly enhance the user experience, leading to increased public trust and engagement with the platform.

Another critical criterion is efficiency, which includes the system's ability to process tasks quickly and accurately. Efficiency can be measured by examining the time taken to complete various processes, such as submitting applications, retrieving information, or processing payments. This aspect also involves evaluating the system's uptime and reliability, as frequent downtimes or errors can deter users. Performance metrics, such as transaction times and system response times, provide valuable insights into the operational efficiency of the e-governance project. Efficient systems reduce the workload on government staff and provide quicker services to the public, thus improving overall service delivery.

Transparency and accountability are also fundamental in evaluating e-governance projects. These systems should make government processes more transparent, providing citizens with clear information about procedures, requirements, and status updates. Transparency is often enhanced through features like real-time tracking, public dashboards, and clear communication channels. Additionally, accountability mechanisms, such as audit trails and user feedback systems, help ensure that government actions are traceable and that any misconduct can be identified and addressed promptly. These features build public trust and encourage responsible governance.

Impact assessment is another crucial component of evaluating e-governance projects. This involves measuring the tangible and intangible benefits of the system on society and governance. Evaluators look at how these projects have improved public service delivery, increased citizen participation, and reduced corruption. Social and economic impacts, such as increased access to services for marginalized communities or cost savings for both the government and citizens, are also considered. Long-term impact studies can provide insights into how e-governance initiatives have contributed to broader developmental goals, such as enhancing education, healthcare, or economic development.

User satisfaction is a vital indicator of the success of e-governance projects. Surveys, feedback forms, and user reviews provide direct insights into how citizens perceive the system. High levels of user satisfaction often correlate with increased usage rates and positive public perception. Evaluators should consider both qualitative and quantitative feedback to get a comprehensive understanding of user experiences. Continuous monitoring and responsiveness to user feedback are essential for ongoing improvement and adaptation of the system to meet evolving needs and expectations.

Finally, the sustainability and scalability of e-governance projects are key factors in their evaluation. A sustainable project has a clear plan for long-term operation, including financial viability, technical support, and continuous updates. Scalability refers to the system's ability to expand and accommodate a growing number of users and additional functionalities without compromising performance. Evaluators assess whether the project has the resources, infrastructure, and planning necessary to sustain and scale effectively over time. Projects that are both sustainable and scalable can serve as models for other regions or sectors, amplifying their positive impact.

In the subsequent section various national and state level projects have been mentioned on which students may prepare their mini project reports on evaluation of the projects. However, these projects have already been discussed in detailed in the previous chapters.

5.1.1 Various national e-governance projects

In this section few national e-governance projects are mentioned on which students may prepare their mini project reports related to the primarily evaluation. Here are some key national e-governance projects.

a) Aadhaar **:** A unique identification number issued to residents of India, serving as proof of identity and address.

   Agency: Unique Identification Authority of India (UIDAI).

b) Digital India: An umbrella program aimed at transforming India into a digitally empowered society and knowledge economy.

   Components: Digital infrastructure, digital literacy, and delivering services digitally.

c) GSTN (Goods and Services Tax Network**):** A comprehensive IT infrastructure for implementing Goods and Services Tax (GST).

   Objective: To enable smooth registration, return filing, and tax payment.

d) MCA21: An e-governance initiative of the Ministry of Corporate Affairs for providing easy and secure access to corporate entities.

   Objective: To improve the ease of doing business in India.

e) Passport seva project: The Passport seva project is an important e-governance initiative by the Government of India, aimed at transforming the passport issuance system by making it more efficient, transparent, and user-friendly.

   Objective: To provide passport services to citizens in a timely, transparent, more accessible, reliable manner, and in a comfortable environment through streamlined processes and innovative use of technology.

f) Income Tax: The Income tax Department of India has implemented several e-governance initiatives to streamline tax administration and make it easier for taxpayers to comply with tax laws.

   Objective: To enhance taxpayer convenience, ensure greater transparency, and improve the efficiency of tax administration through the use of technology.

g) SWAYAM: An online education platform for courses from school to post-graduate level.

Objective: To make learning resources accessible to all learners.

h) National e-Governance Plan (NeGP): An initiative to make all government services accessible to common people in their locality through common service delivery outlets.

i) e-Courts: A project to provide efficient and time-bound citizen-centric service delivery by courts.

Components: Case management systems, e-filing, and court records digitalization.

j) e-Kranti: A major pillar of the Digital India initiative focused on delivering all government services electronically to citizens.

5.1.2 Various state level e-governance projects

In this section few state-level e-governance projects have been mentioned on which students may prepare their mini project reports related to the primarily evaluation of these projects. Here is some key state-level e-governance projects are as follows:

a) Land Record Project: State-level e-governance projects for land records are crucial for improving the management and accessibility of land-related information. These projects typically aim to digitize land records, make them available online, and streamline processes related to land ownership, transfers, and other transactions.

b) Property Registration Project: State-level e-governance projects for property registration are designed to modernize and streamline the property registration process, making it more efficient, transparent, and accessible to citizens. These initiatives typically involve the digitization of property records, the development of online services, and the integration of various government departments involved in property transactions.

c) Transportation Project: State-level e-governance projects in the transportation sector aim to improve the management, efficiency, and transparency of transportation services and infrastructure. These projects leverage technology to streamline processes, enhance service delivery, and provide citizens with easy access to transportation-related information and services.

d) Bhoomi Project (Karnataka): Digitize and provide online access to land records to ensure transparency and reduce land disputes and provides Online portal for land records, automated land registration, integration with GIS for accurate mapping.

e) e-District Project (Various States): Deliver high-volume citizen services at the district level through a common portal. Online application and issuance of various certificates (birth, death, income), grievance redressal, service tracking.

f) e-PDS (Public Distribution System) (Chhattisgarh): Improve the efficiency and transparency of the public distribution system in food and civil supplies. It reduced leakage and corruption, ensured delivery of food grains to eligible beneficiaries.

5.2 Preparing mini project report by students

Preparing a project report on the evaluation of various national-level e-governance projects involves several key steps to ensure a comprehensive understanding and analysis.

Here is a structured approach to help you create a comprehensive and detailed report:

i. Title Page

- Title: Assessment of Various National-Level E-Governance Projects
- Subtitle (if any)
- Your Name
- Institution Name
- Date of Submission

ii. Table of Contents

- List of all sections and sub-sections with page numbers.

iii. Executive Summary

- A brief overview of the project, objectives, methodology, key findings, and conclusions.

iv. Introduction

- Background: Introduction to e-governance and its importance.
- Objectives: What the project aims to achieve.
- Scope: The extent of the study, including what is covered and what is not.

v. Literature Review

- Overview of existing research and literature on e-governance.
- Key theories, models, and frameworks in e-governance.
- Previous assessments and findings on national-level e-governance projects.

vi. Methodology

- Research Design: Description of the research design and approach.
- Data Collection: Methods used for data collection (e.g., surveys, interviews, secondary data).
- Data Analysis: Techniques and tools used for analyzing the data.

vii. Overview of National-Level E-Governance Projects

- Selection Criteria: Criteria used for selecting the projects for assessment.
- Project Descriptions: Brief descriptions of the selected e-governance projects (e.g., Digital India, e-Seva, UIDAI, GSTN).
- Objectives and Goals: Goals of each project and their intended impact.

viii. Assessment Criteria

- Parameters: Criteria used for assessment (e.g., efficiency, transparency, user satisfaction, impact on governance).
- Indicators: Specific indicators used to measure each parameter.

ix. Data Analysis and Findings

- Project-wise Analysis: Detailed analysis of each e-governance project based on the assessment criteria.
- Comparative Analysis: Comparison of the projects to highlight strengths and weaknesses.
- User Feedback: Summary of feedback from users and stakeholders.

x. Discussion

- Interpretation of findings.
- Implications for policy and practice.
- Challenges and limitations faced during the assessment.

xi. Conclusion and Recommendations

- Summary: Summarize key findings and conclusions.
- Recommendations: Provide actionable recommendations for improving e-governance projects.

xii. References

- List all sources, including books, articles, reports, and websites, cited in the report.

xiii. Appendices

- Include any additional material such as questionnaires, interview transcripts, detailed data tables, etc.
- Tips for writing the report:
- Be Clear and Concise: Ensure that your writing is clear and to the point.
- Use Visual Aids: Include charts, graphs, and tables to illustrate key points and data.
- Provide Evidence: Support your analysis and findings with concrete data and examples.
- Follow Guidelines: Adhere to any specific guidelines provided by your institution or organization.

Note: It is recommended that students must prepare their mini project report in accordance with the guidelines provided in section 5.2.

UNIT SUMMARY

This unit delves into the evaluation of various e-governance projects, highlighting both national and state-level initiatives in India. It covers key national projects such as the National e-Governance Plan (NeGP) and central government initiatives like e-Procurement Exchange, as well as significant state-level projects including e-Seva in Andhra Pradesh and Tamilnilam in Tamil Nadu. The unit emphasizes the impact of these projects on citizen services and public administration. Additionally, students are encouraged to prepare a mini project report, applying their understanding of e-governance concepts and evaluating real-world implementations. This practical exercise aims to deepen their grasp of e-governance strategies and their outcomes.

EXERCISES

Q1 Which of the following is a primary objective of the National e-Governance Plan (NeGP)?

a) To increase the number of government employees

b) To improve the delivery of public services through electronic means

c) To develop new physical infrastructure

d) To reduce the use of digital technology in governance

Q2 What does the term "Government to Citizen" (G2C) initiatives refer to in the context of e-governance?

a) Services provided by the government to other government agencies

b) Services offered by businesses to government bodies

c) Services provided by the government directly to citizens

d) Services offered by citizens to businesses

Q3 Which project aims to computerize the land records and provide online access to them in Tamil Nadu?

a) e-Kosh

b) Tamilnilam

c) Akshaya

d) e-Procurement Exchange

Q4 The 'e-Seva' initiative is primarily associated with which state in India?

a) Karnataka

b) Andhra Pradesh

c) Kerala

d) Uttar Pradesh

Q5 Which of the following is a central government initiative designed to facilitate e-procurement in India?

a) e-Kosh

b) KAVERI

c) e-Procurement Exchange

d) Nagarpalika

Q6 What is the focus of the Akshaya project implemented by the Kerala government?

a) Land record digitization

b) IT literacy and digital inclusion

c) Agricultural marketing

d) Treasury computerization

Q7 Which initiative aims to facilitate digital access to government services in Chhattisgarh?

a) e-Seva

b) Tamilnilam

c) e-Kosh

d) Lokvani

Q8 The 'Lokvani' project is an initiative of which state government?

a) Uttar Pradesh

b) Gujarat

c) Madhya Pradesh

d) Karnataka

Q9 Which e-governance initiative was introduced to streamline agricultural marketing in Madhya Pradesh?

a) e-Procurement Exchange

b) e-Kosh

c) EKVI

d) Nagarpalika

Q10 The 'Common Service Centers' (CSC) is part of which type of e-governance initiative?

a) Government to Government (G2G)

b) Government to Business (G2B)

c) Government to Citizen (G2C)

d) Business to Government (B2G)

Answers

Q.N.	1	2	3	4	5	6	7	8	9	10
Option	B	C	B	B	C	B	C	A	C	C

Short Answer Type Questions

1. What factors are crucial for evaluating the success of an e-governance project?
2. Identify two major national e-governance projects and describe their primary objectives.
3. How does the e-Governance project 'Aadhaar' improve public service delivery in India?
4. What are the main objectives of the e-Seva project implemented in Andhra Pradesh?
5. Describe the purpose of the 'KAVERI' project in Karnataka.

6. What impact does the Tamilnilam project have on land record management in Tamil Nadu?
7. Explain the significance of the 'e-Kosh' initiative in Chhattisgarh.
8. What is the role of Common Service Centers (CSC) in the e-governance framework?
9. How does the 'Lokvani' initiative in Uttar Pradesh benefit citizen engagement with local government?
10. What are the key features of the 'e-Procurement Exchange' initiative at the national level?

Long Answer Type Questions

1. What are the key benefits and challenges associated with the implementation of national e-governance projects like Aadhaar and GST?
2. How have state-level e-governance initiatives, such as Karnataka's Bhoomi project, improved land record management?
3. In what ways has the Digital India initiative impacted citizen access to government services across different states?
4. What role does public-private partnership play in the success of state-level e-governance projects?
5. How do national e-governance projects differ in their implementation and impact compared to state-level initiatives?
6. What are the primary objectives of state-level e-governance projects like Mee Seva in Andhra Pradesh?

Dynamic QR Code for further reading

REFERENCES AND SUGGESTED READINGS

1. Prabhu, C. S. R. (2013), "E-Governance: Concepts and Case Studies", PHI Learning Pvt. Ltd.
2. Sharma, P (2009), "E-Governance in India: Initiatives and Issues", Global India Publications Pvt Ltd
3. Arora, R. C. (2020), "Digital India: Understanding Information Communication Technology (ICT) in Government", New Century Publications

4. Kumar, A. (2011), "E-Governance and Indian Society: An Impact Assessment", Regal Publications
5. Muttoo, S. K. and Rajan, B. S. (2018), "E-Governance in India: Problems, Prototypes, and Prospects", Cambridge Scholars Publishing
6. Johnston, E. W. and Gil-Garcia, J. R. (2015), "Governance in the Information Era: Theory and Practice of Policy Informatics" Routledge India

REFERENCES FOR FURTHER LEARNING

1. "E-Governance in India: Theories and Practices", by Dr. S. P. Gupta, 2nd edition, 2020.
2. "Digital Governance: New Directions in e-Government", by Dr. R. K. Arora, latest edition, 2021.
3. "Digital India: Understanding E-Governance and Its Applications", by Dr. S. R. Mahalingam, latest edition, 2021.
4. "E-Governance: Concepts and Case Studies", by Parag Kulkarni, latest edition, 2021.
5. https://www.meity.gov.in/divisions/national-e-governance-plan
6. "E-Governance in India: A Vision for the 21st Century", by Dr. S. P. Bansal, latest edition, 2021.
7. "Digital Transformation of Government and Public Services", by Dr. A. R. Natarajan, latest edition, 2020.

CO AND PO ATTAINMENT TABLE

Course outcomes (COs) for this course can be mapped with the programme outcomes (POs) after the completion of the course and a correlation can be made for the attainment of POs to analyze the gap. After proper analysis of the gap in the attainment of POs necessary measures can be taken to overcome the gaps.

Course Outcomes	**Expected Mapping with Programme Outcomes** (*1- Weak Correlation; 2- Medium correlation; 3- Strong Correlation*)						
	PO-1	**PO-2**	**PO-3**	**PO-4**	**PO-5**	**PO-6**	**PO-7**
CO-1							
CO-2							
CO-3							
CO-4							
CO-5							
CO-6							

The data filled in the above table can be used for gap analysis.

INDEX